GUIDE TO

NAPLES

AND BAY AREA

GW00402185

PAUL BLANCHARD

© C.P.M.
Creative Publishing Marine s.a.
C.so S. Gottardo, 32
CH 6830 Chiasso – SWITZERLAND
Edito in Italia a cura di Kiven Editrice s.a.s.
C.so Trapani, 48 – Torino

Stampa: Istituto Grafico Bertello – Borgo San Dalmazzo (CN)

Foreword

"When I would write words, only images start before my eyes-the beautiful land, the free sea; the hazy islands, the roaring mountain, powers to delineate all this fail me."
- Johann Wolfgang von Goethe, in March 1787.

Naples possesses a subtle magic that is difficult to describe. Even Goethe, the great German poet, fell prey to its Circean charm. "Naples is a paradise", he exclaimed, "in it everyone lives in a sort of intoxicated self-forgetfulness. It is even so with me; I scarcely know myself - I seem quite an altered man." For foreign visitors of all ages, Naples and its lovely environs have been an oasis of peace, the ideal place to go to escape the tensions, or the monotony, of day to day life. But it is important to remember that Naples is very much more than a fabulous resort, "full of gardens, of fountains, and of rich men," as Boccaccio, writing in the fourteenth century, described it.

During the Roman age Naples became an important center of learning (Virgil wrote his exquisite *Georgics* here), and the intellectual tradition of the city seems to have continued unbroken up to the present day. During the Middle Ages, St. Thomas Aquinas taught theology at the university, Petrarch and Boccaccio enjoyed the patronage of the Angevin kings, and the native poet Jacopo Sannazaro brought distinction to the humanist court of Alfonso of Aragon. In the sixteenth century the Sorrentine Torquato Tasso (1544-95) composed his immortal *Gerusalemme liberata*, Giambattista Basile (1575-1632) established the Neapolitan satire as a genre in its own right, and Giambattista della Porta (1535-1615) gave form to the *Commedia dell'arte*, that peculiar form of comedy, improvised from standardized situations and stock characters, made famous throughout the world by the mask of Pulcinella. In the eighteenth century, while Giovan Battista Vico gave a new impetus to Western thought, Neapolitan composers devoted their energies to the development of the *opera buffa*, a form of comic opera - exemplified by Pergolesi's *Serva Padrona* (1733), Paisiello's *Socrate immaginario* (1775), and Cimarosa's wonderful *Matrimonio segreto* (1792) - where poetry was submitted to the most outlandish caprices of music. At the same time charitable institutes, called "conservatories", where Neapolitan orphans received a musical education, grew up throughout the city; they were later joined together to form the Conservatory of San Pietro e Maiella, the oldest and most famous in the world. In our own century Benedetto Croce (1866-1952) played a major role in determining the course of modern thought; the *canzone napoletana*, immortalized by a variety of performers from Enrico Caruso to Elvis Presley,

3

became the popular symbol of Naples in Italy and abroad; and Eduardo de Filippo won universal acclaim as the greatest modern Italian playwright after Pirandello.

Thus it is clear that Naples is something other than a sun-baked, sea-washed Mediterranean town. Today Naples (*Napoli* in Italian) is one of the more populous cities in Italy (1.3 million inhabitants), an important port, and the intellectual and commercial center of the south. The animated and noisy metropolis enjoys one of the more wonderful situations in the world, spread out fanwise above its beautiful gulf. This characteristic charm, which of course extends from Naples itself to its far-famed environs, helps offset the artistic and architectural supremacy of the cities of the north; and it must not be forgotten that innumerable treasures of the Greek and Roman age, as well as many memorable works of medieval, Renaissance, and baroque art, are to be seen in and around the city.

This book is intended for the first-time visitor to Naples. It gives information about the main things to see and the main places to visit, and it explains why they are interesting. It considers the Naples area in terms of its historical development, each chapter dealing with a major period of which there are visible remains. Where possible, the historical subject matter is hung on a certain number of people and events everybody knows about; while the carefully-planned site visits take readers to the most beautiful and representative monuments. There is a special section devoted to Neapolitan cookery, and another providing up-to-date information about hotels, restaurants, shopping, entertainment, popular festivals, etc. As the book is intended for the general reader, such distracting paraphenalia as footnotes have been dispensed with.

An essential bibliography has been provided for those interested in the principal sources used in preparing the guide.

The author owes particular gratitude to Italian National Tourist Agency (E.N.I.T.) and to the local tourist boards of the Naples area. Acknowledgment must also be made to Laura and Antonio Rotulo, and to Mimma and Salvatore Califano, whose friendship and advice have proven invaluable. Thanks are also due to Lauretta and Daniele Lombardi, for their companionship and hospitality. Recognition for help and advice during the author's travels also goes to the *Soprintendenza alle Gallerie* in Naples, and to the local people, too numerous to name, whose generosity and kindness vastly facilitated the work of editing on the spot.

Suggestions for the correction or improvement of the guide will be gratefully welcomed.

Florence, January 1989

I Greeks and Romans

Today we know with certainty that the region of Campania was inhabited as early as the Stone Age, the first known period of prehistoric human culture (before 3500 B.C.). Human remains and stone tools have been found on the Island of Capri (the first of these were discovered in the time of the Roman Emperor Augustus), as well as along the coast and in the hills and valleys of the Neapolitan hinterland. Artefacts dating from the Bronze Age (after 3500 B.C.) and the Iron Age (after 1100 B.C.) are also common.

Many of these early inhabitants came to Italy by sea from the Eastern Mediterranean: traces of the Bronze Age cultures of Crete and Mycenae, for instance, are visible in burial artefacts from around the fifteenth century B.C. onward. In the period, around 1000 B.C., when archaeological deduction gives way to recorded history, references to our area may be vaguely glimpsed in the myths and legends of ancient Greece. On the northern shore of Naples' crescent-shaped bay, for instance, we find *Cumae*, home of that ancient prophetess, the Sibyl; and the *Phlegraean* or *Burning Fields* where the Olympian gods defeated the Giants (and in order to keep them down, buried them beneath the earth which stirs, in the earthquakes characteristic of the region, whenever the imprisoned monsters try to free themselves). To the south lie the *Isole Sirenuse*, the rocks into which the Sirens were metamorphosed after they had swum in pursuit of Ulysses' ship and vainly enticed him to land.

The Greeks came to Southern Italy from Ionia, a region of western Asia Minor from which they were driven by the non-Greek peoples who inhabited the neighboring regions. The earliest Greek colonies in our area were *Cumae* and *Pithecusae* (Ischia), founded by Chalcis in the eleventh century B.C., according to tradition. These were soon followed by the neighboring centers of *Dikaearchia* (Pozzuoli), *Parthenope* (Naples), and a little farther to the south, *Poseidonia* (Paestum).

Greek colonization of the Mediterranean eventually extended as far afield as France and Spain, but the Bay of Naples marked for all practical purposes the outer edge of what came to be called *Magna Graecia* or Greece Beyond the Sea. Sybaris, Croton, Taranto, and Naples on the mainland; and Messina and Syracuse on the island of Sicily, became the chief centers of a flourishing Hellenistic civilization that attracted distinguished visitors from the homeland and gave rise to a splendid local culture as well.

Except on Sicily, the Greeks rarely ventured into the interior of the areas they settled. They were not colonialists in the pioneer sense of the term, but a seafaring people interested above all in securing safe and dependable lines of communication between their more distant outposts and their home ports in the Aegean. In Southern Italy they also traded with the native tribes of farmers and herdsmen who inhabited the plains and mountains in isolated settlements much like the Indian villages of pre-Columbian America. These Italic peoples, though considerably less civilized than the Greeks, were quick to realize the mutual advantages of cooperating with the newcomers. In the coastal areas of Campania, where the contacts between the two cultures were particularly intense, the indigenous peoples profited by their acquaintance with the foreigners, picking up their customs and passing them on to their neighbors further inland. For centuries both sides enjoyed the fruits of this relationship.

Campania may have continued to flourish under Greek domination for the next four hundred years, had it not been for the Etruscans, a powerful ethnic group that lived in the area coextensive with modern Tuscany and Umbria. Like the Greeks, the Etruscans had migrated to Italy (it is still not known whence, when, or how); and their civilization had reached a comparable degree of political, social, and artistic development.

Attracted by the mild climate and lucrative trade, they established their first colonies in Campania in the ninth century. Later, as their northern homeland was invaded by the Celts, they migrated to the region *en masse*.

The Etruscans were more warlike than the Greeks, and per-haps more actively colonialistic. As the years passed, they gradually consolidated their foothold in the South, conquering one Greek city after another. At one point their influence was so strong that new houses in Campanian towns were built almost exclusively in the Etruscan manner. The tide finally turned against them, however, as a consequence of two Greek victories at Cumae in 525 and 474 B.C. The resulting decline in their power was so rapid that between these dates the Etruscan kings were also chased out of Rome. Eventually, the expanding Roman Republic interposed itself between the Etruscan homeland to the north and its extension in Campania; deprived of a land connection, the southern settlements were left to wither on the vine.

The expulsion of the Etruscans and the involvement of the Greek colonies in the fraticidal Peloponnesian Wars created a power vacuum in Campania, which was filled when the indigenous Samnites rose up and conquered the region, with relative ease, around 420 B.C. The Samnites were a simple people who dwelled in the hills of eastern Campania. They were so keenly aware of the inferiority of their own civilization with respect to those they had conquered, that instead of governing the occupied territory according to Samnite law and custom they created a federation of city-states, each governed by its own magistrate and faithful to its own traditions. In this manner they managed to maintain their hold over the area even while they were themselves gradually being conquered by the Romans in the series of conflicts generally referred to as the Samnite Wars (343-290 B.C.).

Under the Romans, who occupied it after the Social War (88 B.C.), Campania rose again to great prosperity, and it soon won the appellative *Campania Felix* on account of its beauty and fertility. The alluvial plains and fruitful hills produced the finest grains, vegetables, olives, and wines. From Paestum came the famous roses whose essence, regarded as one of the more delightful and luxurious scents in the Roman world, was sold at the celebrated perfume market at Capua. The fertile slopes of Mount Vesuvius produced the highly prized Falernian wine, as well as the more common *vinum vesuvium*. The forests yielded wood in abundance, the mountains provided numerous varieties of building stone, and the sea supplied fish from which the ancients made the sauces *garum, liquamen,* and *muria*, which Pliny says were a special treat.

In the first century A.D. Campania developed its character as a rich man's playground. It became a place where Romans went to escape the tensions of the capital, to retire in their old age, or simply to vacation. The main resort centers were Cumae, Baiae, Sorrento, the Island of Capri, and the coast around Puteoli, Naples, and Pompeii. Herculaneum was known as a particularly healthful place, due to its position on a pleasant promontory. Pompeii was a bustling commercial, agricultural, and resort town receiving gentle sea breezes in the day and cool mountain breezes from Vesuvius at night. The whole of the coast along the Bay of Naples was adorned by towns, residences, and plantations, which spread out in unbroken succesion, presenting the appearance of a single city, as indeed is still very much the case today.

Naples is the modern successor of two ancient towns that even before Roman times had merged to form a single metropolis. The colony of *Parthenope*, the most ancient forerunner of Naples, was founded by Rhodian navigators in the ninth century B.C. It stood on Mount Echia, a volcanic hill on which the quarter of Pizzofalcone now stands. This site was chosen because it was easy to defend, it was surrounded by the sea on three sides, with steep cliffs, and was separated from the hinterland by a deep valley, today Via Chiaia. After the Greek victory over the Etruscans, however, the population of Parthenope grew rapidly, and it soon became clear that the city would have to be enlarged. This posed some serious problems: the lay of the land, which made Parthenope impregnable, also made urban development virtually impossible. For this reason it was decided to build a new town, *Neapolis* (from which the Italian name *Napoli* derives) on a hillside on the other side of the harbor, with its highest point, the acropolis, in the area that would later become Caponapoli. Neapolis soon surpassed the older city in importance due to the arrival around 450 B.C. of Greek colonists from Chalcis, Pithecusa, and Athens. Both towns were conquered by the Samnites around 400 B.C. and by the Romans in 326 B.C.

Under the Romans Neapolis grew in population, and it held on more tenaciously perhaps than any other city in Magna Graecia to its Greek customs, culture, and institutions. The population remained mainly Greek. Greek games, in which musical competitions alternated with gymnastic events, were held by the Neapolitans every five years; and Greek was preserved as the official language. The Emperor Nero was particularly fond of Naples' Hellenic character, and he sang there several times before going to Greece.

Due to its Hellenic culture, Naples was regarded as the city of learning. Roman youth flocked there to cultivate the arts of rhetoric, poetry, and music. Although the city lacked an amphitheater it did have a famous covered theater, and the Neapolitan actors were renowned throughout the Roman world. Plutarch, the Greek biographer and moralist, tells that Brutus came personally to Naples to beg one of these actors, Canuzio, to come and recite in Rome. The theaters of Naples offered plays in Latin and in Greek; among the latter that written by Claudius to honor his brother Germanicus. The great masters included the orator Polemone, whose pupils included the Roman emperor and Stoic philosopher, Marcus Aurelius. Virgil, not yet famous, came to Naples in search of that atmosphere that his spirit demanded and that the hustle and bustle of the capital precluded. Here he wrote his exquisite *Georgics*. And when he died at an early age in Brindisi, on his way back from a fateful journey to Greece, he wished to be buried in Naples. Augustus ordered that his wish be fulfilled, and tradition initiated by Dante places his tomb on the hill of Posillipo.

For the Romans, Naples and its splendid surroundings, the slopes of Vesuvius, the Capodimonte hill, the Phlegraean Fields, the harbors of Pozzuoli, Baia, Pompeii, Stabia, and Herculaneum, afforded an extraordinary oasis of peace. Horace, the famous poet and satirist, wrote of "restful Naples," and another poet, Ovid, claimed that "Parthenope was born in idleness." Although modern Naples is anything but tranquil, the city and its magnificent environs still offer the visitor spectacles of immense cultural interest and unparalleled natural beauty.

Site Visits

a Naples

Walking tour, 2 miles, with bus and taxi service along much of the way.

This route takes us into the center of Naples, along the straight, perpendicular streets whose layout still follows that of the Graeco-Roman town.

Unfortunately, there are no ancient ruins in Naples to speak of, nothing, at least, as extensive as the Forum in Rome or as impressive the Colosseum: most of Naples' ancient treasures lie buried beneath the fabric of the modern city. The few remains that can be seen have been ably camouflaged by time: incorporated in later structures, they crop up in unexpected places. The church of San Paolo Maggiore, for instance, stands over a temple of the Dioscuri, of which two fine columns survive; the church and convent of San Lorenzo Maggiore occupy the site of the Basilica (something like the ancient town hall) and the Curia (court of justice); and some imposing ruins of the Theater and the adjacent Baths can be seen along the via dell'Anticaglia. The Cathedral is built over a Temple of Apollo, and the church of the Santissimi Apostoli rises on the ruins of a Temple of Mercury; but their outward appearance gives no clue to these noble antecedents. The Castel dell'Ovo has supplanted the spendid Roman villa of Lucullus on the Isle of Megaris; and the suburban homes and high-rises on the hill of Posillipo have canceled all trace of "those Graeco-Roman pleasure houses... so well calculated to banish melancholy and exhilarate the mind" (Harold Acton) that the epicure Pollio and other Roman patricians built there. Luckily, something of the spirit of the ancient city survives in the crowded lanes around the via dei Tribunali, which follows the course of the old *decumanus maximus*, the main street of the Graeco-Roman town.

Our starting point, in this as in the following chapters, shall be the centrally located Castel Nuovo. This is strictly a matter of convenience.

To reach the church of *San Paolo Maggiore* (Map 2, 2) the first stop on our visit to ancient Naples, take the via San Carlo past the celebrated San Carlo Theater to piazza Trento e Trieste. Turn right and walk up the via Roma, modern Naples' main shopping street, to the semicircular piazza Dante. This is quite a hike-about a kilometer and a half, or just under a mile-and if you're not feeling up to it, you might want to take a bus (no. 24) or a taxi, which you can find at the taxi stand in the adjacent piazza del Plebiscito.

From the piazza Dante, pass under the Port'Alba to enter the via San Pietro a Maiella. To the right, in the former convent of the same name, is the *Conservatorio di Musica*, the oldest in existence, described in Chapter IV, b. Across the street we glimpse the Policlinico, a vast hospital complex with a seventeenth-century chapel; and, just beyond, the ruined church of Santa Maria Maggiore. From here on we are in the colorful and animated via dei Tribunali, the *decumanus maximus* of the Graeco-Roman city, today one of the principal thoroughfares of downtown Naples. A little farther along, this narrow street opens up on the left to form the piazza San Gaetano, where a flight of steps mounts to our destination. Formerly part of a convent established by St. Gaetano de Thienne in 1538, this church was built between 1583 and 1603 over a ninth century church that in turn stood on the site of a Roman temple dedicated to the *Dioscuri*-Zeus's twin sons Castor and Pollux, who were reunited after Castor's death by Zeus' decree that they live in the upper and lower worlds on alternate days. The front of the temple originally included six fluted Corinthian columns. It was used as the façade of the church until 1688, when it was destroyed in an earthquake. Today little remains of the ancient temple. There are two tall columns with their architrave and the bases of two more columns in front of the church; another column along the right side; and, beneath the statues of St. Peter and St. Paul, some weathered sculptures of the Dioscuri. The Chiostro di San Paolo (entrance in via San Paolo, 14) incorporates twentytwo ancient granite columns which, however, did not belong to the Temple of the Dioscuri.

Almost opposite, on the site of the Roman basilica, stands the Franciscan church of Sa*n Lorenzo Maggiore* (Map 3, 3), one of Naples' most important medieval churches, described at length in Chapter 2. Here it is not so much the details of the church that interest us, as the form of the building as a whole. A *basilica* was originally an oblong building ending in a semicircular apse used in ancient Rome as a court of justice and place of public assembly. During the first centuries of the Christian age, the Roman basilican form was taken by the Christians as the prototype for their meeting places, and architectural historians now use the term to refer to an early Christian church building consisting of nave and aisles and a large, high transept from which an apse projects. San Lorenzo Maggiore is, in this sense, a Christian basilica. But what is more interesting is that its form corresponds almost perfectly to that of the Roman basilica. Its builders used the massive walls of the pre-existing edifice as the foundation of their own building-a common practice in the Middle Ages, and not only the Middle Ages, as anyone who has visited Atlanta, Georgia, can attest. The proof of this relationship may be had in the cloisters where archaeological excavations have brought to light the massive walls of the treasury in the basement of the basilica; the remains of a Roman street flanked by shops; traces of Greek buildings made of large square blocks of tufa; and the ruins, on a higher level, of a medieval public building.

Across the street from San Lorenzo Maggiore, and running along the right flank of San Paolo Maggiore, is the narrow vico Cinquesanti. This brings us to the via Anticaglia, which corresponds to the *decumanus superior* of Roman Neapolis. The street is crossed by two massive brick arches, the remains of the walls that joined the Baths, which were located on the far side of the street, with the ancient Theater, which stood in the area between the vico Giganti, the via dell'Anticaglia, the via San Paolo, and the former Convento dei Teatrini. The Theater was built to accomodate 11,000 spectators. Here Claudius had the play he had written in honor of his brother Germanicus performed, and Nero sang to an enthusiastic audience.

We turn right along the via dell'Anticaglia to the busy via del Duomo, and then turn right again. Inside the Cathedral (left, Map 3,3), the piers of the nave incorporate no less than 110 antique columns of Oriental and African granite which, however, have nothing to do with the temple of Apollo over which the church was built. The sacrestan will show, on request, a stretch of ancient street pavement in a courtyard in the Curia building, and other Graeco-Roman remains (including fragments of mosaic pavement) in the basement.

b Paestum and Velia

Road, 300 km (180 miles) round trip. Autostrada A3 to Battipaglia (73 km, 44 miles), then Highway 18 and Highway 267. Bus, from Naples to Paestum and back daily, leaving from the piazza del Municipio, next to the Castel Nuovo.

Railway, 2.30 hours one way. A change is required at *Salerno* or *Battipaglia*, as only local trains stop at Paestum.

This route takes us to two of the best preserved Greek colonies in the Mediterranean, set in a natural environment whose beauty rivals that of the ancient ruins.

Paestum has been for a thousand years a romantic ruin in the midst of a solemn wilderness. Its Doric temples, unsurpassed even by those of Athens in noble simplicity and good preservation, produce an incomparable effect of majesty and grandeur. **Poseidonia**, the City of Neptune, was founded by Greeks from Sybaris in the sixth century B.C., its name being latinized to Paestum when it came into the hands of the Lucanians in the fourth century. In 273 B.C. it was taken by the Romans. Paestum was famed in antiquity for its roses, which flowered twice a year, and also for its violets. Malaria gradually killed or drove off much of the population, and about A.D. 877 the city was destroyed by the Saracens. All but overgrown by tangled vegetation, it was rediscovered during the building of the coach-road in the eighteenth century.

The ancient ruins comprise remains of numerous public, private and religious buildings, including four major temples, a forum, and an extensive residential quarter. The town walls measure about three miles in circumference. Their extant ruins rise to a height of 15-50 ft and include four gates (of which the most impressive is the Porta Sirena on the east side) and several towers. The town is crossed by a *cardo* and a *decumanus*, both of which preserve paved segments. Recent excavations have shown that the temples belong to two groups, that to the south (dedicated to Hera) comprising the so-called Basilica and Temple of Neptune, and eleven smaller temples; that to the north (dedicated to Athena) includes notably the Temple of Ceres. Between the two ran the via Sacra, now brought to light. In the middle, immediately east of the via Sacra, are the forum and other neighboring buildings, while the residential area develops to the north and west.

Enter the city by the porta della Giustizia (adjacent to the Ristorante Nettuno, where an excellent lunch may be had). From here the ancient via Sacra, a paved road, leads past the three great temples (right). The first of these is the *Basilica*, the earliest temple at Paestum, misnamed by its discoverers in the eighteenth century. Like most Greek temples, it stands on an east-west axis, and is reached by a brief flight of steps. Its outer colonnade has fifty fluted columns, nine at the ends and eighteen along the sides. The colonnade is still standing, as are the entablature and part of the inside of the frieze. The columns belong to the Doric order and show distinct features of the early style: rapid tapering, a marked *entasis* (or swelling profile, and a bulging moulding of the capital). These and other features enable archaeologists to date the temple to around 550 B.C.

Inside the colonnade stands the *cella*, or sanctuary, preceded by a porch-like structure formed by three columns standing between two great pilasters at the ends of the *cella* walls. A colonnade at the center of the *cella* divides the interior into two small naves; three columns are still standing and the capitals of two others are lying on the ground. There were probably seven in all, and also perhaps a half-column against the end wall, which separated the *cella* from the treasury. It is probable, though not entirely certain, that the temple was dedicated to Hera.

About 50 yards farther north stands the so-called **Temple of Neptune**. This temple, built in the majestic style of the fifth century B.C., is the largest in Paestum and ranks with the Theseion at Athens and the Temple of Concord at Agrigento as one of the three best-preserved temples in Europe. It stands on a basement of three steps, and it has thirty-six fluted columns (fourteen at the sides, six at the ends). These are 30 ft high and taper from 108" at the base to 59" at the top. The *cella* is divided into three aisles by two rows of two pilasters and seven columns, with smaller columns above, of which three remain on the north side and five on the south. The entablature is well preserved, and the pediments are almost intact. The roof, however, has gone. Shelley, the English romantic poet, wrote that "the effect of the jagged outline of the mountains through groups of enormous columns on one side, and on the other the level horizon of the sea, is inexpressibly grand." To the east are the remains of a large sacrificial altar.

Continuing to the north, the via Sacra crosses the *decumanus maximus* (which joins the porta Sirena to the porta Marina) on the site of the *forum,* the marketplace and chief public square of the ancient Roman town, which replaced the earlier Greek *agora.* The *forum*, which measures 488 x 185 ft, was surrounded on all four sides by a fine Doric portico, of which some fragments are still visible on the three remaining sides (the fourth, to the east, is hidden by the modern highway that unfortunately still cuts through the excavations). Behind this stood numerous public buildings and shops: on the south side are the remains of Baths of the Imperial age, of the *Curia*, and of an early Greek Temple. On the north side are a Roman Temple of an early period with later additions, a Greek Theater, and farther to the right and partly under the modern road, a Roman Amphitheater.

Adjoining the via Sacra just north of the forum is the underground *Sacellum*, a tomb-like structure of dubious significance. It is generally believed to have been a sacred edifice consecrated to the deities of fertility; but it might also have been an empty tomb dedicated to Is, the mythical founder of Sybaris, erected in Paestum by the Sybarite refugees after the city was destroyed in 509 B.C.

Still following the via Sacra to the north, we come to the Temple of Ceres (more accurately an *Athenaion*, a temple dedicated to the goddess Athena), of a date intermediate between the two surviving southern temples. It is the smallest of the three, and presents six fluted columns on the short sides and thirteen along the flanks. It stands on a basement of two steps. The *cella* is quite simple, and the porch of unusual depth. The architrave is the only remaining part of the entablature, but much remains of the pediments. Near the south wall of the *cella* are three Christian tombs of the early Middle Ages when the temple was used as a church. To the east of the temple are traces of a large sacrificial altar and of a votive column, which suggest that the temple once stood at the center of a small sanctuary.

Regaining the modern road we turn south to the **Museum** (open as the archaeological area; a ticket to one gives admission to the other) designed in 1952 to display many fine objects from recent excavations, including prehistoric and protohistoric material, burial treasures, an important group of tomb paintings, architectural and sculptural fragments, and votive terracottas, of Greek, Lucanian, and Roman provenance. Most notable are the collection of archaic sculpture from the sanctuary of Argive Hera at the mouth of the Sele, including thirty three Metopes with Homeric and other scenes; and the truly extraordinary cycle of mural paintings from the so-called Tomb of the Diver, perhaps the only extant examples of Greek painting (ca. 480 B.C.). The four panels forming the coffin are decorated with a funeral banqueting scene in which singing, games, lovers, and music accompany the deceased into the other world. The fifth panel, the lid, shows the Diver from whom the tomb takes its name-a nude youth who executes a perfect dive into a blue sea, in an unusual allegory of death.

The atmosphere of Paestum may best be appreciated by a tour of the Walls. The lower and outer courses are of the fifth century B.C., the inner parts are later. The porta Sirena retains

Paestum, Museum. This remarkable painting shows the deceased plunging wide-eyed into the Beyond. It is part of a cycle of mural paintings from the so-callled Tomb of the Diver, which receives its name from this image.

its arch, and the porta Marina its towers and bastions. From the latter the *Torre di Pesto*, a medieval watch-tower, lies about half a mile southwest. It commands a good view of the magnificent sandy unfortunately marred by bathing establishments extending in both directions. In the area outside the walls, particularly to the north and south of the city, extends the *Necropolis*, or cemetery. Many of the tombs, which judging from the finds of the last few years contain considerable treasures, have yet to be excavated.

About 4 km (2 miles) beyond Paestum, Highway 18 crosses the Solofone. Here turn right onto Highway 267, a scenic road that follows the coast of the Cilento region to Velia. The Cilento, a broad mountainous peninsula between the Gulfs of Salerno and Policastro, is one of the more beautiful and unspoiled areas of Campania, where local journeys are still made by mule or by the traditional cart. Known in ancient times for its unpredictable winds and currents, the coast is particularly rich in literary allusions. The Punta Licosa (the ancient *Enipeum* or *Posidium Promontorrium*) takes its name from the siren Leucosia, who threw herself into the sea from the headland after failing to enchant Ulysses; and Capo Palinuro recalls Aeneas' pilot Palinurus who, overtaken by sleep, fell into the sea and drowned, and here appeared to the hero asking to be buried.

At **Agropoli**, a popular resort, is believed to have stood, the acropolis of Paestum although no ruins have been found to support this theory. The medieval town stands on a headland above a small, picturesque bay. On the hill seaward of the town stands a fifth century A.D. castle, reached by narrow alleys among village houses and churches. A helpful custodian may be summoned by a bell in the gatepost. The castle commands magnificent views, both along the coast and inland.

San Marco, a fishing village and a growing resort, has remains of ancient walls and, in the sea, of a Roman breakwater carved out of the rock. Opposite the point stands the tiny isle of Licosa, containing remains of ancient walls and the modern light, visible at a distance of 12 miles.

Acciaroli, on a lovely promontory, was a favorite resort of Hemingway.

The ruins of **Velia** stand on a headland overlooking the valley of the Alento (the Hales of the ancients). *Elea*, as the city was called by the Greeks, was founded in the mid-sixth century by Phocaean colonists driven from their homeland by the attacking Persians. The town derived its livelihood from fishing and commerce, as the rocky and arid hinterland was unsuitable to agriculture. Its ties with Massalia (the modern Marseilles) developed to such an extent that at one time Elea was considered a sub-colony of the latter. In the third century B.C. the inhabitants threw in their lot with Rome; nevertheless it retained its Hellenistic culture, language and customs, supplying the capital with priestesses of Ceres, who tradition dictated must be Greek. Although it never attained great civic or economic importance, Elea became a leading intellectual center, giving its name to the Eleatic school of philosophy of Xenophanes, Parmenides and Zeno. Its decline became evident in Roman times, as its harbors (there were apparently two, on the north and south sides of the headland, which initially projected into the sea) filled with silt. By the twelfth century it had disappeared altogether and the medieval town of Castellammare della Bruca had grown up its place. This in turn was abandoned in the seventeenth century.

The ruins of Velia can be seen comfortably in about one hour. After passing the promontory, leave the main road on the right and proceed by foot to the excavations. Entering from the south, we pass a sea wall (later fortified when the area beyond filled with silt) and remains of Roman tombs, and arrive shortly at the porta Marina Sud, one of the two gates (the other is at the north end of the town) which initially opened onto the harbors. Within, we enter the south quarter, the center of residential and political life. On the right lies the *Palaestra*, with its enclosed portico; note, near the entrance to the latter, the collection of bricks, of a type peculiar to Velia, impressed with the town's mark. Here were found numerous statues, including a portrait of Parmenides. In an olive grove to the east are Roman Baths dating from the second century A.D, of which some rooms preserve their mosaic pavements. Farther on, on the right, is the *Agora*, the central square and marketplace of the Greek town, dating, as it is to be seen today, from the third century B.C. Along the right side stalls were attached to the walls and pillars on market days. The main street now ascends more sharply, the paving stones (which are laid end-wise in the characteristic Greek fashion) being staggered somewhat to provide a better foothold. Near the top of the hill there come into view the *porta Archaica*, built in the sixth century B.C., in a position of obvious defensive importance; and the *porta Rosa*, a remarkable structure of the fourth century B.C. brought to light in 1964. Toward the end of the same century the lofty arch was walled up and this tract of the road, threatened by landslides, was replaced by another road that runs along the viaduct above to the *Acropolis*. Here remains of a medieval tower overlie the foundations of an Ionic temple dating from the second half of the fifth century B.C. Excavations in the area have revealed a small Hellenistic temple and an open sanctuary dedicated to Poseidon. At the north-east corner of the site the walls come together to form the *Castelluccio*, a tall tower dating from the fourth century B.C.

From Velia the coast road continues, in a series of curves,

through wild valleys and groves of giant olives, past the villages of Ascea and Pisciotta to **Palinuro,** a fishing center and a popular resort splendidly set in a small bay. An *Antiquarium* contains finds from nearby Molpa, originally an outpost of the Greek colony at Velia, later made over into a castle, where the Emperor Maximian withdrew after renouncing his title. At the entrance to the harbor can be seen the ruins of what popular belief holds to be the cenotaph erected to Palinurus (*Aeneid*, V, 838-871 ; VI, 337-383). An excursion (1 mile) to the ruins of Molpa may be made in about 30 minutes; the path, which runs through olive groves and along the beach, is difficult in places.

This headland also contains numerous caves accessible from the sea (boats may be hired at the harbor), of which some were occupied in prehistoric times. Also of interest are the natural arches at **Foce del Mingardo** and **Archetiello**.

c Pompeii

Road, Autostrada A 13, 44 km (26 miles) round trip.
Bus, tours daily: see your travel agent.
Train, "Circumvesuviana" Railway (Sarno line) to Pompei Santuario, Pompei Scavi, or (Sorrento line) Pompei Villa dei Misteri, in 35-50 min, service alternately at about half hour intervals; day return tickets valid by either route. The State Railway (FS) is more useful for visitors arriving from Salerno and the south.

Pompeii is one of the Campanian towns that were buried by the Vesuvian eruption of A.D. 79. Painstakingly brought back to light, it provides the foundation of our knowledge of the domestic life of the ancients. Here we see the greater part of a town as it was when disaster overtook it more than 1900 years ago, and in a setting sufficiently isolated from modern surroundings to preserve the illusion of antiquity. The contrasting beauties of white stone seen against a background of azure sky, and the ever-changing patterns made by sun and clouds on the slopes of the volcano, combine with the ruins' intrinsic interest to make this one of the most fascinating archaeological sites in the world.

Admission to the ruins. The excavations may be entered either on the south, by the *porta Marina*, or on the north, by the *porta Nolana*. They are open daily from 9 until one hour before sunset. The official custodians, stationed in different quarters of the town, open the closed houses on application and give all necessary information. They are not supposed to accept gratuities or accompany visitors.

At least four hours are necessary for an adequate visit.

Lunch may be obtained at the *Posto di Ristoro* (near the Forum). In hot weather the absence of shade is noticeable; flat shoes, preferably rope-soled, are the most comfortable for the uneven paved streets. Although much of the site was closed after the 1980 earthquake, the more frequently visited areas remain open. The other areas will be opened again as restoration work proceeds.

History. Although it is not known exactly when Pompeii was first settled, an Oscan village probably existed on the site as early as the eighth century B.C. (the name *Pompeii* is of Oscan derivation, it seems). There is no archaeological or documentary evidence to support this date, however, and the oldest building that can be identified and reconstructed from its ruins-the Doric Temple in the Triangular Forum-dates from the sixth century, when Pompeii was already a flourishing commercial center and one of the chief ports on the coast of Campania. Like the Greek coast-towns of Cumae and Neapolis-of which it was first a rival, then an ally-Pompeii fell under the domination of the Etruscans around 530 B.C. Certain aspects of the ruins, such as layout of the oldest section and the design of the sixth-century city wall, as well as some family names (the Cuspii, for instance) are thought to be of Etruscan origin.

This influence, however, must have been of short duration; for as we have seen the Greeks soon drove the Etruscans out of Campania.

Pompeii fell to the Samnites around 425 B.C., and remained under their dominion for more than two centuries. In 200 B.C. it became a subject ally of Rome, but with the outbreak of the Social War it joined the Italic League and was besieged in 89 B.C. After the war's end Pompeii sank back into the near anonymity of provincial life. As a token of Romanization it was now called *Colonia Cornelia Veneria Pompeiianorum*, after the clan name of its conqueror L. Cornelius Sulla and the Venus Pompeiiana, patron deity of the city. In A.D. 59, in consequence of a conflict in the Amphitheater between the Pompeians and the citizens of Nuceria, the gladiatorial spectacles were suspended for ten years. It was possibly in compensation for this that in A.D. 62 it was allowed to call itself *Colonia Neroniana*.

The following year Pompeii was devastated by an earthquake, an unwelcome token of the renewed activity of Mount Vesuvius. Heedless of this warning, however, the town continued to flourish, and even increased its wealth and influence. The final catastrophe took place on August 24, A.D. 79, when the famous eruption of Vesuvius overwhelmed Pompeii, Herculaneum, and Stabiae. Pompeii, like Stabiae, was covered with a layer of fragments of pumice-stone (lapilli), mostly very minute, and afterwards by a similar layer of ashes. The flow of lava stopped at the base of the mountain and did not reach the inhabited quarter. All who had not left the city in the first hours died from the accumulation of volcanic debris, the collapse of buildings, or in many cases, the poisonous vapors. It is estimated that of an approximate population of twenty thousand, two thousand, who were trapped in the city, or who for some reason chose to remain, perished. Among the victims of the catastrophe the most illustrious was Pliny the Elder, a distinguished naturalist and commander of the Roman fleet at Misenum. Warned by his sister of the appearance of an ominous cloud in the east and by a letter from Popilla Rectina, wife of the magistrate Cn. Pedius Cascus, he hurried to the help of the fugitives, but could not reach Pompeii on account of the huge mounds of lapilli. He therefore sailed to Stabiae, where he found his friend Pomponianus, but was here overtaken and suffocated by the stifling vapors. (The story of his heroic journey is preserved in two letters written by his nephew, Pliny the Younger, to the historian Tacitus some twenty years later; see p. 39).

When the fury of the volcanic conflagration was over, the site of Pompeii was a sea of ashes and lapilli, from which emerged the upper parts of the buildings that had not been totally destroyed. These, later, served as guide-posts to the inhabitants who returned to dig amid the ruins, and, still later, to the searchers for treasure and building material. By the third century a number of buildings had been erected at *Civita*, to the north of Pompeii. This second Pompeii was, however, abandoned in the eleventh century on account of the frequent earthquakes, the eruptions of Vesuvius, and the incursions of the Saracens. Between 1594 and 1600 Domenico Fontana, the Roman architect, in constructing an aqueduct from the sources of the Sarno River to Torre Annunziata, tunneled through the Pompeian mound and discovered some ruins and inscriptions. But it was not till 1748 that antiquarian excavations were begun and which, continued since with more or less activity, have laid bare the larger and more important half of Pompeii. In 1860 a regular plan of excavation was organized by the Italian Government; however, a chronic shortage of funds has made the task of unearthing and preserving the city a slow and arduous one. The site has now been systematically photo-graphed, and the first comprehensive catalogue of its artistic assets is in preparation. Despite these efforts to protect and preserve the city, however, the greatest threat to Pompeii remains that of the thievery and clandestine resale of artworks and artefacts, of which the most clamorous recent example, the removal of three marble and two bronze statues from the House of the Vetii, is only too typical.

The Ruins. The elliptical form of Pompeii reflects that of the prehistoric lava flow on which it is built, the southern fortifications following the natural bulwark made by the limit of the flow. The town is divided (though not very regularly) into a chessboard of streets, the main thoroughfares being the

via Stabiana, via di Nola, and *via dell'Abbondanza.*
Archaeologists have devised a street plan which divides the
town into nine Regions, with varying numbers of *Insulae,* or
blocks. These generally consist of a group of dwellings but may
be wholly occupied by one building. Thus the location of any
building may be designated by three figures-those of the
region, the insula, and its entrance-and is so indicated in the
account below.

The streets in Pompeii are paved with large blocks of
Vesuvian lava and bordered by kerbed foot-pavements. In
nearly all the roadways, at regular intervals, stepping-stones
have been provided for pedestrians. The streets are generally
well preserved, so much so that even the wheel-ruts of the
heavy vehicles that passed along them (Pompeian ladies and
gentlemen, when they did not want to walk, used litters;
wagons served almost exclusively for transporting goods) can
still be seen. A distinguished nineteenth century visitor, Mark
Twain, in *The Innocents Abroad* complains about "how ruts
five and even ten inches deep were worn into the thick
flagstones by the chariot-wheels of generations of swindled
taxpayers," concluding from these signs that "the street
commissioners never attended to their business."

Pompeian houses differ considerably from modern
dwellings. They rarely had windows or openings facing the

Via dell'Abbondanza. In this view of the main thoroughfare of Pompeii, the raised stepping-stones for pedestrians, and the public fountains that stood at all major crossroads, are prominent. Note also the deep wheel ruts worn in the roads.

street, but presented a nearly solid façade to the outside, while gathering light and air from interior courts. Upon entering the house and passing through a vestibule, the visitor arrives at a large, high room, called the *atrium*. This is surrounded by a roofed arcade, at the center of which is the *impluvium*, a basin receiving the rain-water from the inward-sloping roof and passing it on to a cistern beneath the floor. On the side opposite the entrance is the *tablinum*, or chief living room, where the family dined and received their guests. To the right and left are the bedrooms and other chambers used for various purposes. This, at least, was the early Italic plan, introduced by the Etruscans. Later, however, the chambers adjoining the main façade, and sometimes also those at the sides, were converted into shops, opening on the street. A *peristyle*, a colonnaded corridor passing around an inner court or garden open to the sky, was added to the earlier house, and the *tablinum* ceased to be the general living room. Its former place was taken by the *triclinium*, one of the rooms opening off the *peristyle*. A *lararium* or domestic sanctuary, often in the form of a small temple, stood in the *atrium*, in an adjoining chamber, or in the *peristyle*; sometimes, reduced to a mere painting, even in the kitchen. Nearly every house had a second floor and some had a third; these were narrower than the first floor and were usually occupied by slaves or tenants. The number of shops lent great animation to the main streets, and the lamps hung at the doors, together with those of the municipal altars at the street-corners, furnished the chief source of the town's lighting.

Among the more striking attractions of Pompeii are the frescoes painted on its stuccoed walls. These are disposed in three horizontal bands. The colors are very vivid, red and yellow predominating. The central field is occupied by small pictures, groups of flying figures, or isolated figures. Four manners or periods may be distinguished in Pompeian wall painting. In the first or Samnite Period the stucco ornamentation imitates the marble panelling of important Greek or Roman mansions; there are no human figures. In the second period (first century B.C.) the marble decoration is imitated in painting and figures are introduced in scenes depicting mythical, heroic, or religious subjects. In the third and best period (first half of the first century of the Roman Empire), the architectural framework takes on a distinctly decorative quality, and figures become more numerous. In the fourth period the figures are accompanied by bizarre architectural effects, the coloring is less delicate, and the ornamental details are coarser.

The entrance to the excavations for travelers arriving by road, or by railway from the Sorrento or Salerno lines, is the *porta Marina*, the gate toward the sea. Travelers arriving at the "Circumvesuviana" station at *Pompei Scavi* may join the itinerary described below by following the via di Nola straight to the Temple of Fortune and then turning to the left for the Forum, about half a mile. Arriving from *Pompei Santuario*, proceed past the Amphitheater to the via dell'Abbondanza, then turn left to the Forum.

The Antiquarium, adjoining the porta Marina, was designed to show the historical development of the city, but is now closed to the public (it is used as a restoration laboratory). We walk up the via Marina, which leads to the *Forum*. To the right can be seen the remains of the **Temple of Venus Pompeiana**, guardian deity of the town. This building had been partly destroyed by the earthquake of A.D. 63, and was being restored and enlarged when overtaken by the final catastrophe. Farther on, on the same side, is the *Basilica* (VIII, 1) or court of law, the most monumental of the city's public buildings. This probably dates from the second century B.C. It is divided into nave and aisles by twenty-eight Ionic columns of brick, covered with stucco. The Corinthian capitals in tufa, now leaning against the wall, adorned the upper story. At the end of the hall, badly damaged by the earthquake, was the raised tribunal for the judges.

Across the street from the Basilica stands the **Temple of Apollo** (VII, 7), built during the Samnite period on the site of a sixth century sacellum. The forty eight columns of the portico were originally Ionic, with a Doric entablature, but after the earthquake they were converted into Corinthian columns by means of stucco, while the entablature was embellished with animal forms. The stucco has now fallen off and the original design has come to light. The portico was formerly decorated with paintings of scenes from the *Iliad*. The large tripod, painted on the first pilaster of the east wing, is one of the tributes to Apollo. A travertine altar stood in the middle of the uncovered area, and the Ionic column to the left of the steps bore a sundial, emblematic of Apollo in his role of sun-god. The bases placed against the columns of the portico supported statues, now in the *Museo Archeologico Nazionale* in Naples. At the sides are two copies representing Apollo and Diana with bows and arrows. It is interesting to notice that the actual temple stands on a high podium, accessible by steps in front which lead to the Corinthian *pronaos*. This enclosed the *cella*, which contained the statue of Apollo and the conical *Omphalos*, the symbol of the god. The latter is still in its place. An Oscan inscription on the pavement of the cella records that it was laid at the instance of Oppius Campanius, a public official. Beside the rear door is the priest's chamber.

The **Forum** (VII, 8), the most perfect example known to us of a Roman central square, is so planned that Vesuvius dominates its major axis. This was the commercial and administrative center of the town, and the favorite meeting place of the Pompeians. Its great open space (462 ft long and

124 ft wide), paved with flags of limestone and adorned with statues of officials and other distinguished persons, was closed to vehicular traffic, and was reserved for stalls on market days, which as we know from an inscription fell on Saturday. Originally a colonnade ran round the east, south, and west sides, the north side being enclosed by the Temple of Jupiter. Above this colonnade was a gallery, reached by small staircases (traces of which remain) designed to accomodate spectators of the fêtes and games held in the Forum before the construction on the Amphitheater. The conversion of the colonnade from tufa to travertine, begun at a fairly late date, was interrupted by the earthquake. Many of the statue pedestals are extant, some with inscriptions. The larger base halfway down the west side is the orator's tribune.

On the west the Forum is adjoined by the Basilica and the Temple of Apollo, already described. We walk along the colonnade, to the north (left). In a niche at N° 31 is a travertine tablet showing the standard measures of capacity. Adjacent is the entrance to an inner court, and at N° 29 is a portico, possibly used as a vegetable market. N° 28 was a public latrine, and N° 27 the municipal treasury.

At the north end of the Forum stands the **Temple of Jupiter** (VII, 8) built in the Italic manner, with a wide *cella* and *pronaos* enclosed by Corinthian columns. Later, it became the *Capitolium* of the Roman town. The *pronaos* is reached by a flight of steps originally flanked by equestrian statues and

Pompeii, the Forum. In Roman towns, the forum was a large open space used as a market and a meeting-place. It was surrounded by the city's major civil and religious buildings. The forum of Pompeii was closed to vehicles, and it was lined on three sides by colonnades that formed covered walkways for the populace and porticoes for the buildings behind.

interrupted by a platform on which stood an altar. The *cella*, with its Ionic columns, had a marble pavement bordered by mosaics. Apertures in the flooring of the *pronaos* and *cella* admitted light to some lower chambers (such as the treasury), which communicated directly with the Forum. The podium against the back wall, reached by steps, is believed to have borne statues of Jupiter, Juno and Minerva. When, however, the temple was reduced to ruins by the earthquake the cult of these deities was carried on at the small temple of Zeus Meilichios.

To the right and left of the main steps were two triumphal arches. That on the right was demolished by the ancients to open up the view of the arch behind, which had an equestrian statue of Tiberius on its top and statues of Nero and Drusus in its niches.

Return by the east side of the Forum, which was built in the first century A.D. The **Macellum** or provision market, was preceded by a graceful colonnade with the shops of the *Argentari* or money-changers. The interior court was enclosed by another colonnade, destroyed by the earthquake. The walls were adorned with frescoes, the survivors of which include *Io Guarded by Argus* and *Ulysses and Penelope*. On the frieze are

The only building to intrude into the forum proper was the Temple of Jupiter at the north end, crowned in this view by Vesuvius, which has developed its distinctive double peaks since the days of Pompeii. On market days, which fell on Saturday, the great square was filled with stalls. The many empty plinths held commemorative statues now lost or removed for safekeeping to the National Museum of Naples.

fish, game, amphorae of wine, and the like. On the south are shops, with an upper story. In the open center of the court was a dome borne by twelve columns, of which the bases remain; it probably sheltered a tank or basin for fish. At the back is a chapel which contained statues of the imperial family. To the right and left of this are the shops of a fishmonger and of a butcher.

The **Sacrarium of the Lares** (N° 3) is preceded by a marble colonnade and was originally paved and lined with marble slabs. In the apse is a podium, which bore several statues. Round the walls are niches for eight other statues, probably representing the tutelary deities of the town.

The **Temple of Vespasian** (VII, 9; N° 2) was begun after A.D. 63 but was never completed. In front was a columned portico. In the middle of the open court is an altar, with bas-reliefs of the sacrifice of a bull, the sacrificial utensils, and a civic crown between two laurels (the symbol of the Imperial house).

The **Building of Eumachia** (N° 1) was erected by the priestess Eumachia, acting also for her son, M. Numistrius Fronto. It was occupied by the bleachers of linen, who probably used it as a sales room. In front is a vestibule with a portico of two rows of columns, at the ends of which are four niches for statues of Aeneas, Romulus, Julius Caesar, and Augustus. Round the other three sides runs a covered corridor. A marble doorway with splendid acanthus-leaf decoration gives access to an open court surrounded by a colonnade with two rows of columns superimposed on each other without the intervention of a second storey. At the back stood the Statue of Eumachia now in the *Museo Archeologico Nazionale* in Naples.

On the other side of the via dell'Abbondanza stands the *Comitium* or polling booth for the election of the civic magistrates. At the south end of the Forum are three large halls: the Chambers of the Duoviri, the principal municipal officers who exercised a mayoralty power; the Hall of the City Council; and the Office of the Aediles, who supervised public works, markets, streets, and civic services. All these officials were elected annually by vote of the qualified electors.

Now descend the *via dell'Abbondanza*, the name of which is due to a misinterpretation of the bust of *Concordia Augusta*, on a fountain at the back of the Eumachia Building. To the right a steep quarter spreads down the slope of the lava flow; this represents one of the last expansions of the Augustan age (27 B.C. - A.D. 14), when the now superfluous walls on this side were demolished to make way for terraced houses. At the end of the block is the **House of the Wild Boar** (VIII, 3; N° 8), named from the mosaic on the entrance floor. Farther on, at the corner of the via dei Teatri, stands the **House of Holconius Rufus** (VIII, 4; N° 4), one of the more prominent citizens of

Pompeii, honored by a statue at the neighboring crossroads. The rich decoration of his elegant dwelling is unfortunately much faded.

The via dei Teatri (right) leads to the **Triangular Forum.** This is reached by a fine Ionic portico (N° 30), giving access to two gates opening on the forum proper, which is surrounded by a Doric colonnade. Obliquely set within are the ruins of a Doric Temple of the sixth century B.C., 98 ft in length and 65 ft in width, with eleven columns on each side. The remains include the elevated *stylobate*, a few capitals, and fragments of the *cella* walls. The temple was apparently dedicated to Hercules. It seems to have been already a ruin in the second century B.C., and was used as a public dumping ground and as a quarry of building material. Toward the end of that century, however, this area appears to have been cleared for the erection of another sacred edifice dedicated to Athena.

Near the left rear of the temple was placed a semicircular seat, on the back of which was a sundial. Opposite the steps leading to the porch is a enclosure, perhaps a heroön to Hercules. To the left are three altars and (further back) a cistern, formerly covered with a cupola raised on eight Doric columns.

Adjoining the Triangular Forum, near the corner of the via del Tempio d'Iside, lay the **Samnite Palaestra** (N° 29), where the young men trained for the games. To the south of this is a

House of Holconius Rufus. The remains of this patrician house include the impluvium (or basin for collecting rain water), the walls of the triclinium (where the family dined and received guests), and two tall columns of the peristylium (or garden arcade).

large reservoir for the water used in the theater.

Pompeii has two theaters, the larger open to the sky, the smaller with a roof. The **Large or Uncovered Theater** (VIII), which could contain 5000 spectators, dates from the second century B.C. Built on the model of the Greek theaters and especially resembling that of Antioch, it was provided with large tanks or basins, installed in the orchestra and communicating with the reservoir mentioned above, thus making it at once a theater and a *nymphaeum*. The water below the stage is said to have acted as a sounding-box. The *Cavea*, or auditorium, is divided into three tiers: one, placed above a corridor and accessible by several staircases; another, with fifteen rows of seats arranged in five wedges, all also reached from the corridor; and the third, accessible from the orchestra only, consisting of four broad, low tiers with the chairs of the city councillors. Later seats for distinguished spectators were placed in the orchestra, too. The stone rings at the top of the wall were for the poles supporting the *Velarium*, or awning for protecting the audience from the sun. The whole of the upper part overlooking the *Foro Triangolare* is a modern restoration. Above the entrances to the orchestra are two small boxes, one of which was reserved for the President of the Spectacle, the other (perhaps) for the Priestesses. The stage, which had a wooden flooring, was reached from the orchestra by flights of steps. Between the stage and the orchestra was a narrow slit for the curtain. The *scena* or wall at the back of the stage represented the façade of a palace with three doors, the usual backdrop of an ancient theater.

The **Small or Covered Theater** (VIII), the roof of which was probably pyramidal, could hold an audience of 1000. It was constructed soon after 80 B.C. by the councilmen C. Quintius Valgus and M. Porcius (Roman public officials often financed public building projects out of the their own pockets with a view to winning votes), and was used, as an *Odeion*, for concerts. The *cavea* is traversed by one corridor. The lower part consists of four wide tiers, the upper of seventeen tiers arranged in five sections. The marble pavement was presented by the councilman M. Oculatius Verus. Behind was a vast, square piazza, surrounded by an arcade of seventy four columns, that served originally as a foyer to the theater. Later this was converted into gladiators barracks, with two rows of cells. A wooden gallery, part of which has been reconstructed, gave access to the upper cells. Here were found the fine weapons now in the *Museo Archeologico Nazionale* in Naples, as well as iron fetters and sixty-three skeletons. The *palaestra* of this building, the walks and colonnades of the Triangular Forum, and the *palaestra* mentioned on p. 19 collectively formed the gymnasium of the Samnite period.

From the Small Theater the via Stabiana leads left to the

Temple of Zeus Meilichios (Jupiter the Placable), on the corner at the end of the block. This is the smallest temple in Pompeii. The dedication indicates a Greek cult probably imported from Sicily. The temple had a four-columned vestibule, and a large altar in front of the steps. The *cella* had a small portico of two columns; at the back were found the terracotta statues of Jupiter, Juno, and Minerva, now in the Naples Museum.

Turn left, along the side-street, to reach the **Temple of Isis** (N° 28), almost entirely rebuilt, after the earthquake, by Numerius Popidius Celsinus. Agreeably to the mysterious character of the cult of Isis, this temple is somewhat curious in form, with its lateral entrance provided with a triple door. The sacred enclosure was surrounded by a colonnade, the front walk of which has its central intercolumniation, formed of two pilasters with half-columns, wider than the others. Opposite was a recess, the back of which bore a painted figure of Hippocrates (now in the Museo Archeologico Nazionale). In the open court is a small shrine, from which steps descend to a subterranean reservoir, intended for the lustral water. More steps ascend to the porch, the roof of which is borne by six Corinthian columns. To the right and left of the entrance to the *cella* are niches for statues, and in front of that to the left is an altar. At the back, to the left, is a small staircase by which the priests entered the *cella*. Underneath this temple runs Fontana's aqueduct.

Now return to the via Stabiana, in which, to the right (N° 5), is the large **House of the Lyre Player** (I, 4), or House of Popidius Secundus Augustianus, with two atriums and three peristyles. Here was found the statue of *Apollo* playing the lyre now at the Museum of Naples.

On reaching the intersection of the via Stabiana with the via dell'Abbondanza (once adorned with a statue of Holconius Rufus; see above), turn to the right. N° 20 (left) is the **House of Cuspius Pansa**, and N° 22 that of **Epidius Sabinus** (IX, 1).

At this point begin the **New Excavations**, first undertaken in 1911. They stretch east for some 500 yards, to the porta di Sarno or porta Urbulana, and comprise some of the most sriking remains in the town.

The original aim of these excavations was to trace the general line of the thoroughfare and to restore to their proper places the roofs, balconies, windows, stalls, doors, and the like which formed the street-front. On the north side little further has been done and though the façade is complete for much of the distance, we cannot penetrate far into any building. To the south, however, every block has now been excavated back to the next parallel street. The characteristic feature of the new excavations is that the fittings and articles of domestic use, frescoes, mosaics, statues, and stucco ornamentation have all been restored; some of the gardens have been replanted in accordance with what is known of classical horticulture; water plays once more in the private and public fountains, some of the latter having several jets. Mural inscriptions, including unauthorized scrawls relating to the games or elections, are seen in full force. Here we come nearest to capturing the atmosphere of everyday urban life in the Roman era.

Note that excavations since 1951 have served to modify the old conception of the Regions, with some consequent renumbering of insulae; current excavations are opening up much of the area at the east end of the via dell'Abbondanza, which should be accessible to visitors by 1985.

The **House of Popidius Montanus** (N° 9) was a great resort of chess-players, who were responsible for the motive to the left of the portal. The door, studded with large-headed bronze nails, was wide open at the moment of the catastrophe (plaster cast). Note also the cast of the closed door of N° 10 (left). N° 7-5, in front of which was a projecting penthouse, show the façade of the **Workshops of Veredundus**, maker of cloth, woolen garments, and articles in felt. The entrance on N° 7 is flanked by four paintings. Two of these show the patron deities of the work-rooms, namely, Venus Pompeiana, in a chariot drawn by elephants, and Mercury; the others represent the factory in full activity (right) and the sales room for its products (left). The plaster cast of the door shows the iron mechanism for fastening it. At N° 2, also with a penthouse, and surmounted by a pillared loggia, are the **Workshops of the Dyers**. To the right of the threshold is one of the vats used in dyeing, projecting from a furnace bearing phallic emblems. N° 1, above which is a large balcony used as a drying-room, was also (as a notice tells us) occupied by felt-makers. The painted frieze shows busts of Apollo, Mercury, Jupiter, and Diana, and the processional figure of Venus Pompeiana which was carried through the town.

The greater part of Insula 6, on the south, belonged to one owner who lived at N° 11 and converted the neighboring houses (N° 8-9) into domestic quarters. The fragments of a marble table, bearing the inscription P. Casca Longus, probably belonged to the fat conspirator who dealt the first blow at Julius Caesar, and may have been acquired at auction after his banishment.

N° 7, known as the **Fullonica Stephani** (I, 6), was a laun-dromat. The double door was closed at the time of the eruption, but the small hatch in the right wing had been left open, as is shown by the position in which its fastenings were discovered. Through this hatch were handed in the cloth and garments to be washed (in the *impluvium* or in the three tanks at the back), to be bleached (by sulphur vapor), to be dried (on the wide terraces of the first floor), or to be pressed (in the clothes-press by the wall to the left, on entering).

The house at N° 4 was being redecorated during the last days of Pompeii. This is proved by the heaps of material for making stucco in the *peristyle* and the *triclinium*, by the plinths still waiting for their roughcasting, by the state of the rooms adjoining the entrance, and by the one completed frieze, in the chamber at the southeast corner of the atrium. The decorations of the cabinet (perhaps a *lararium*) to the right of the *tablinum* are amazingly fine. The small vaulted roof, reconstructed of hundreds of minute fragments, is adorned with scenes from the last books of the *Iliad*, executed in a band of white stucco against a blue background. At the top: Hector, driven by a Fury, resists the appeal of his parents at the Scaean Gate of Troy; Hector's combat with Achilles; Hector's corpse dragged at the chariot-wheels of Achilles. At the sides: Priam loading his treasures on the car and setting out, under the guidance of Hermes, to offer them to Achilles as a ransom for the body of Hector. On the south are a large hall and a bedroom with the red coloring of the second style. The hall has a magnificent mosaic floor, and its walls show traces of extensive frescoes.

N° 3 is the **Shop of Verus the Blacksmith** , who dealt in bronze ware. The lamp and other objects on view here are just a small part of those that were found. Among the technical instruments were the valuable fragments in bronze and iron, probably brought for repair, which enabled a reconstruction to be made of the theodolite of a Roman surveyor.

By passing through House N° 2 we reach the **Underground Portico**, with its semicircular vaulting and elaborate decoration in white stucco. The walls, in the second style, are divided into vertical sections by female and phallic hermae. The frieze showed upward of fifty pictures of scenes in the Trojan War, taken from the *Iliad* and other poems. Only about twenty of these have been preserved. At some point the underground portico had been degraded to the status of a wine-vault. The existing chamber is just a fragment of the whole, the rest having been filled up to enlarge the garden. In a glass case are shown plaster casts of the impressions made by the bodies of several occupants of this house. During the eruption they took refuge under the portico, but when the rain of lapilli ceased they climbed up to the garden with the aid of a ladder. Here, however, the showers of ashes overtook them, and they were all suffocated in one huddled group. Adjoining the east wing are some well-preserved rooms, including a striking *triclinium*, the vaulting of which, with fine white stucco-work, rested on painted caryatids. In the frieze are remains of paintings in which heroic or mythical scenes alternate with banquets.

The door at the southwest corner of the Underground Portico opens on a little street containing the **House of L. Ceius Secundus** (N° 15), notable for its beautiful façade with white rustication, protected by the original overhanging roof. In the vestibule are a plaster model of the door and a ceiling reconstructed from fragments: the *atrium*, admirably preserved, contains a plaster cast of a wooden cupboard. Beyond it is a false *peristyle*, the walls of which are adorned with hunting scenes and Nile landscapes.

Across the little street is the **House of the Menander** (I, 10: N° 4), a fine dwelling belonging to a kinsman of the Empress Poppaea, where the silver plate now in the Naples Museum was found. At the time of the catastrophe the house was being redecorated. At the onset of the eruption the family and their the slaves took refuge in the room with the strongest roof, in which they were trapped by the fall of part of the *peristyle* and eventually killed when the roof collapsed about their heads. The beautifully appointed *atrium* contains a *lararium* in the form of a tiny temple. In an *exedra* to the left, three Trojan scenes. The peristyle has stuccoed columns, and in the center of the mosaic floor a panel depicting a Nile scene. On the north side are two elegantly decorated rooms for the reception of guests. A series of other guest rooms contain a rich selection of paintings, including the seated figure of the poet Menander, from which the house takes its name. The warm room of the private bath is well preserved.

N° 11 on the southwest corner of the block is the **House of the Lovers**, a charming little house with a splendid inscription beneath the portico; "lovers, like bees, desire a honeyed life."

Return by the side lane between Insulae 6 and 7 to the crossing, and continue along the via dell'Abbondanza. On the north side (IX, 10), N° 2 is a **Tavern** that served hot and cold drinks on the ground floor, while on the floor above the wares included the favors of such complaisant young women as Asellina, Smyrna, Maria, and Aegle. The objects found, including a phallic lamp, have been placed in their proper positions in the interior. The sign, to the right of N° 4, represents large wine-jars, goblets, and a wine-funnel. In contrast the opposite side of the street (I, 7) consists of a series of residences of middle-class respectability. N° 1 is the imposing **House of P. Paquius Proculus**, with rich mosaics in its vestibule, *atrium*, *tablinum*, and a room adjoining the *peristyle*. The restoration of the first floor, behind the *tablinum*, is noteworthy. A room on the north side of the *peristyle* contains the skeletons of seven children caught together at the catastrophe. Beyond the modest but tasteful **House of Fabius Amandio** (N° 2-3), is the **House of the Priest Amandus** (N° 7), where the *triclinium* is decorated in the third style, the panels show Polyphemus with the ship of Ulysses and Galatea riding a dolphin, Perseus and Andromeda, Hercules in the garden of the Hesperides, and the Fall of Icarus. The charming garden was shaded by a tree, the stump of which remains.

Entered from the side lane is the **House of the Ephebus** (N° 10-12) where the rich decoration added to an agglomeration of modest dwellings indicate the rise to wealth of its owner, the shop-keeper L. Cornelius Teges. Here was found the *ephebus* now in the Naples Museum. Opposite (I, 8; N° 19) is a **Dyeworks** with four boilers, washing vats, and pressing-tables.

On the corner of the main street is the **Shop of Felix the Fruiterer** (Pomarius; I, 8, N° 1). The sales room, in which the fruit was exhibited on wooden shelves, is adorned with Bacchic motives. Opposite, on the north side, are weavers, workshops, with a high columned upper story. N° 6, the **Workshop of Crescens**, has a painted figure of Hermes-Priapus to the right of the entrance. We continue on the north side to the next block (IX, 13). The plain façade of the **House of C. Julius Polybius** (N° 1-3) has carved lintels over the side doors. Adjoining the entrance of N° 5 are paintings of Aeneas, Anchises, and Ascanius (r.) and of Romulus with the spoils of King Acron (1.).

On the opposite side of the street excavations behind the frontage were resumed in 1951, revealing (I, 9) three interesting dwellings. The **House of the Beautiful Impluvium** (entered from N° 2) has well-preserved decoration in the *atrium* and *tablinum*. In the **House of Successus** (N° 3) the painting of the boy being chased by a duck and the statue of the boy bearing a dove probably portray a favorite child of the house. We enter the **House of the Fruit Orchard** (N° 5) through the adjacent shop, as a plaster model of the original door closes the main portal. The walls of two bedrooms are finely painted in the third style with pictures of fruit trees, including the then rare lemon. In the alley beyond is the public altar of the serpent Agathodoemon.

We pass a tavern of the next block and, at the crossroads, we return to the north side.

The **House of C. Trebius Valens** (III, 2; N° 1) has no shops on its front. Among the interesting features of this large house are the black-walled room at the southeast corner of the *atrium*; a bedroom, in the second style, to the left of the *atrium*; the *tablinum*, with its fine frieze (north wall) and its reconstructed east wall; the bathroom behind the kitchen, to the right of the *tablinum*; and the reconstruction of the east door in the portico. The garden has been replanted, and the twelve jets of the fountain again spout. At the end of the garden is a summer *triclinium*. The skeletons of the occupants were found under the portico (reconstructed).

On the same side, at N° 5 of insula 3, many carbonized fragments of mats are preserved. The **Schola Armaturarum** (N° 6) was probably the headquarters of a military organization, and the decorations of the building all refer to its function. On the exterior are two trophies of arms. On the doorjambs are two palm-trees, the leaves of which were the

Paestum, Archaeological Excavations. The temple of Neptune, built in the fifth century B.C., is one of the best-preserved Greek temples in Europe. It is admired for its intrinsic beauty as well as for the magnificence of its settiing.

House of the Faun. This house, belonging to the prominent Casti family, occupies a whole city block. Its popular name comes from the celebrated bronze statuette of the Dancing Faun, found near the impluvium (now at Naples). There are two atria and two peristyles, the first (5) with a fine mosaic pavement, the second (6) in the form of a large garden .

Amphitheater. The amphitheater of Pompeii stands in a beautiful position at the eastern end of town, adjoining the palaestra and oriented in such a way that Vesuvius dominates its major axis. Begun ca. 80 B.C., is the most ancient structure of its kind known to us. It held 12,000 spectator, in three tiers of seats, the uppermost being reserved for women and children.

This bird's-eye view gives an idea of Pompeii's beautiful setting, and of the city's distance from Vesuvius, the peaks of which are lost in the clouds in the background. At the bottom of the picture is the marble bar of a tavern.

Street in Herculaneum. More of the upper stories of buildings survive in Herculaneum than in Pompeii, partly because official excavators have been more careful here than were the early excavators of Pompeii. This is a view of Cardo IV, looking toward the sea. The house in the right foreground, presents a unique example of the wood and plaster construction called opus craticium, used for plebeian dwellings.

Herculanean Baths. The baths of Herculaneum were erected early in the reign of Augustus on a plan similar to that used at Pompeii and decorated somewhat later. They survive almost as they were planned. Here we are in the women's dressing room, whose mosaic shows a Triton surrounded by dolphins and cuttle-fish. Clothes were deposited in the bins around the walls.

Samnite House. The main features of the Herculanean (and Pompeian) house was the atrium, or interior court, surrounded by a roofed arcade. Here the traditional atrium designs has been modified for the addition of a blind gallery of graceful proportions. The impluvium, at the center of the floor in the foreground, collected rain-water from the roof and conveyed it to a cistern.

Baia, Archaeological Excavations. Baia was the fashionable bathing resort for the Roman aristocracy. The extensive ruins unearthed on this site, including the baths shown here, comprise an imperial palace built beetween the first and the fourth century A.D.

Pompeii, Via dell'Abbondanza.

Cumae, Cave of the Cumaean Sybil. Here Aeneas came to consult the sibyl (Aeneid, VI, 42-51), or prophetess, who met here visitors in the dark chamber situated at the end of this corridor. The famous sanctuary remained buried for centuries beneath the acropolis of the ancient city. It was brought to light in 1932.

reward of victory in the gymnasium. Inside are the Ten Female Genii, each holding a buckler and some kind of weapon. By the west wall is a plaster model of one of the cupboards which contained the gymnastic apparatus and fencing gear. The modern fastening was made from a cast of the ancient one.

Here cross the narrow via Nuceria, which enters the city by the porta Nuceria (see below). In this street to the left is the entrance (right) to the small but charming **House of Pinarius Cerialis**, identified from 114 gems found here (some uncut) as that of a lapidary. The fine decorations of a little room on the north side depict a theatrical representation of Iphigeneia in Tauris. On the corner is the **Tavern of Zosimus** ; the rest of the block, known as the **House of the Moralist**, consists of two intercommunicating houses belonging to the related families of T. Arrius Polites and M. Epidius Hymenaeus. In N° 2 two ceilings have been reconstructed: a coffered black ceiling in the triclinium, a yellow one in a bedroom. The garden has been replanted. A wooden staircase {reconstruction) ascends to the rooms on the upper floor, the details of which have been reproduced as far as possible. The remains of the ornament-ation have been affixed to the walls and ceilings. A small porch, giving on the inside garden, is almost intact. At the southeast corner is a perfectly preserved windowledge. From the foot of the staircase, pass (without returning to the street) into N° 3, skirting a black-walled room with flying female figures (left) and a small garden court (right). Below the porch already noted, in immediate contact with the garden, is a summer triclinium in masonry, with the usual table in the middle. On the three black walls were painted, in white, three maxims for polite conduct at table. Today two of these remain; the third was destroyed in the Second World War.

At the south corner of the crossroads is the **Hermes Tavern** with the customary bar-room and a first-floor balcony (reconstructed). To the left is a private cistern, the only one yet discovered. It retains the leaden tank from which pipes con-veyed the water to the neighbor-members of the Consortium, or fellowship. On the walls of the next alley to the north are inscriptions in large white letters, almost literally fulminating against committers of nuisance, by invoking the thunderbolts of Jove against offenders.

On the right (II, 2; N° 5), between two taverns, is the **House of Loreius Tibertinus**, one of those that give a perfect idea of patrician Pompeian life. A special charm is lent by the beautiful garden, now flourishing again after a rest of nearly 2000 years. A wide doorway, closed by a door of bronze and flanked by benches, opens into the atrium where the water-jet of the impluvium plays again. A bedroom in the east wing contains a Rape of Europa and a charming Medallion of a Girl. To the left is a room with two rows of paintings. The first, on a black ground, presents a summary of the *Iliad* in a series of 12 pictures. The other shows the Labors of Hercules, taken from a Hercules cycle. The peristyle is bordered on the garden-side by the north arm of a *euripus,* a series of communicating basins. At the east end is a cascade where the water gushes out between paintings of Narcissus and of Pyramus and Thisbe. Below is a dining room, the table of which seems to rise from the water. On the right arm of the couch is the signature of the artist Lucius who executed the adjoining paintings. When the north arm of the euripus was full, it overflowed through conduits, passing under the little temple in the middle, into another branch, traversing the garden from north to south. Beneath the temple are ornamental carvings from which issued the water for a second cascade. In the large garden numerous plaster casts have been taken of roots of ornamental plants, shrubs, and trees. The euripus makes its final exit near the back door of the house, in the south alley.

The small house at N° 4 has over its entrance a painted stucco relief of the imperial emblem-a civic crown between two laurels.

The **House of the Marine Venus** (II, 3; N° 3) was damaged by a bomb in 1943 and not completely excavated until 1952, when the great painting of Venus was brought to light. The stuccoed decoration of the portico round the garden was completed just before the eruption. The whole of the next block is occupied by the **Villa of Julia Felix** (II, 4) and its magnificent garden. The villa seems to have been a luxury hotel. It has three sections: the residential quarter of the proprietess; a bath for public use; and an inn, a shop, and a series of rooms, some with independent street doors. The fine private rooms have big square windows overlooking the garden, but they lost their decoration in the eighteenth century, when the villa was first excavated; that of one room (Apollo and the Muses) is now in the Louvre. The portico has slender rectangular marble columns with delicate capitals; the tiled roof is a copy of the antique. Below in the couches of the triclinium look out across the marble fish-ponds in the middle of the garden to the rustic stucco colonnade opposite. The baths are the most complete and perfect in Pompeii; their charming vestibule communicates by a hatch with the adjacent inn. The rented apartments, one still displaying its "to let" notice, were on two floors.

Behind the villa rises the **Amphitheater** (I, 6), the most ancient structure of its kind known to us. Begun about 80 B.C. through the munificence of the city councilmen C. Quintius Valgus and M. Porcius, it was not completed until the time of Augustus. The inscriptions beneath the north entrance probably refer to restorations undertaken by C. Cuspius Pansa after the period of disuse that followed the fatal brawl of A.D. 59 and the earthquake. The axes of the amphitheater measure 438 x

348 ft, and it held 12,000 spectators. The cavea was divided into three tiers, containing five, twelve, and eighteen rows of seats. A space on the east side, as wide as two rows, was reserved for the President of the Games. In construction it differs from later amphitheaters in that the gallery from which the first and second tiers are reached is constructed in four unconnected sections, while the upper gallery, reserved for women and children, is entered from a corridor reached only by an external staircase. There are no subterranean chambers beneath the arena.

To the west lies the **Great Palaestra**, a space of about 1600 ft, once shaded by great plane-trees; surrounded by a portico in the center is a large swimming pool. Here, after the Samnite palaestra had proved inadequate, the youth of the city exercised themselves and held their gymnastic competitions. In the latrine at the southeast corner were found many skeletons of youths who fled in vain to its shelter.

From the west side we may pass between Insulae 8 and 9 and, by turning left, descend to the **Nucerian Gate**. Outside the gate modern excavations, removing an enormous quantity of earth, have exposed a street (Via Nuceria) running east-west and flanked by sumptuous tombs that date mainly from the second half of the first century B.C. Particularly worthy of note are (right) the painted announcements of games at neighboring cities (Nuceria, Herculaneum, etc), tombs with portrait statues and busts, and the **Sepulchre of Eumachia**, the builder of the cloth-market in the Forum.

Now return along the via dell'Abbondanza to its intersection with the via di Stabia. To the right lie the **Stabian Baths** (VII, 1), the largest in Pompeii. They date originally from the Samnite era, but were enlarged soon after the establishment of the Roman colony and again under the Empire. We first enter the *palaestra*, enclosed by a portico, some of the beautiful decorations of which are seen to the left. Along this stretch the bowling alley and the swimming pool, with its appurtenances. Opposite are another bowling alley, a latrine, and some private baths. To the right are the Men's Baths. These include the dressing room, two chambers with marble floors, stuccoed vault, and recesses for the clothes; the circular cold bath; the tepid room, with a plunge-bath; and (at the back) the warm room, whith a plunge-bath and a basin for washing. Hot air circulated below the rooms containing the tepid and warm baths. Adjacent are the Women's Baths. From a corridor enter the dressing room, with two entrances from the street and the usual recesses. Beyond the cold and tepid rooms is the warm room, with hollow walls and flooring for the passage of the hot vapor. Between the tepid and warm rooms was the heating apparatus, of which the furnace and the position of three cylindrical boilers are recognizable.

Beyond, to the right, diverges the vico del Lupanare, in which (right) stands the **House of Siricus** (N° 47; VII, 1; closed) composed of two communicating apartments. On the threshold is the inscription *Salve lucru (m)*, a candid salute to lucre. The handsome *triclinium* contains paintings of Neptune and Apollo helping to build the walls of Troy; Hercules and Omphale; and Thetis with Vulcan. Opposite the entrance is a painting of two large serpents, with a poorly preserved nscription which, roughly translated, means "loitering forbidden."

Farther on, to the left, is the **Lupanar Africani et Victoris**, the obscene paintings and inscriptions on the ground floor of which place its character beyond a doubt. The first floor has a balcony (restored). Opposite is the **Inn of Sittius**, the sign of which was an elephant.

The vico del Lupanare ends at the via degli Augustali, where, almost opposite, is the **House of the Bear** (VII, 2), so called from the mosaic at the entrance. To the right is a **Shoemaker's Shop**. Keeping to the right, we regain the via Stabiana, which we follow to the left.

To the right (N° 12) is a restored **Mill.** N° 5, on the same side, is the **House of Marcus Luretius** (IX, 3), priest of Mars and decurion of Pompeii, once one of the more luxuriantly decorated houses in the city. In the atrium, to the right, is a small shrine dedicated to the two tutelars of the house. Opposite is the tablinum. At the back is a pretty little garden, with a fountain and some marble figures amid its flowers. The best of the well-preserved paintings, in the fourth style, are now at Naples.

The whole of the next block on the right is occupied by the **Central Baths** (IX, 4), built between the earthquake and the eruption, with the usual features on a more sumptuous scale and, in addition, a hot-air chamber of circular shape with domed vaulting. The building was unfinished at the time of its destruction.

Leaving the Baths by the north side we find ourselves in the via di Nola. On the right side of the lane opposite is a **Tavern** in which were discovered three large bronze trumpets, apparently deposited here by the gladiators of the Amphitheater fleeing from the shower of lapilli. Farther on, to the right, is the entrance to the **House of the Silver Anniversary** (V, 2), so called because the excavations were made in the presence of King Humbert and Queen Margherita in 1893, the year of their silver wedding anniversary. This is a real Pompeian palace, with a spacious atrium. The front colonnade of the well-preserved *peristyle* is higher than the others. The *triclinium* is a large and handsome room. The bedrooms on the south side have well-preserved decoration in the third style, and their private baths have been wonderfully restored. The garden, with its stonework *triclinium*, is noteworthy.

Returning to the via di Nola and following it to the left, we soon reach (right; N° 3) the large and magnificent **House of the Centenary** (IX, 6), so named because excavated in 1879, the 1800th anniversary of the eruption. It has two atriums (that on the left handsomely decorated) and a spacious *peristyle*. A graceful fountain plays in a small court, now covered in and adorned with paintings of gardens, a fish pond, and hunting scenes. To the west are the bathrooms and two chambers adorned with paintings. From one opens a secret chamber with obscene decoration. Of interest also are the decorations of two rooms entered from the front walk of the colonnade, one with white walls, the other with black.

Off the alley opposite stands the House of Marcus Lucretius Fronto (V, 4), which dates from the early Imperial period. The roof of the atrium is a modern restoration. Among the notable paintings in this house are Neoptolemus Slain by Orestes (first room on the right), Theseus and Ariadne, the Toilet of Venus (second room on the right), the Wedding of Mars and Venus, the Triumph of Bacchus, landscapes (in the tablinum), Pyramus and Thisbe, and Bacchus and Silenus (first garden room to the right).

Farther on in the via di Nola, to the left, is the **House of the Gladiators**, with a four-sided portico. The **Nola Gate**, at the end of the street, dates from the Samnite era. It is decorated, on the side facing the city, with the head of Minerva.

Return to the via Stabiana, and turn to the right. At the corner on the left are a fountain, an altar to the lares of the crossroads, and a pillar of an acqueduct. N° 20 (left) is the **House of M. Vesonius Primus** (VI, 14), known as the **House of Orpheus** from the large painting in the peristyle. In the atrium is a portrait-herm of Vesonius. N° 22 is Vesonius's **Laundromat**. The *impluvium* contains a marble table and a fountain, and there are three tanks behind the atrium. Opposite (N° 26) stands the **House of L. Coecilus Jucundus** (V, 1), the banker, where the famous receipts now in the Museum of Naples were discovered. In the atrium is a portrait-herm of the master of the house, a copy of the original in Naples; also two bas-reliefs representing respectively the north side of the Forum and the overthrow of the Vesuvius Gate by the e arthquake of A.D. 63. The *tablinum* has good decorations.

The sign of the **Taberna Lusoria** (N° 28), a vase between two phalli, indicates its business, a gambling house below with rooms for hire above. Beyond the next crossroads we have on our left (N° 7) the **House of the Gilded Cupids** (VI, 16), which belonged to Nero's in-laws, the Poppaei, and which demonstrates the refined tastes of its age. The portico has been restored to its old lines. The marble sculptures in the garden remain as they were. The marble bas-reliefs in the south wing of the colonnade represent Satyrs, Maenads, and so forth.

At the southeast corner of the *peristyle* is a shrine devoted to the cult of Egyptian deities. The *lararium* in the north colonnade has the conventional form of a small temple. The mosaic on the floor of the interesting bedroom to the right indicates the place occupied by the beds. On the walls, under antique glass, are the flying and gilded Cupids that give the house its name. In the east colonnade is a large room with paintings of Thetis and Vulcan, Jason and Pelias, Achilles in his tent with Patroclus and Briseis. The stucco ceilings of two bedrooms in the west colonnade are unusually fine.

The street ends at the **Vesuvius Gate**, adjoining which is a conduit-head where water entering from an aqueduct was distributed to three channels. Outside the gate, beneath cypresses, is the **Tomb of the Aedile Vestorius Priscus**, with scenes from his life painted on the inner walls.

Return by the vicolo dei Vetii. N° 1 is the **House of the Vettii** (VI, 15), belonging to Aulus Vettius Restitutus and Aulus Vettius Conviva, two wealthy merchants of the Roman colony. Its beautiful paintings (still in their original positions) and the skillful reconstruction of its apartments make it one of the more interesting houses to visit in the whole town. To the right of the entrance, under lock and key, is a characteristically obscene image of Priapus. The *atrium* has delightful paintings of cupids and putti. To the right and left are strong-rooms. On the right is the doorman's room. In the corresponding little room to the left are paintings of Ariadne deserted, Hero and Leander and a Fish Pond. The larger room to the left of the entrance has pictures of Cyparissus, Amor and Pan wrestling for the entertainment of Bacchus, and Ariadne, Leda and the Swan, and Jupiter enthroned. Opening off the *atrium* are two bedrooms and other rooms, in one of which (left) is a clever little picture of a cock fight. To the right of the main *atrium* is a small rustic *atrium* (with a *lararium*), from which we pass into the kitchen, with its fire-grate and boilers. Adjoining is a closed room with equivocal pictures and a statuette of Priapus. The *peristyle* offers an enchanting spectacle. Against the columns surrounding it are statuettes, from which jets of water spouted into marble basins. Two other jets rise in the middle of the gaily colored garden. In the east colonnade are two handsome rooms. In one of them are paintings of the Infant Hercules and the Serpents, Pentheus torn limb from limb by the Bacchantes, and Dirce and the Bull; in the other, Daedalus showing Pasiphaë the wooden bull, Ixion on the wheel, Bacchus and the sleeping Ariadne, and beautiful arabesques. In the north colonnade is a separate group of *triclinium*, bedroom, and small garden. The *triclinium* is the exquisite Painted Room, probably used for banquets on special occasions. On a black band round the room are charming little cupids at work and play (right to left): hurling at a target, weaving and selling wreathes, distilling perfume, driving a biga, forging metal, bleaching cloth, celebrating the Vestalia, harvesting grapes, worshipping Bacchus, and selling wine. On the black panels below are winged nymphs gathering flowers; Agamemnon forcing his way into the temple of Artemis to slay the sacred hind; Apollo as conqueror of the Python; Orestes and Pylades with Thoas and Iphigeneia. Below, Amazons and women with sacrificial vessels, and a Bacchante and Satyr. On the large red panels, separated by candelabra-pilasters corresponding to the small black panels, are flying groups of Perseus and Andromeda, Dionysis and Ariadne, Apollo and Daphne, and Poseidon and Amymone. On the doorjambs, Hermaphroditus and Silenus.

Follow the vicolo di Mercurio to the right; at the corner on the left are the pillar of an aqueduct and some lead pipes. N° 10 (right) is the **House of the Labyrinth** (VIII, 11), dating from the Samnite era and taking its name from a mosaic of Theseus and the Minotaur. Turn south by the via del Fauno to reach the via della Fortuna. Here, to the right (N° 2-5), is the entrance to the famous **House of the faun** (VI, 12). This house, belonging to the Cassii, is 260 ft long and 114 ft wide, occupying a whole block. Its popular name comes from the celebrated bronze statuette of the Dancing Faun, found near the *impluvium* (now in Naples, and replaced here by a copy). On the pavement in

House of the Faun. This house, belonging to the prominent Casti family occupies a whole city block. Its popular name comes from the celebrated bronze statuette of the dancing Faun, found near the impluvium (now at Naples). There are two atria and two peristyles, the first with a fine mosaic pavement, the second in the form of a large garden.

39

front of the house is the salutation *Have* (welcome). There are two *atriums* and two *peristyles*. The beautiful stucco decoration need not fear comparison with marble. The fine pavement of the first peristyle has, unfortunately, been much injured. The mosaic pavements of the four *tricliniums* (one for each season of the year) are now at Naples. The twenty eight Ionic columns of the peristyle are coated with stucco. The well-known mosaic of the Battle of Alexander was found in the red-columned room. The second peristyle is in the form of a large garden, with a Doric portico.

Continue to follow the via della Fortuna. To the left, at its intersection with the strada del Foro and the via di Mercurio, stands the **Temple of Fortune** (VII, 4), constructed in 3 B.C. by M. Tullius, and restored after the earthquake. The Corinthian *pronaos* has two columns on each side. An architrave in the *cella* bears the name of the founder. At the north (right) corner is a Triumphal Arch, also used as a reservoir. It bore an equestrian statue of Caligula. Refreshments are sold in the adjoining building.

Beyond the crossroads, to the left (N° 2), are the **Baths of the Forum** (VII, 5), built by the city councilman L. Cesius and the Aediles C. Occius and L. Niremius. The general arrangement resembles that of the Stabian Baths. The shelves for clothes in the dressing room are decorated with a frieze of *telamones*. The large bronze brazier in the tepid room and also the benches were presented by M. Nigidius Vaccula. The marble basin in the warm room was placed here in 3 or 4 A.D. and cost (according to the inscription) 5250 esterces. Within are plaster casts of victims of the eruption, in glass cases.

N° 5, opposite the Baths, is the **House of the Tragic Poet** (VI, 8), adopted by Bulwer Lytton, in his *Last Days of Pompeii*, as the dwelling of Glaucus. Among the valuable mosaics found here was one of a theatrical rehearsal, now in Naples. On the threshold is a mosaic dog, with the inscription "beware of dog." Beyond the *peristyle* is the household sanctuary. In the *triclinium* are paintings of a youth and maiden looking at a nest of cupids, Marsyas teaching Olympus the flute, Theseus and Ariadne, Dido and Aeneas, and personifications of the seasons. Another picture found here was the Sacrifice of Iphigeneia.

A little farther on, to the right, is the large **House of Pansa** (VI, 6), notable for the regularity of its construction. Along the entrance wall and the wall to the left were rows of shops, the rooms on the right side were rented.

We next follow the vicolo di Modesto to the right and, taking the first turning on the left, find ourselves opposite the misnamed **House of Sallust** (VI, 1; N° 4), more properly known as the House of A. Casius Libanus, a fine mansion of the Samnite period damaged by a bomb in World War II, when its well-known picture of Diana and Actaeon was destroyed. A partial restoration was paid for by American funds. Following the via Consolare, which bears to the left, we pass a storehouse for salt (N° 13; right) and the **House of the Surgeon**, a massive structure of Sarno stone, notable as a unique example of an Etruscan dwelling. Several surgical instruments, now at the *Museo Archeologico Nazionale* in Naples, were found here.

The **Herculaneum Gate**, at the end of the via Consolare, dating from the close of the second century B.C., is the most recent and most important gate of the town. In antiquity, it seems to have been called porta Salina or Salinienis. Of its three archways that in the center, for vehicles, was vaulted at the ends only; the lateral openings for pedestrians were vaulted throughout.

Outside the gate runs the via delle Tombe, or street of Tombs, which leads down a gently sloping hill to the two suburban villas. The famous **Villa of Diomedes** is so called on the slender ground that the burial place of M. Arrius Diomedes is on the opposite side of the road. The villa had the largest garden in Pompeii, with a colonnade containing various chambers. In the middle are a fountain and an arbor borne by six columns.

The main entrance was on the west side. In a vaulted cellar extending below three sides of the garden-colonnade were found amphoras of wine and eighteen skeletons of adults and children who had vainly taken refuge in it. The owner of the villa, probably a wine merchant, was found near the garden door, with the key in his hand; beside him was a slave with money and valuables. A small staircase with two columns formed the main entrance from the via delle Tombe and led directly to the *peristyle*. To the left are the private baths and a wide gallery giving access to the *tablinum*.

About 200 yards to the west of the Villa of Diomedes stands the **Villa of the Mysteries**, a complex dwelling that started in the third century B.C. as a town house, developed into a manor, and declined into a farmhouse. It takes its name from a hall with twenty-four life-size painted figures, thought to have been executed by a Campanian painter of the first century B.C., on a background in the second style.

The paintings form a cycle, the meaning of which, although still under discussion, is probably connected with the rite of initiation into the Dionysiac mysteries, a practice which was common in Southern Italy despite prohibitory measures adopted by the Roman Senate. According to the leading interpretation, the scenes, starting on the wall to the left of the door, represent (1) a child reading the rite before a young bride and a seated matron; (2) a priestess and three female assistants making a sacrifice; (3) sileni playing musical instruments in a pastoral setting; (4) the flight of the frightened initiate and a group of two satyrs and a silenus with a mask; (5) the marriage of Dionysus and Ariadne (damaged); (6) a kneeling woman unveiling (or, by a different interpretation, protecting) the sacred phallus while a winged demon raises a flagellum to strike the young initiate, who seeks refuge in the lap of a companion; (7) the orgiastic dance of Dionysus; (8) the dressing of a bride for initiation and a seated woman who has undergone the initiation rite.

Among the sixty rooms note also a bedroom, with two alcoves with a cupboard in stone work, another room with good paintings, a huge kitchen with two fireplaces; and the beautiful peristyle.

Villa of the Mysteries. This complex dwelling takes its name from a hall with 24 life-size painted figures thought to have been executed by a Campanian painter of the first century B.C. The paintings form a cycle, the meaning of which is probably connected with the rite of initiation into the Dionysiac mysteries.
Here we see (left to right) a kneeling woman unveiling (or, by a differing interpretation, protecting) the sacred phallus while a winged demon raises a flagellum to strike the young initiate, who seeks refuge in the lap of a companion, and the orgiastic dance of Dionysus.

d Vesuvius and Herculaneum

From Naples the expedition to Mount Vesuvius is most easily made, by car or by public transport, via the modern town of *Ercolano*, and is thus conveniently combined with a visit to Herculaneum.

Road, 23 km (14 miles), via Ercolano to the lower station of the Seggiovia (chair-lift), which ascends in 6 minutes to the crater (continous service 9 a.m. - dusk; strong winds may cause interruption of service); or (5 1/2 km, 3 miles more; toll) to within 10 minutes walk of the summit. Ercolano is reached by Highway 18 (10 km), by the Autostrada (12 km), or by the Circumvesuviana Railway (25 - 30 minutes). A bus runs four or five times daily from Pugliano Station, near Ercolano, to the Seggiovia. An official guide (fee) of the comune of Ercolano, conducts parties by a path to the edge of the crater.

I Vesuvius

Mount Vesuvius, the most familiar feature in the Neapolitan landscape, is one of the smallest active volcanoes in the world (4150 ft; 3906 ft before 1944), but certainly the most famous. It is the only active volcano on the continent of Europe. It consists of a truncated cone, Monte Somma, which rises to the height of 1152 m in Punta del Nasone on the north side. Within is an enormous crater, broken on the west, called the Atrio del Cavallo and Valle dell'Inferno. (Here Spartacus and the rebel slaves took refuge in 73 B.C., escaping by an unguarded rift from the besieging force of Clodius Pulcher.) From the center of this crater rises a smaller cone, variable in size and shape, which is Vesuvius proper.

Vesuvius and Monte Somma are the most thoroughly known volcanoes in the world, their development having been studied since Roman times. The volcanic activity started about 10,000 years ago. Ever since, periods of frequent eruption have alternated with periods of absolute tranquillity sometimes lasting more than 2000 years; before the disastrous eruption of A.D. 79 the volcano had been quiet for more than 1200 years.

In ancient times the lower slopes of Vesuvius were planted with vineyards, above which was a thick belt of woods noted for their wild boars. The famous author Pliny the Elder maintained that no region on earth was more joyously touched by nature. Vesuvius's volcanic nature was unsuspected save by men of science; and even they did not see any particular danger in this. One writer mentions the existence of hot springs near

Vesuvius; another reports that in the dim past, the mountain had rained fire on the surrounding countryside; and a third, in an account of the legendary battle between Hercules and the giants, adds that Vesuvius once was an active volcano much like Mount Aetna. The most qualified of these early observers, the geographer Strabo, wrote that "in early times this district was on fire and had craters of fire, and then because the fuel gave out, was quenched" (*Geog.*, V, 4). To this he attributed the fruitfulness of the lands around the mountain, saying that it had already been shown at Mount Aetna that volcanic ash was particularly suited for the vine. Strabo's view, based on an actual ascent of the mountain and an examination of the burnt rocks at its summit, seems to have been universally held. Even the great earthquake of A.D. 63, now considered to have been a kind of dress rehearsal for the eruption of A.D. 79, does not appear to have caused any apprehension that the mountain might once more burst forth in fury. And as there was no reason to be fearful, there was no reason to avoid the beautiful region, though judging from the settlements that crowd the area today, it is doubtful that even the knowledge of danger would have kept people away. In his *Naturales Quaestiones* (VI, De Terrae Motu), Seneca describes the tremor of A.D. 63 in some detail:

> We have heard that Pompeii, the very lively city in Campania where the shores of Surrentum and Stabiae and that of Herculaneum meet and hem in a lovely, gently retreating inlet from the open sea, has been destroyed by an earthquake which also struck the entire vicinity. This occurred in winter, a time which our forefathers always held to be free from such perils... The region had never before been visited by a calamity of such extent, having always escaped unharmed from such occurrences and having therefore lost all fear of them. Part of the city of Herculaneum caved in; the houses still standing are in ruinous condition.

But he draws no warning from it. Despite the nonchalance of Seneca and his contemporaries, the earthquake of 63 was followed by other shocks, and in the space of just a few years the entire cone blew out and Pompeii, Herculaneum, and Stabiae were destroyed, the first and last buried in cinders and lapilli, or small pumice stones, while Herculaneum was drowned in a torrent of mud. The catastrophe struck on the morning of August 24, 79 ironically only a day after the annual celebration of the Volcanalia, the festival of the Italian god of fire and forge, Volcanus. History owes an inestimable debt to Pliny the Younger, who witnessed the event, and left a description of his observations in two letters addressed to the historian Tacitus. This is altogether the oldest realistic description, in Western literature, of a major natural disaster. Pliny was staying with his uncle, Pliny the Elder, at Missenum on the Bay of Naples (about fourteen miles by water from Herculaneum and twenty from Pompeii), where the latter was stationed as admiral of the fleet. The letters are exciting to read, for they are seasoned with a touch of immediacy. More important than their literary value, however, is their truthfulness. They are brief enough to be reproduced here with only minor omissions:

To Tacitus:

Your request that I would send you an account of my uncle's end, so that you may transmit a more exact relation of it to posterity, deserves my acknowledgments; for if his death shall be celebrated by your pen, the glory of it, I am aware, will be rendered for ever deathless...

He was at that time with the fleet under his command at Misenum. On the 24th of August, about one in the afternoon, my mother desired him to observe a cloud of very unusual size and appearance. He had sunned himself, then taken a cold bath, and after a leisurely luncheon was engaged in the study. He immediately called for his shoes and went up an eminence from whence he might best view this very uncommon appearance. It was not at that distance discernible from what mountain this cloud issued, but it was found afterwards to be Vesuvius. I cannot give you a more exact description of its figure, than by resembling it to that of a pine tree, for it shot up a great height in the form of a trunk, which extended itself at the top into several branches; because I imagine, a momentary gust of air blew it aloft, and then falling, forsook it; thus causing the cloud to expand laterally as it dissolved, or possibly the downward pressure of its own weight produced this effect. It was at one moment white, at another dark and spotted, as if it had carried up earth or cinders.

My uncle, true savant that he was, deemed the phenomenon important and worth a nearer view. He ordered a light vessel to be got ready, and gave me the liberty, if I thought proper, to attend him. I replied I would rather study, and, as it happened, he had himself given me a theme for composition. As he was coming out of the house he received a note from Rectina, the wife of Bassus, who was in the utmost alarm at the imminent danger (his villa stood just below us, and there was no way to escape but by sea); she earnestly entreated him to save her from such deadly peril. He changed his first design and what he began with a philosophical, he pursued with an heroical turn of mind. He ordered large galleys to be launched, and went himself on board one, with the intention of assisting not only Rectina, but many others; for the villas stand extremely thick upon that beautiful coast. Hastening to the place from whence others were flying, he steered his direct course to the point of danger, and with such freedom from fear, as to be able to make and dictate his observations upon the successive motions and figures of that terrific object.

And now cinders, which grew thicker and hotter the nearer he approached, fell into the ships, then pumice-stones too, with stones blackened, scorched, and cracked by fire, then the sea ebbed suddenly from under them, while the shore was blocked up by landslips from the mountains. After considering a moment whether he should retreat, he said to the captain who was urging that course, "Fortune befriends the brave; carry me to Pomponianus". Pomponianus was then at Stabiae, distant by half the width of the bay (for, as you know, the shore, insensibly curving in its sweep, forms here a receptacle for the sea). He had already embarked his baggage; for though at Stabiae the danger was not yet near, it was full in view, and certain to be extremely near, as soon as it spread; and he resolved to fly as soon as the contrary wind should cease. It was full favorable, however, for carrying my uncle to Pomponianus. He embraces, comforts, and encourages his alarmed friend, and in order to soothe the other's fears by his own unconcern, desires to be conducted to a bathroom, and after having bathed, he sat down to supper with great cheerfulness, or at least (what is equally heroic) with all the appearance of it.

In the meanwhile Mount Vesuvius was blazing in several places with spreading and towering flames, whose refulgent brightness the darkness of the night set in high relief. But my uncle, in order to soothe apprehensions, kept saying that some fires had been left alight by the terrified country people, and what they saw were only deserted villas on fire in the abandoned district. After this he retired to rest, and it is most certain that his rest was a most genuine slumber; for his breathing, which, as he was pretty fat, was somewhat heavy and sonorous, was heard by those who attended at his chamber-door. But the court which led to his apartment now lay so deep under a mixture of pumice-stones and ashes, that if he had continued longer in his bedroom, egress would have been impossible. On being aroused, he came out, and returned to Pomponianus and the others, who had sat up all night. They consulted together as to whether they should hold out in the house, or wander about in the open. For the house now tottered under repeated and violent concussions, and seemed to rock to and fro as if torn from its foundations. In the open air, on the other hand, they dreaded the falling pumice-stones, light and porous though they were; yet this, by comparison, seemed the lesser danger of the two; a conclusion which my uncle arrived at by balancing reasons, and the others by balancing fears. They tied pillows upon their heads with napkins, and this was their whole defence against the showers that fell round them.

It was now day everywhere else, but there a deeper darkness prevailed than in the most obscure night; relieved, however, by many torches and diverse illuminations. They thought it proper to go down upon the shore to observe from close at hand if they could possibly put out to sea, but they found the waves still ran extremely high and contrary. There my uncle having thrown himself down upon a disused sail, repeatedly called for, and drank, a draught of cold water; soon after, flames, and a strong smell of sulphur, which was the forerunner of them, dispersed the rest of the company in flight; him they only aroused. He raised himself up with the assistance of two of his slaves, but instantly fell; some unusually gross vapour, as I conjecture, having obstructed his breathing and blocked his windpipe, which was not only naturally weak and constricted, but chronically inflamed. When day dawned again (the third from that he last beheld) his body was found entire and uninjured, and still fully clothed as in life; its posture was that of a sleeping, rather than a dead man.

Meanwhile my mother and I were at Misenum. But this has no connection with history, and your inquiry went no further than concerning my uncle's death. I will therefore put an end to my letter. Suffer me only to add, that I have faithfully related to you what I was either an eye witness of myself, or heard at the time, when report speaks most truly. You will select what is most suitable to your purpose; for there is a great difference between a letter, and an history; between writing to a friend, and writing for the public. Farewell.

To Tacitus:

The letter which, in compliance with your request, I wrote to you concerning the death of my uncle, has raised, you say, your curiosity to know not only what terrors, but what calamities. I endured when left behind at Misenum (for there I broke off my narrative).

Though my shock'd soul recoils, my tongue shall tell.

My uncle having set out, I gave the rest of the day to study, the object which had kept me at home. After which I bathed, dined, and retired to short and broken slumbers. There had been for several days before some shocks of earthquake, which the less alarmed us as they are frequent in Campania; but that night they became so violent that one might think that the world was not merely shaken, but turned topsy-turvy. My mother flew to my chamber; I was just rising, meaning on my part to awaken her, if she was asleep. We sat down in the forecourt of the house, which separated it by a short space from the sea. I know not whether I should call it courage or inexperience, I was not quite eighteen, but I called for a volume of Livy, and began to read, and even went on with the extracts I was making from it, as if nothing were the matter. Lo and behold, a friend of my uncle's, who was just come to him from Spain, appears on the scene; observing my mother and me seated, and that I have actually a book in my hand, he sharply censures her patience and my indifference; nevertheless I still went on intently with my author.

It was now six o'clock in the morning, the light still ambiguous and faint. The buildings around us already tottered, and though we stood upon open ground, yet as the place was narrow and confined, there was certain and formidable danger from their collapsing. It was not till then we resolved to quit the town. The common people follow us in the utmost consternation, preferring the judgement of others to their own (wherein the extreme of fear resembles prudence), and impel us onwards by pressing in a crowd upon our rear. Being got outside the houses, we halt in the midst of a most strange and dreadful scene. The coaches which we had ordered out, though upon the most level ground, were sliding to and fro, and could not be kept steady even when stones were put against the wheels. Then we beheld the sea sucked back, and as it were repulsed by the convulsive motion of the earth; it is certain at least the shore was considerably enlarged, and now held many sea animals captive on the dry sand. On the other side, a black and dreadful cloud bursting out in gusts of igneous serpentine vapour now and again yawned open to reveal long fantastic flames, resembling flashes of lightning but much larger.

Our Spanish friend already mentioned now spoke with more warmth and instancy: "If your brother, if your uncle," said he, "is yet alive, he wishes you both may be saved; if he has perished, it was his desire that you might survive him. Why therefore do you delay your escape?" We could never think of our own safety, we said, while we were uncertain of his. Without more ado our friend hurried off, and took himself out of danger at the top of his speed.

Soon afterwards, the cloud I have described began to descend upon the earth, and cover the sea. It had already begirt the hidden Capreae (Capri), and blotted from sight the promontory of Misenum. My mother now began to beseech, exhort, and command me to escape as best I might; a young man could do it; she, burdened with age and corpulency, would die easy if only she had not caused my death. I replied, I would not be saved without her, and taking her by the hand, I hurried her on. She complies reluctantly and not without reproaching herself for retarding me. Ashes now fall upon us, though as yet in no great quantity. I looked behind me; gross darkness pressed upon our rear, and came rolling over the land after us like a torrent. I proposed while we yet could see, to turn aside, lest we should be knocked down in the road by the crowd that followed us and trampled to death in the dark. We had scarce sat down, when darkness overspread us, not like that of a moonless or cloudy night, but of a room when it is shut up, and the lamp put out. You could hear the shrieks of women, the crying of children, and the shouts of men; some were seeking their children, others their parents, others their wives or husbands, and only distinguishing them by their voices; one lamenting his own fate, another that of his family; some praying to die, from the very fear of dying; many lifting their hands to the gods, but the greater part imagining that there were no gods left anywhere, and that the last and eternal night was come upon the world.

There were even some who augmented the real perils by imaginary terrors. Newcomers reported that such or such a building at Misenum had collapsed or taken fire, falsely, but they were credited. By degrees it grew lighter; which we imagined to be rather the warning of approaching fire (as in truth it was) than the return of day: however, the fire stayed at a distance from us: then again came darkness, and a heavy shower of ashes; we were obliged every now and then to rise and shake them off, otherwise we would have been buried and even crushed under their weight. I might have boasted that amidst dangers so appalling, not a sigh or expression of fear escaped from me, had not my support been founded in miserable, though strong consolation, that all mankind were involved in the same calamity, and that I was perishing with the world itself.

At last this dreadful darkness was attenuated by degrees to a kind of cloud or smoke, and passed away; presently the real day returned, and even the sun appeared, though lurid as when an eclipse is in progress. Every object that presented itself to our yet affrighted gaze was changed, cover'd over with a drift of ashes, as with snow. We returned to Misenum, where we refreshed ourselves as well as we could, and passed an anxious night between hope and fear; though indeed with a much larger share of the latter, for the earthquake still continued, and several enthusiastic people were giving a grotesque turn to their own and their neighbours' calamities by terrible predictions. Even then, however, my mother and I, notwithstanding the danger we had passed, and that which still threatened us, had no thoughts of leaving the place, till we should receive some tidings of my uncle.

And now, you will read this narrative, so far beneath the dignity of a history, without any view of transferring it to your own; and indeed you must impute it to your own request, if it shall appear scarce worthy of a letter. Farewell.

On August 25 and 26 a thin white ash fell on Rome, borne by winds driven from Vesuvius, 180 miles to the south. The Emperor Titus, when told of its cause, appointed two former consuls to oversee rebuilding in Campania. A year later, in A.D. 80, a great famine struck the capital, followed by a plague which, according to contemporary sources, was as bad as any that could be remembered. It was probably brought on by a crop failure in Campania.

With reference to the tragic end of Pompeii, Herculaneum, and the other Campanian towns destroyed in A.D. 79, the poet Statius asked, *"Will future centuries, when new seed will have covered the waste, believe that entire cities and their inhabitants lie under their feet, and that the fields of their ancestors were drowned in a sea of flames?"* As memory of the event waned and other misfortunes befell the Empire, future generations did not believe because they did not know of the catastrophe. Pompeii was discovered inadvertently in 1592, and Herculaneum in 1602; but a systematic program of excavation was not undertaken until the middle of the nineteenth century.

Meanwhile, Vesuvius has been active at irregular intervals, but has seldom remained quiet very long. A violent eruption of 1631 destroyed nearly all the towns at the foot of the mountain; the lava reached the sea near Portici and killed over 3000 people. During the next 300 years there were 23 eruptions at intervals from 1 to 30 years. Sir William Hamilton (who we shall properly introduce in his capacity as English ambassador to the Bourbon court in Chapter 4) forecast that of 1767, and went up to mountain while it was in progress. The most serious were those of 1794, which destroyed Torre del Greco; of 1871-72, which damaged San Sebastiano and Massa di Somma, and of 1906, in which Ottaviano and San Giuseppe suffered severely. In August 1928 and in June 1929 the lava descended into the Valle dell'Inferno, menacing Terzigno. The last major eruption occured in 1944, but activity may start again at any moment. Today the fertile volcanic soil of Vesuvius produces the excellent wine called "Lacrima Christi." At Boscoreale, overlooking Pompeii, several Roman villas were unearthed in 1870 - 1907; they yielded a large find of silver ware (now in the Louvre) and frescoes, some of which may be seen in Naples, others in the Metropolitan Museum of New York.

II Herculaneum

In Ercolano Highway 18 passes the entrance to the excavations; travelers arriving by the Circumvesuviana Railway descend the wide road to seaward of Pugliano station (10 minute walk).

Herculaneum, destroyed with Pompeii in A.D. 79 and rediscovered in 1709, was a residential town without Pompeii's commercial importance, surrounded by villas of wealthy Romans. Though the excavations are small in extent compared with those of Pompeii and, because of the proximity of modern structures, less immediately striking, the better state of preservation of domestic buildings, above all of their upper stories, together with the successful use of modern techniques for preserving woodwork and the replanting of gardens, combine to give a feeling of life and humanity not always achieved at Pompeii. In addition Herculaneum has the interest of a richer artistic life, of its contrasted styles of house construction, and above all of its attractive terraced site.

The foundation of Herculaneum, originally called *Herakleia* by its Greek settlers, was attributed to its patron deity, Hercules. The town passed through periods of Oscan and Samnite domination before falling to the Romans in 89 B.C., after which a colony of veterans seems to have been established there. The damage done by the earthquake of A.D. 63 was being repaired, under the patronage of Vespasian, when the catastrophe of A.D. 79 overwhelmed the town. Unlike Pompeii, Herculaneum was submerged by a torrent of mud , containing sand, ashes, and bits of lava, which raised the level of the soil by between 39 and 81 ft and hardened into a sort of tufa, preserving many timber features and household objects which were burnt at Pompeii. Subsequent layers of volcanic matter buried the ruins to a depth of 123 ft, and the town remained untouched for 1630 years.

The first discoveries were made in 1709 when Emmanuel de Lorraine, Prince of Elbeuf and cavalry commander of the Kingdom of Naples, came upon the back of the stage of the theater while sinking the shaft for a well, and distributed a large group of statues and much of the scena among various museums. Charles III of Bourbon continued the exploration (1738-65), without any very clear plan, but not until 1927 was systematic excavation begun on any scale. This still continues, and not the least interesting part of a visit is provided by the opportunity of watching a "dig" in progress. A large proportion of Herculaneum still remains to be excavated.

The division into Regions used at Pompeii is unnecessary here, and houses are designated by insula and street numbers only. The extent of the city is still uncertain, but in both area and population it probably attained only one-third of the size of Pompeii. With decumani running parallel with the coast (then much nearer the town than it is today), and cardines at right angles to the shore, the town suggests a Greek rather than a Roman plan and has affinities with Neapolis. The streets are paved with local volcanic stone, but are noticeably free from both the wheel-ruts and the stepping-stones so characteristic of Pompeian streets. On the seaward side the town ended in a terraced promontory, lined with patrician villas, beneath which the cardines descended abruptly through narrow archways to the harbor.

Unlike Pompeii, which was entirely dominated by the commercial classes, Herculaneum was a city of wealthy citizens, small artisans, and fishermen. The Herculean house differs somewhat from the Pompeian house. The Samnite type of construction described in our introduction to Pompeii exists also at Herculaneum, but frequently with the *atrium* daringly modified for the addition of an extra floor. In the richer type of dwelling the Greek plan of building round a *peristyle* is frequently followed, but the *peristyle* itself is often modified to a closed corridor with windows overlooking the central garden. In many middle-class houses the traditional plan has been abandoned and a central courtyard, more akin to the modern "well," has been substituted. Finally there are apartment houses of several floors in Herculaneum (though not on the scale developed, say, in Ostia), in which the poorer artisans lived the crowded life of their modern Neapolitan counterparts.

The avenue that leads down from the entrance-gate commands a wonderful view across the excavations to the sea. To the west stands the newly completed **Antiquarium**, which will soon house many of the objects now visible in the houses themselves, as well as a wealth of material currently in storage.

We descend to Cardo III at the west corner of the site. To the left are Insula II and, beyond the *decumanus inferior*, Insula VII, both brought to light in 1828-35 when much of their interest was spoiled by inexperienced excavators. The **House of Argus** (II, 2), indeed, must have been one of the finest mansions in the town. Some idea of its grandeur may still be gained from the wall fronting the street and the noble columns of its *peristyle*. To the left of Cardo III is the back entrance to the house usually but wrongly designated the **Hotel** (II, 1). Occupying well over half the block, this was the largest and perhaps the richest dwelling in the southern quarter of the city. At the time of the catastrophe it had already fallen on bad times, and was undergoing modification: the whole south wing had been converted into a self-contained dwelling, and a room on the north side into a shop; the private bath of the Augustan period had been abandoned. The house was badly damaged in the eruption and further mutilated by Bourbon excavators, but even in decay its extent is impressive.

Emerge by the main entrance (19) into Cardo IV. Opposite is the **House of the Mosaic Atrium** (IV, 1-2), another panoramic house beautifully disposed for the enjoyment of the view. From the street (N° 2) we pass through an entrance hall to the *atrium*, both of which retain their pavements of geometric mosaic, though the floors became corrugated under the weight of the invading tufa. Fom the *atrium* leads the unusual *basilican tablinum*, and, at right angles, a closed gallery formed by partially filling in the intercolumnar spaces of *peristyle*. The door and window frames are remarkably well preserved. Off the narrow east walk are four bedrooms with red walls, and a raised central guest-room, adorned with mythological scenes, with a wooden table. This room enjoys a charming view of the garden with its marble fountain. The main living-rooms beyond, including a lofty *triclinium* paved in marble, open on to a terrace, formerly shaded by a colonnaded roof, with a sun room, at either end of which is a siesta room, with low windows for the enjoyment of the view.

Continuing up Cardo IV, we visit on the left the **House of the Bronze Herm** (III, 16), with typical though diminutive characteristics of the Samnite house. The bronze portrait presumably represents the owner. The base of the stairs leading to an upper floor can be seen in the blind corridor leading off the atrium. On the other side of the street is the **House of the Alcove** (IV, 3), its façade in *opus reticulatum* (masonry arranged in squares or diamonds so that the mortar joints make a network pattern) pierced with iron gratings and overhung by the remains of a first-floor balcony. The smaller door (N° 4) gave on to the stairs. The ground floor comprises two separate dwellings thrown into one, that to the left modest; and that to the right more distinguished with a mosaic atrium and a richly painted room with wooden couches. At the end of a long corridor is a small court with the alcoved room that gives the house its name.

The **House of Opus Craticium** (III, 13-15) presents a unique example of the wood and plaster construction, called *opus craticium*, used for plebian dwellings. The building, which consists of a shop with a back-parlor or work room, and two self-contained apartments, preserves complete its upper floor with a balcony over the pavement.

Next on the left is the **House of the Wooden Partition** (III, 11-12), whose façade, rising to the second story, gives a striking picture of the external appearance of the Roman private house. The open gallery above the cornice belonged to a second floor, added to the structure when the house declined in status; this was reached from a separate entrance in the *decumanus*. In the imposing *atrium* the double lining of the *impluvium* tank should be noted; also the dog's-head spouts (some original) of the roof. The most striking feature, giving its name to the house, is the wooden partition that closes the *tablinum*, reconstructed here with its ancient hinges and lamp brackets. Glass cases preserve remains of toilet articles, beans, etc., found in the house. The bedroom to the right of the entrance hall has a geometrical pavement and a marble table, the farther room on the left a well-preserved frieze. Behind the house is a charming small garden. The side of the house abutting on the *decumanus* inferior was occupied by shops that, with one exception, communicate directly with the house. The corner shop (N° 10) was a dry cleaner's: it contains a unique example of a wooden clothes-press in an astonishing state of preservation.

Cross the *decumanus inferior*, passing a shop selling postcards. The greater part of Insula VI (left) is occupied by the **Baths**, erected in the first century B.C. on a plan similar to that used at Pompeii, and decorated somewhat later; they survive, finely preserved and without modification, almost as they were planned. In the center is the **Palaestra**, to which the main entrance was in Cardo IV (N° 7). To the south, with separate entrances from the *decumanus*, was a covered hall with a penthouse roof, probably a **Sphaeristerium**, where the ball-game of *pila* was played. A second entrance to the palaestra from Cardo III (N° 1), flanked by a porter's lodge and a latrine, led also to the Men's Baths. From the corridor we enter the dressing-room, with a convex pavement in *opus segmentatum*, shelves for clothes, and vaulted stucco. In an apse stands a *cipollino* marble basin. A vestibule, to the left, leads down marble steps to the circular cold room, the domed ceiling of which is painted with fish on a blue ground and pierced by a skylight. From the other side of the dressing room, we pass through the tepid room to the warm room, with the usual plunge-bath and a scalloped apse for a hand basin; the fall of the vault has exposed the heating pipes and smoke vents. The **Women's Baths**, entered from Cardo IV (N° 8), though smaller and simpler, are even better preserved. We enter a waiting room and pass through a small linen room to the dressing room, whose mosaic, like that in the men's tepid room, shows a Triton surrounded by dolphins and cuttlefish. Beyond, the small tepid room and warm room are virtually complete. Behind (N° 10) are the service quarters, where there is a well, and a staircase leading up to the attendant's living quarters and down to the boiler room, of which the heavy iron door and the poker survive, though the boilers were removed by Bourbon excavators.

Farther along (N° 11) is the **House of the Black Hall,** still largely buried, with an elegant portico. The paintings of the little vaulted rooms and of the black hall are particularly lively. The model temple, with wooden columns surmounted by marble capitals, was a shrine for the lares.

We next visit the houses on the other side of Cardo IV, starting at the crossroads. The **Samnite House** (V, 1), preceded by a stretch of fine paving, has an imposing portal and an open gallery (approached by a stair from N° 2) that led to a separate apartment added at a later date. The interior decoration is beautifully executed; that of the entrance hall in the first style of architectural imitation. The *atrium* has a blind gallery of graceful proportions.

Beyond a simple weaver's house (V, 3-4) and workshop, is the small but dignified **House of the Caronized Furniture** (V, 5), in the Samnite style, with an elegantly decorated *triclinium* and a delightful little court. The *lararium* is placed to be seen from the window of an inner room, the couch and table of which survive. Some furniture remains also in the upper rooms of the **House of the Neptune Mosaic** (V, 6-7), which stand open to the street. Below is the best-preserved **Shop** in the town, its goods and fittings as they were at the moment of catastrophe (note the coil of rope; right). A fine wooden partition separates the shop from the attractive living quarters behind, where a little court is enlivened by the fresh blues and greens of the mosaic of Neptune and Amphitrite that gives name to the house, and of the **Nymphaeum**. The **House of the Beautiful Courtyard** (V, 8) has an unusual plan grouped round a wide hall that precedes the court. Within are displayed everyday objects of Herculanean life. The *cardo* continues between high pavements (once arcaded, as may be seen from the remaining columns) to the crossing, with the usual public fountain and altar. A painted inscription on a pillar records rules of the street police.

We turn into the broad *decumanus maximus*, reserved to pedestrians, the left side of which still lies beneath the tufa. On the right is a **Shop** (V, 10) with a little room over the pavement. Built into the counter and sunk into the floor are the large jars in which foodstuffs could be preserved at an even temperature. This and the adjoining shops originally formed part of the **House of the Bicentenary** (Vn 15-16), a rich dwelling disinterred in 1938, two hundred years after Charles III initiated the excavations. Despite later modifications the ground floor preserves its original plan. The fine *atrium* still has its lattice partition and the *tablinum* is decorated with mythical scenes and paved in mosaic. The outline of a cross on the wall of an upstairs room postulates the existence here of a private Christian oratory, though other evidence is lacking to suggest the general adoption of the crucifix as a Christian symbol as early as A.D. 79.

Cardo V is admirably paved in limestone. To the left is a public fountain with a masque of Hercules; turn toward the sea. The corner shop (V, 21) is interesting for the wooden window-fittings remaining in the dwelling above (cntered from N° 22). Beyond on the right the houses continue to be in styles already familiar; three of them, preceded by a stretch of marble pavement once shaded by a portico, have features worthy of note.

In the **House of the Corinthian Atrium** (V, 30), small but in good taste, the *atrium* roof, supported by six tufa columns faced with stucco, feeds a graceful fountain. A mosaic, in a room to the right, shows in its pattern the sacred two-edged axe. A glass case contains a wooden table and a small basket. Note also the elegant decoration of the bedroom, lighted by three skylights. Next door is the **House of the Lararium** (V, 31), an earlier and smaller dwelling showing good examples of decoration in the first and third styles. Most wonderfully preserved is a wooden sacellum, which consists of a cupboard surmounted by a shrine in the form of a small temple with Corinthian columns, where the lares were kept. Beyond is the so-called **House with the Garden** (V, 33), though the garden probably belonged to one of the more distinguished houses in the *decumanus*.

The other side of the street is quite different, foreshadowing the style developed at Ostia a hundred years later. The whole block (Insula Orientalis II), ca. 290 ft long, is of uniform construction in *opus reticulatum* and was apparently planned as a unit. The street frontage consists of shops with flats above, on a plan having no resemblance to the traditional Campanian house, but such as might be seen today. The chief interest of the plain rectangular shops is in their use and contents: N° 16 contains a marble casket and an almost perfect wooden partition door; N° 13 has a counter with remains of its vegetable wares; N° 9 preserves its stove and sink and a little painting of Hercules pouring a libation between Dionysus and Mercury. N° 8 was a bakery; it contains the two mills for grinding flour, twenty-five bronze baking pans, the seal of the proprietor, and the oven carved with a phallic emblem. At N° 7 was the main staircase to the flats. Behind this workaday façade a series of finely decorated and vaulted rooms overlook a huge open space surrounded by a portico, of which only the north and west sides have been unearthed. This area, the **Palaestra** where the public games were held, is approached by two great entrance halls (N° 19 and N° 4), each with a porch. N° 4, by which we enter, had a black mosaic pavement, white walls and vault, a fitting entrance to the impressive colonnade within. Bourbon tunnels beneath the avenue give a vivid impression of the difficulties of excavation as well as of the size of the cruciform swimming pool which occupied the center of the palaestra. Here has been re-erected its central fountain, of bronze cast in the form of a five-headed serpent entwined round a tree-trunk.

Rejoin Cardo V by the Neptune fountain, whose rectangular basin is formed, as was customary, of limestone slabs joined at the corners by lead clamps. On the right side of the *decumanus inferior* is the imposing entrance to the **House of the Great Portal** (V, 35), its engaged brick columns surmounted by Corinthian capitals carved with winged Victories and an architrave decorated in terracotta; within are several good paintings, and, in the pavement, a picture executed in marble *opus sectile*. The other side of the street is occupied by shops; N° 14, a tavern well stocked with amphoras; the largest, on the corner (IV, 15-16), has an impressive counter, faced with polychrome marble and containing eight earthenware jars for the storing of cereals.

Continuing the descent of Cardo V, note a small **Shop** (right, IV, 17) with a Priapic painting next to the counter, and remains of nuts, lamps, utensils, etc. In the lane to the left, flanking the palaestra, is another bakery, where the iron door of the oven remains closed despite the collapse of the vault, and with a stable for the asses that turned the mills. In the **House of the Cloth** (IV, 19-20) are preserved pieces of ancient fabric in which the design is still discernible. The unusual arrangement of the stairs deserves notice. Beyond, we again approach the terraced quarter occupied by the houses of the rich. On the right is the **House of the Deer** (IV, 21), the grandest dwelling yet discovered at Herculaneum, with a frontage of 43 meters. The entrance leads into a covered atrium, from which opens the spacious *triclinium*, painted with black and red panels having architectural motifs, and paved in marble intarsia. Within are the two delicately executed groups of Deer at Bay, after which the house is named. Behind in an equally elegantly decorated room stands a statuette of a Satyr with a wineskin. The kitchen, latrine, and pantry form a compact little block to the right. The garden is surrounded by an enclosed corridor, lighted by windows and decorated with panels of cupids playing (most of these have been removed to the *Museo Archeologico Nazionale* in Naples); in this, the latest development of the *peristyle*, the columns have finally disappeared. In the center is a summer *triclinium* flanked by two lovely smaller rooms, in one of which is a vigorously indelicate statue of the drunken Hercules. The far walk opens on to a terrace where an arbor, flanked by flower beds and siesta rooms, overlooks a sun balcony. Originally, this terrace opened directly on to the sea, commanding a view from Posillipo to Sorrento and Capri.

Cross the street to Insula Orientalis I. This consists of only two houses, both planned in an individual manner dictated by their situation; some of their rooms lie at a lower level and have yet to be explored. The **House of the Gem** (N° 1), named from an engraved stone found in it, has an unusual atrium with buttresslike pilasters and a side door that opens toward the irregular sunken garden. The kitchen preserves its kettle, and the latrine an inscription (perhaps the work of a servant) recording a visit by a famous doctor. The floor of the *triclinium* is "carpeted" in fine mosaic.

The **House of the Relief of Telephus** (N° 2-3), the most extensive of Herculanean mansions, is built round two sides of the House of the Gem and at two levels on the hillside. The walls were partially overthrown by the rush of mud that brought down from some higher public building the Quadriga reliefs that we see on either side of the entrance. The atrium has colonnades on three sides; between the columns have been rehung the original *oscilla*, circular marble panels depicting satyrs. On the north side small doors lead to the servants' quarters and stables. Descend a steep passage to the *peristyle*, which surrounds the garden, at the center of which is an azure basin. Off the south walk are the ruins of a once grand room (8.5 x 6 m), with a polychrome marble pavement; the reconstructed marble base of one wall demonstrates the palatial standards of this rich dwelling. In an adjacent room is a relief of the myth of Telephus, a late work executed academically.

Below the terrace are the public baths known as the **Terme Suburbane**, probably of late construction and surviving in a good state. Because they are subject to continuous flooding, they are often unvisitable. The **Theater** lies partially buried to the west (entrance at N° 119 corso Ercolano: apply at the office). The visit is interesting less for the theater itself, the best of which was rifled by d'Elbeuf, than for the impression it gives of the daring eighteenth century excavators. The great suburban **Villa of the Papyri**, from which came many works of art in the Naples Museum, is inaccessible.

e The Phlegraean Fields

Road, 60 km (36 miles) round trip. Highway 7 quarter and subsidiary roads. This route takes us across some truly unusual countryside, past the chic Imperial Roman watering holes of the coast north of Naples to Cumae, home of the Sibyl. By car a tour of the principal sights may comfortably be made in half a day; but the more leisured traveler will do well to spend a day or two on foot exploring this delightful country. I have done this many times, and the reward is well worth the effort. Beyond Pozzuoli the roads are fairly free from traffic. The countryside is fairly wild; and the hiker is accompanied throughout his journey by birdsong and the buzz of cicadas.

Frequent trains of the Cumana Railway connect Naples Montesanto Station with Pozzuoli, Baia, and Torregaveta. From Piazza Garibaldi the Metropolitana (FS) runs to Pozzuoli about every half hour.

The **Phlegraean Fields**, or *Campi Flegrei* (burning fields), is the name given to the volcanic region between Naples and Cumae. Its eruptive activity is apparently extinct, but has left its trace in thirteen low craters, some filled with water, which give the country its distinctive appearance, full of beauty and variety. It still abounds in hot springs (those at Agnano are particularly famous) and *fumarole* (such as the Solfatara at Pozzuoli). The most recent of the craters is the *Monte Nuovo*, formed in 1538.

The history of the region takes its origin in the Homeric and Virgilian myths. The whole character of the district fullfils the description of the Greek Infernal Regions; the subterranean murmurs suggested the horrors of Tartarus, and the natural beauty of the countryside inspired the idea of the Elysian Fields. The beauty of the seaboard attracted the first Greek colonists to the Italian mainland, and the Romans were quick to appreciate the glorious climate and delightful surroundings. Innumerable villas sprang up at Baiae and Puteoli, and under the Empire they became a byword for unbridled luxury and the scene of the excesses of the Imperial court. Of all this nothing remains save a few ruined buildings and the names that evoke the memory of past glories.

Agnano lies about 1 km (1/2 mile) south of Agnano Terme, a spa on the south side of the crater of Agnano. The latter abounds with mineral springs of varying composition and temperature. Not the least of its attractions is the unusual **Dog Grotto**, in which carbon dioxide covers the floor to the height of two feet, instantly extinguishing lights held in it and stupefying and killing animals, as was formerly demonstrated to thoughtless visitors at the expense of an unhappy dog. Adjacent to the modern spa are the ruins of the Roman **Thermae Anianae**, a six-storied building with passages leading to the vapor-chambers, hollowed out in the hillside. Excavations have revealed some interesting mosaics and pipes for water and steam.

The road climbs among the hills anciently called *Colles Leucogaei* on account of their white earth, which was used for bleaching barley. Out to sea appears the island of Nisida with Capri behind, and ahead is Capo Miseno backed by Monte Epomeo on Ischia. In the convent of san Gennaro, built in the sixteenth century on the supposed site of the beheading of St. Januarius, is preserved a stone stained with the martyr's blood, which turns bright red on the occasion of the liquefaction of his blood in Naples. The view from the convent over the Gulf is very fine.

We reach the **Solfatara di Pozzuoli**, the crater of a half-extinct volcano known to the ancients as *Forum Vulcani*. The Solfatara is today the most active volcano on the Italian mainland, after Vesuvius. Its huge elliptical crater extends over an area of 2 sq. km. Twenty five fields of *fumaroles* (vents from which gases and vapors are emitted, characteristic of a late stage of volcanic activity) are known in the area, nine of them in the crater itself. The ground here consists of lightly packed ashes, and makes a hollow sound when stamped on. The temperature of the gases that the fumaroles expel-steam, carbon dioxide, and hydrogen sulphide-is about 100° C (212° F) and the sulphur sublimates at the edges of the fumaroles. A phenomenon often demonstrated by guides is the apparent increase of the steam activity if a lighted cigarette or something similar is held next to a vent. The activity is not really increasing, but the overheated steaming gases condense on the smoke particles and become visible. The same phenomenon can be repeated at every steam well in the world. The barren northwest part of the crater is at the lowest level and was probably covered with hot muddy water until the eighteenth century. At various dates since funnel-shaped cavities containing hot mud have appeared here. Sometimes a mud volcano is formed: the mud starts to boil violently, and if the temperature of the fumarole increases, mud particles may be thrown out and deposited at the edge of the hollow. Beyond the Solfatara the road curves back toward the sea and town, passing the entrance to the Amphitheater (see below).

Pozzuoli is the Greek *Dikaearchia*, founded by colonists from Samos. It became a trading post subject to Cumae, and was afterwards conquered by the Samnites. The Romans established a colony here in 194 B.C. The Romanized town, renamed *Puteoli*, soon became the principal Italian port for trading with the East, and was adorned with buildings appropriate to its wealth. Puteoli was the end of St. Paul's perilous voyage from Caesarea in A.D. 62. The fall of Rome, the barbarian invasions, the eruption of Monte Nuovo, and the increase of malaria reduced the once prosperous port to the level of a fishing village, and today only its ruins remain to testify to its former glory.

At the east end of the town, just beyond the seagirt Capuchin Convent where the composer G.B. Pergolesi (1710-36) died, is the piazza Matteotti (porta di Città), where the buses from Naples terminate. From here the via del Duomo ascends to the **Cathedral** (San Procolo), which incorporates a temple erected in honor of Augustus by the architect Cocceius. The church was completely rebuilt in 1643, but a fire in May 1964 destroyed the baroque structure, revealing the Roman building, in marble, as well as remains of a Samnite temple, in tufa, of the third or second century B.C. Within the church is the tomb of Pergolesi, undamaged by the fire.

From the porta di Città the corso Garibaldi runs northwest, then bears right to the Public Garden. To the left extends the harbor that has engulfed the surviving remains of the Roman port. This consisted of a breakwater of twenty five piers connected by arches, cleverly arranged to prevent the silting up of the harbor. At the end was a triumphal arch dedicated to Antoninus Pius, who restored the harbor in A.D. 120 after a disastrous storm. In calm weather from a boat the foundations of a double line of piers and a number of columns can be discerned below the surface. The mooring rings by which ships were attached are now covered by more than a fathom of water owing to the subsidence of the land. Offshore, on the south side of the town, are the remains of three submerged docks.

Continue beyond the Cumana Station to the so-called **Serapeum**, set in a park along the waterfront. This was not a temple of Serapis, but really a *macellum* or rectangular market-hall of the first century A.D. Opposite the entrance on the seaward side there was an apse, preceded by four Corinthian columns, three of which are still standing. These columns have been eaten away and perforated, from 11 to 18 ft above ground, by a species of shellfish (Lithodomus lithopphagus) which still abounds in the Tyrrhenian Sea. It has been argued from this that the columns were at one time buried for 11 ft and submerged for another 7 ft, since when (perhaps during the eruption of 1538) they were again raised above the sea until they became dry early in the present century. Today water again covers the floor, although the "slow quake" of 1970 raised the ground level by nearly 3 ft. Within is a courtyard, 340 ft square, surrounded by a gallery of forty eight *cippolino* and granite columns beneath which were thirty five booths and two marble-lined public latrines. A second story probably existed on the same plan. The domed circular edifice at the center, was supported by sixteen columns of giallo antico, which are now at Caserta. Only their bases remain here.

Cross the railway and mount by steps (5 minutes) to rejoin the via Domiziana. The **Amphitheater** is the best preserved of the monuments of Puteoli, and the third in size in Italy after the Colosseum in Rome and that of Capua. The present building, finished under Vespasian, replaced an older amphitheater whose ruins may be seen near the railway bridge to the northeast. It is built on three rows of arches, and was originally surrounded by a brick arcade. The *cavea* had three ranges of seats divided by stairs into *cunei*. The arena has an open corridor along its greater axis, below which are substructures (dens for wild beasts and rooms for stage machinery) in a remarkably good state of preservation. These were added under Trajan or Hadrian. Sixty openings connecting the substructures with the arena served for letting loose the wild beasts, for ventilation, and for erecting the wooden scaffold on which the gladiators fought, and which could be run up very quickly. In Vespasian's time a conduit supplied water for flooding the arena on the occasion of a *naumachia*, or mock naval battle. St.

Januarius and his companions were imprisoned in the amphitheater under Diocletian before their executions near the Solfatara. Here too Nero amazed the Armenian king Tiridates by his exploits among the beasts in the arena.

To the northwest are remains of what was probably a Roman villa, the ruined **Temple of Honor**, and some fragments of baths, known as the **Temple of Neptune**, dating from the time of Nero. Around the amphitheater were reservoirs of water, the largest of which, the **Piscina Cardito**, still exists on the right of the Solfatara road.

From the via Domiziana above the town, the via Campana (the Roman *via Consularis Puteolis Capuam*) diverges inland, lined on either side with sepulchral monuments. About 1 mile beyond Pozzuoli we leave the new road and descend to the left, joining the old road. This, with the Cumana Railway, follows the lovely coast of the Gulf. To the right rises Monte Nuovo (457 ft), a volcanic cone of rough scoriae and tufa, formed during the earthquake of 29 September 1538, when the Lucrine Lake was half filled up, and Pozzuoli deluged with mud and lapilli.

The **Lucrine Lake** (Lago Lucrino) is separated from the sea (fine beach) by a narrow strip of land, the via Herculea, by which the hero drove the bulls of Geryon across the swamp. The lake is much shrunken since the time (ca. 100 B.C.) when the Romans began the cultivation of the famous oysters. Cicero's villa, which he called "Academia," stood on the shore nearby.

Lake Avernus (Lago di Averno) is reached by a road running straight inland from here. It is a volcanic crater entirely surrounded by hills save for a narrow opening on the south side. It has been encircled by a stone edging to prevent the formation of malarial swamps. Surrounded, in the heroic age, by dense forest which invested it with a dark and gloomy atmosphere, Avernus was said to be the abode of the Cimmerians (Homer, *Odyssey*, XI) who lived in eternal darkness, and the entrance to Hades. The Greek name Aornus (wrongly held to mean "without birds") gave rise to the legend that birds flying over the lake fell suffocated by mephitic fumes. Hannibal, in pretended respect for local superstition but really for a reconnaissance of Puteoli, visited Avernus and offered a sacrifice; and the custom of making a propitiatory sacrifice to the Infernal deities of Avernus endured until after the days of Constantine.

Agrippa, however, completely altered the appearance of the countryside. To counter the threat of Sextus Pompeius' fleet (37 B.C.) he cut down the forest and united Lake Avernus with the sea by a canal via the Lucrine Lake, and to Cumae by a tunnel (see below), thereby construcing a military harbor of perfect security, the Portus Julius. This was afterwards abandoned, and finally wrecked by the eruption of 1538.

Despite Agrippa's improvements the legend, sung by Virgil and kept alive by Pliny and Silius Italicus, survived even among sixth century Byzantine writers.

On the east shore of the lake are ruins of **Baths**; the most remarkable remains, arbitrarily known as a Temple of Apollo, of an octagonal building with a round interior broken by niches, the dome of which (now fallen) once spanned a space of over 117 ft. The overgrown ruins on the west side probably represent a shipbuilding and repair yard. Agrippa's tunnel to Cumae, a passage more than half a mile long executed by Cocceius leads away from the northwest shore. It is known as the *Grotta della Pace*, after Pietro della Pace, who explored it in 1507. Straight and wide enough for chariots to pass, it is the most ambitious underground work attempted by the Romans and, being lighted at intervals by vertical openings, it could be traversed with ease, even without a light, until it was damaged in the fighting of 1943. A path along the south side of the lake, and rising above it to the left, leads in roughly 3 minutes to a long gallery cut into the rock, off which opens a chamber blackened with torch smoke. Once a rival claimant to be the Sibyl's Cave, this is now thought to be part of Agrippa's defensive works.

Road and railway now follow the via Herculea (see above). The railway then tunnels through the Punta dell'Epitaffio, while the road follows the coast. Here must be placed the site of Bauli, where Agrippina, having escaped the previous day from a planned accident at sea, was done to death by Nero's orders in the bedroom of her villa. On the right of the road are some ruins of baths, called the **Stufe di Nerone** or **di Tritoli**, including a remarkable hot-vapor room hewn out of the tufa. Modern quarrying has destroyed all but vestiges of the Imperial villas of Pompey and Vespasian.

Baia, the ancient *Baiae* extolled by Horace and Martial, is today a large village standing on the bay that bears its name and enjoying a splendid view across the Gulf of Pozzuoli. In the early days of the Roman Empire Baiae, which owed its name, according to legend, to Baios, the navigator of Odysseus, was the fashionable bathing resort of Roman society. Successive emperors rivalled each other in the construction of magnificent palaces, but the reputation of the town was stained by Nero's murder of his mother Agrippina, and his sanguinary suppression of the conspiracy of Pio. Hadrian died here on 17 July 138. The ruin of the Empire was the ruin of Baiae; it was plundered by the Saracens in the eighth century, and gradually deserted on account of malaria. The ruins of its palaces now extend some distance beneath the sea, owing to the subsidence of the ground. Finds made in the harbor in 1923-28 included statues and important architectural fragments.

Behind the station is the so-called **Temple of Diana**, like other "temples" one of the thermal establishments for which Baiae was famous. Octagonal without and circular within, it preserves four niches and part of its domed roof. From the piazza, steps ascend to the *Parco Archeologico*. Systematic excavations, begun in 1941 and completed ten years later, have allowed the identification of a group of buildings, some of which were already known in the Middle Ages, comprising an Imperial palace built between the first and fourth centuries A.D. From the entrance, a long avenue leads to a portico where architectural fragments are displayed. Hence steps lead to the upper terrace, one of several such areas set into the hillside at various levels. A row of rooms extends along the right. In the first of these was found the statue of Cassandra, a marble copy of a fifth century Greek original, now at the *Museo Archeologico Nazionale* in Naples. The second contains a statue of Mercury, beheaded by thieves in 1978. A staircase descends to the central terrace, along one side of which a series of rooms forming a semicircle suggested the existence of a theater-nymphaeum. Hence more steps descend to the lower terrace, occupied by a large (114 x 94 ft) rectangular *piscina* surrounded by a graceful portico. To the east lies the complex of buildings traditionally called the **Temple of Venus**, which includes numerous smaller rooms and a large vaulted hall surrounded by apsidal openings, also believed to be a nymphaeum. Across the street, outside the park, is a hall of circular plan, 94 ft in diameter. Although the vault has collapsed, the rest of the structure is intact. From the north side of the piscina a corridor partially covered by arches leads to the so-called **Temple of Mercury**. These buildings appear to have made up a thermal complex, principal among them is a great circular hall nearly 90 ft diameter, similar in structure to the Pantheon in Rome. Like the smaller halls to the rear, it is filled with water to the base of the dome, creating the acoustic effects from which it derives its nickname, **Tempio dell'eco**.

Beyond Baia the road to Capo Miseno ascends a gentle slope along the shore, passing several Roman tombs (fine view). On the left is the **Castello di Baia**, built by Don Pedro de Toledo in the sixteenth century.

At **Bacoli**, at the end of the descent, the via della Marina, to the left at the entrance to the village, descends to the so-called **Tomb of Agrippina**, really the ruins of a small theater. From the main road the via Ercole and the via sant'Anna ascend to the church of sant'Anna. Walking round this (15 minutes) go on to the **Centro Camerelle** (custodian at No. 16), a two-storied ruin of which the upper part was a reservoir; the function of the lower story is not known. At 16 via Greco may be obtained the key of the **Piscina Mirabile** (gratuity). This, 10 minutes south of the village, is the largest and best preserved reservoir in the district. It is constructed like a basilica with five

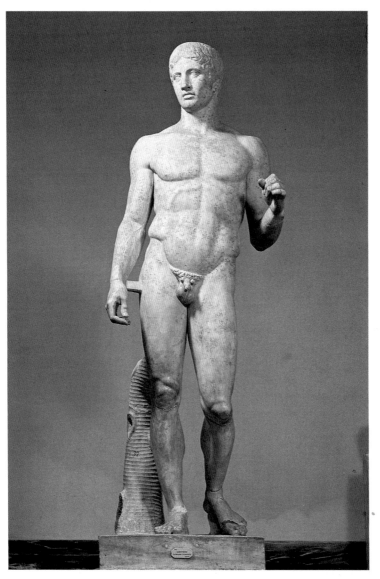

Naples, National Archaeological Museum: The Doryphorus, the most complete copy of the famous spear-bearer of Polycletus (ca 440 B.C.).

Naples, National Archaeological Museum: Toro Farnese, the most famous representation of the torment of Dirce. Found in the Terme di Caracalla in Roma. It is a copy of the sculpture of Apollonio and Taurisco.

Naples, National Archaeological Museum: the lovely mural painting of a young girl with stylus and tablet, found in Pompeii.

Anonymus fifteenth-century artist: View of Naples. In this delightul painting, which shows the fleet of Alfonso the Magnanimous parading before Naples harbor, the city appears as a prosperous port enclosed by imposing fortifications and surrounded, on the landward side, by wooded hills. Many major monuments are recognizable; most prominent is the Castel Nuovo, in the foreground.

Santa Chiara, Chiostro delle Clarisse. This fourteenth-century cloister was transformed into a rustic garden, in 1742, by Domenico Antonio Vaccaro. Its unique character derives from the majolica tiles and terracottas, all of Neapolitan manufacture, which adorn the walkways.

View of Amalfi from the south. In the foreground is one of the huge bouganvillées charactestic of this coast.

Amalfi, Cathedral. The richly colored façade (1203) is a mixture of Norman and Lombard motifs.

Amalfi: Chiostro del Paradiso.

pillared aisles of equal height. It lay at the extremity of an aqueduct and was used for provisioning the fleet stationed at Misenum.

At the end of the town is the Lago di Miseno or Mare Morto. Leave the main road (see below), following, to the south, the causeway separating the lagoon from the picturesque harbor of Miseunum. The harbor of Misenum was built by Agrippa in 41 B.C. as a temporary refuge for the Tyrrhenian fleet during the construction of the Portus Julius (see above); it was while stationed here with the fleet that Pliny the Younger witnessed the fatal eruption of Vesuvius in A.D. 79. The port consisted of two basins, of which the inner, the Mare Morto, is now shut off by the road causeway from the Porto di Miseno proper. The colony of Misenum was founded at the same time as the harbor, and its importance diminished as the Roman naval power declined. It was destroyed by the Saracens in the ninth century.

The by-road goes on to the village of Miseno (1,5 km) beyond which cars cannot proceed. A path turns to the right near the church, to the right again just before a farmhouse, and then to the left, passing various ruins (see below). The tiring ascent (1 hour there and back) leads to **Capo Miseno** (504 ft), a promontory commanding a wonderful view over the Gulfs of Pozzuoli, Naples, and Gaeta, and the surrounding lakes and islands.

Capo Miseno represents a segment of an ancient crater, the rest of which has sunk below the sea. The remaining portion so resembles an artificial tumulus as to have given rise to the legend that it was the burial place of Misenus, the trumpeter of Aeneas. The headland was already covered with villas when the colony was founded, and among its distinguished residents was Caius Marius, whose country house passed into the possession of Lucullus and later to the Emperors. Tiberius died here in A.D. 37. The ruins of Marius's villa are those on the south side of the harbor; near the church are the remains of the circular Baths; to the northwest is a theater commanding a fine view of Ischia. On the west side of the headland is the **Grotta Dragonara**, an excavation supported by twelve pillars, probably a storehouse for the fleet. At the extremity of the cape is a lighthouse.

Hikers may follow the Spiaggia di Miliscola (*Militis Schola*), a narrow sandbar 1 mile long between the Mare Morto and the sea, and rejoin the main road about 1 km before Cappella (see below).

Rejoining the main road, bear to the left along the north side of the Mare Morto, turning sharp to the right to reach Torregaveta (small restaurants), the terminus of the Cumana Railway. Hence another road running south ascends to Monte di Procida (2 miles; bus), a village on a tufa hill covered with ruined villas among vineyards which produce an excellent wine. Acquamorta, on the end of the promontory beyond, commands a fine view of Procida and Ischia.

Leaving the Torregaveta road on the left, we reach the semicircular **Lago di Fusaro**, the ancient Acherusian Swamp, separated from the sea by a sandbar pierced by two canals, one roman and one modern (1858). On the slopes of the tufa hill north of Torregaveta is the ruined villa of Servilius Vatia. Since 1784 the lake has been a center of oyster culture and fish breeding; the establishment, where oysters may be bought, is on the east shore near the road to Cumae. In the lake is a *Casino*, built for Ferdinand IV by Vanvitelli (1782), now a marine biological station (adm. to both establishments on application).

The road crosses the railway near Cuma Fusaro Station. Leaving a road to Baia (1 mile) on the right, follow the lake shore and then pass through vineyards.

Cumae, perhaps the oldest Greek colony in Italy, is now a mass of scattered ruins in a romantic situation where excavation fights a losing battle with nature. By tradition Cumae dates its foundation from ca. 1050 B.C., the first settlers being the Chalcidians and the Aeolians of Kyme. In fact, although it was one of the earliest colonies, there is no proof that it antedated Syracuse. Its prosperity and population increased rapidly, and colonies were dispatched to Dikaearchia (Pozzuoli) and, after the conquest of Parthenope, to found the settlement of Neapolis. Cumae was a center of Hellenic culture, and from its alphabet were derived all the other Italian alphabets. In 474 B.C. the Cumaeans in alliance with Hieron of Syracuse defeated an Etruscan fleet, a victory immortalized by Pindar in the first Pythian Ode. In 421 Cumae was conquered by the Samnites, passing later, with the rest of their possessions, to Rome. In the reign of Nero it was the scene of the voluntary death of Petronius Arbiter. No longer of importance, Cumae was an easy prey to the Saracens in the ninth century, and was utterly destroyed by Naples and Aversa in 1207.

The ruins of the city itself lie for the most part beneath farm land; a visit requires at least three hours. A short distance before a fork, where the main road bears inland to the right, are the ruins of an **Amphitheater**, easily traced through the vineyards and olive groves that cover it. Taking the little road to the left at the fork we pass (right; on cultivated land) the **Temple of the Giants**, and, farther away, the **Temple of the Forum**. As we ascend toward Monte di Cuma (253 ft), the acropolis of the city, traces of many other buildings may be seen over a wide area.

Beyond the entrance to the Excavations, continue to climb; approaching the acropolis we see the massive walls of cyclopean stone, Greek in the lower courses, Roman above.

Traverse a tunnel hewn through the rock. Beyond to the left is the entrance to the **Cave of the Cumaean Sybil**, one of the more famous of ancient sanctuaries, brought to light in 1932. Here Aeneas came to consult the Sibyl; on either side of the entrance marble plaques now recall the lines of Virgil (*Aeneid*, VI, 42 - 51) describing the place and the Sibyl's prophesy. The cave consists of a corridor, about 143 ft long, more than 8 ft wide and about 18 ft high, ending in a rectangular chamber all hewn out of the rock. The corridor, of trapezoidal cross-section markedly Minoan in style, runs due north-south in the shoreward side of the hill, and is lighted by six galleries opening to the west (being thus best visited in the afternoon). From the other side open three lower chambers apparently designed for lustral waters and later used for Christian burials. The secret chamber, at the end, probably designed in the fourth or third century B.C., has three large niches. At a lower level (reached by a path to the left) a huge Roman crypt tunnels through the hill; this lies on the same axis as the Grotta della Pace (see below) and is probably a continuation of it. Many dark passages leading from it show traces of Christian occupation.

A paved via Sacra climbs to the first terrace where (on the right) are the remains of the **Temple of Apollo**, a Greek structure altered in Augustan times and transformed into a Christian church in the sixth or seventh century. On the summit is the so-called **Temple of Jupiter**, a larger work of Greek origin also transformed (fifth or sixth century) into a Christian basilica of five aisles. Behind the presbytery are remains of a large circular piscina for baptism by immersion. Here the beauty of the view and the stillness, broken only by the rustle of lizards and the sea, make an indelible impression.

The chief **Necropolis**, which has provided many interesting additions to the Naples Museum, lies between the acropolis and Licola, to the north, a modern village on the site of a drained lake.

From the ruins a path (not accessible in reverse) leads down to the deserted shore. Towards the sea the outer wall of the town is still traceable. An extension of the railway is planned from Torregaveta which may pleasantly be reached along the beach or by a well-preserved stretch of the Roman road that linked Cumae with Misenum. This was a branch of the via Domitiana, engineered in A.D. 95 to link Rome directly with Puteolo. Along its course to the north lie the Lago di Patria, once the harbor of the Roman colony of Liternum (scanty ruins), where Scipio Africanus died in 184 B.C.; and Sinuessa, near the modern Mondragone, where at the 106 th milestone from Rome it joined the via Appia.

Take the road running northeast (right) from Cumae and in five minutes a path (right) leads to the mouth of the **Grotta della Pace** (closed). The road then passes beneath (about 1 mile from Cumae) the **Arco Felice**, a massive brick archway, 65 ft high and 20 ft wide, in a deep cutting made in the Monte Grillo by Domitian to secure direct communication between Cumae and Puteoli. To the west is a good stretch of Roman paving. Pass the north side of Lake Avernus and the Monte Nuovo, then diverge right to reach (4 km, 2 miles) Arco Felice Station, whence follow the shore road to Pozzuoli. Continue by the sea past thermal spas (hotels) and pozzolana quarries.

Bagnoli is a bathing resort and spa much frequented by the Neapolitans. From here the old road runs straight to Naples. Unhurried travelers may, however, continue round the coast past the huge chemical works of Coroglio, then climb in full view of Nisida to the Rotonda, from which the return to Naples may be made along the Posillipo peninsula.

f Capua, Benevento and Saepinum

Road, 210 km (126 miles) round trip. Autostrada A2 to (28 km, 17 miles) Caserta Nord, then Highway 7 and Highway 17.

This route takes us deep into the Neapolitan hinterland, first through sprawling suburbs then across fertile plains and wooded hills.

Railway, from Naples to Santa Maria Capua Vetere and Capua, in about 1 hour; to Benevento (a change is necessary at Caserta) in about 1 hour more. Buses connect Benevento with Saepinum.

Santa Maria Capua Vetere occupies the site of the ancient *Capua*. Originally an Oscan settlement, it eventually became the most important place in Campania and the richest and most luxurious city in southern Italy. It placed itself under the protection of Rome in 343 B.C., but it opened its gates to the Carthaginian general, Hannibal, in 216 B.C. Retaken by the Romans in 211, its inhabitants, considered guilty of treason, were massacred. In 73 B.C. the revolt of gladiators headed by Spartacus broke out here in the amphitheater. The ancient city was razed by the Saracens in the ninth century, and its inhabitants fled to found the modern Capua. The present town on this site grew from a small settlement that clustered round the church of Santa Maria.

Just outside the town, we pass two interesting and well-preserved **Roman Tombs**, the second of which is the largest in Campania. The imposing **Amphitheater** was built under Augustus and restored by Hadrian and Antonius Pius. It measures 553 x 455 ft, and is second in size only to the Colosseum in Rome. It had four stories and it was surrounded by eighty arches, of which only two survive. Under the arena are three covered galleries, with a fourth round the circumference, and six vaulted passages lighted by square apertures. Fragments of the building's sculptural decoration and other antiquities (notably a second century mosaic pavement with Nereids and Tritons) are set in the park at the south of the monument. Several statues have been removed to the *Museo Archeologico Nazionale* in Naples, and seven of the busts of deities which adorned the keystones of the arches have been incorporated in the façade of the town hall at Capua. Near the amphitheater is an interesting subterranean **Mithraeum**, a cult building dedicated to the Persian god Mithras, with well preserved frescoes; visitors are conducted (10 minute walk) by a custodian.

In the modern city of **Capua**, the **Museo Campano** contains many interesting sculptures, including an extraordinary series of mother-figures from the temple of Mater Matuta; here are also inscriptions from the amphitheater, a fine series of Campanian terracottas, and a colossal head of Capua Imperiale.

Benevento is reached by returning to Caserta, where we pick up Highway 7. A city of ancient importance, it stands on a ridge between the Calore and the Sabato rivers in an amphitheater of mountains. It is the successor of the Oscan or Samni-

Santa Maria Capua a Vetere, Amphitheater. This imposing building, second in size only to the Colosseum in Rome, had four stories and was surrounded by 80 arches, only two of which remain.

te city of *Malies*, which the Romans called *Maleventum*, it is said, owing to the bad air of the place. It changed its name to *Beneventum* on its establishment as a Roman colony in 268 B.C.

Benevento stood at the end of the first extension from Capua of the Appian Way, later continued as far as Brindisium (Brindisi). Today it is famous above all for the **Arch of Trajan**, a triumphal arch 49 ft high erected across the via Appia in honor of Trajan (A.D. 114-166). It is one of the finest and best-preserved arches of its kind; the bas-reliefs depict scenes from the life of Trajan and mythological subjects. The side facing Beneventum and Rome bears a glorification of Trajan's domestic policy, including, in the attic level, Roman consuls receiving Trajan and Hadrian, and Jupiter offering the emperor his thunderbolt; in the middle level, Trajan conferring benefits on the Roman people, in the lower level, the emperor's triumphal return after the Germanic campaign. The façade facing Brindisium and the overseas provinces celebrates Trajan's provincial policy and benefits, including, in the top registers, river gods welcoming the emperor; in the middle level, Trajan recruiting troops and forming new colonies; and in the lower registers, foreign peoples swearing loyalty or bearing gifts. A continuous frieze in the form of a triumphal procession runs round all four sides of the monument, where as beneath the arch are personifications of cities, and scenes of

Fragments of the building's sculptural decoration and other antiquities including this bust of a deity, which adorns the keystone of one of the surviving arches, only two of which remain.

Trajan inaugurating a new road and distributing funds to the poor.

Continuing by the Corso we reach the tiny piazza Papiniano with an Egyptian **Obelisk** of red granite from the Temple of Isis erected by Domitian in A.D. 88 (more material from this temple may be seen in the **Museo del Sannio**, in the cloister of santa Sofia). Below the cathedral to the southwest are the pillaged remains of another triumphal arch, and the **Roman Theater**, built in the reign of Hadrian, and enlarged by Caracalla to accommodate 20,000 spectators. The first and part of the second of three tiers survive, the remainder having been destroyed to make way for the modern buildings that encroach on its perimeter. Beyond the stage ran a *peristyle*, possibly intended as a promenade for spectators, which was reached from the exterior by three flights of steps. A lower corridor behind the auditorium remains intact. Note also the extant fragments of the stage buildings.

From Benevento the return to Naples may be made via Highway 17 and its continuances, or via Autostrada A 16.

A pleasant road of 48 km (24 miles) winds through cultivated upland country to the eastern slopes of the Monti del Matese. Here the Roman **Saepinum**, later named *Atilia*, was founded by survivors from the Samnite Saipins, destroyed in

Capua, Museo Campano: Dea Matre. This image of fertility and motherhood is part of a remarkable serie of Italic statues discovered in the sanctuary of Mater Matuta, at Santa Maria Capua Vetere.

293 B.C. Its history was not particularly eventful. In the ninth century it was sacked by the Saracens, following which the survivors founded the present town on higher ground.

The defensive walls, 4062 ft in circumference, still surround the ancient town. Fortified by twenty seven bastions, they are pierced by four gates, today known as the *porta di Boiano* (northwest), *porta del Tammaro* (northeast), *porta di Benevento* (southeast) and *porta di Terravecchia* (southwest). We enter by the porta del Tammaro and traverse the site to the Porta di Terravecchia, outside which is an improvized parking lot surrounded by low walls in *opus reticulatum*. Within, the *cardus maximus* leads past modern farm houses built with the stones of the ancient city. Farther on, the road preserves its ancient pavement. The **Basilica**, on the left, has a *peristyle* made up of 20 slender Ionian columns. Turning right, follow the *decumanus* past the **Forum** and a series of public buildings that includes the **Curia** or town hall and a temple believed to have been dedicated to the Capitoline triad. Farther on, on the left, are the **House of the Olive Press** (note the brick-lined wells for storing the oil); the **Water Mill** and the so-called **House of the Samnite Impluvium**, a house with a graceful fountain, built to the typical Samnite plan around an atrium with *impluvium*, preceded by shops. Beyond the porta di Benevento stands a monumental tomb with an inscription describing the civic and military career of the defunct. To the left is a small museum with photographs and texts describing the town and its discovery, and a collection of Roman inscriptions.

Returning to the center of the town, we pass behind the Basilica to the octagonal **Market** and to what appears to be a small temple. Beyond are the remains of private dwellings and, at the end of the street, the imposing **porta di Boiano**, in *opus tesselatum*, flanked by cylindrical bastions, another of which can be seen along the wall to the north. At the sides of the arch are statues of prisoners on plinths; that on the right is headless. The keystone is carved with a bearded head, possibly of Hercules; the inscription above the arch tells that the fortification of the town was financed by the future emperor Tiberius and his brother Drusus. Steps ascend to the top of the gate, whence there is a fine view over the excavations; the rectangular **Tomb of the Numisi**, in a field to the north; and the **Baths**, the remains of which extend along the town wall between the *decumanus* and the **Theater**. The latter is reached by a minor gate, an unusual feature that may reflect a combination of theatrical performances with fairs held outside the walls. Surrounded by farm houses, it preserves large portions of the cavea and orchestra. On the stage, another farm building houses a beautiful collection of objects found on the site and in the vicinity, chiefly funerary sculpture from a necropolis brought to light along the portion of the *decumanus* outside the walls. Photographs and texts explain the finds. On the first floor are numerous maps and plans describing the territory, the town, and its monuments.

g The Museo Archeologico Nazionale

Our introduction to the ancient treasures of Naples and its environs now takes us back to the city and the *Museo Archeologico Nazionale* (Map 2, 2), one of the largest and most interesting museums of antiquities in the world. Universally famous for its magnificent series of exhibits of every kind from Pompeii and Herculaneum, the museum is also of prime importance for the study of Greek sculpture. Parts of the collections are periodically closed for restoration; as work proceeds, these rooms are reopened and others are closed.

The **Ground Floor** is mainly devoted to **Sculpture** from the Farnese collection (inherited by King Charles of Bourbon from his mother, Elisabeth Farnese), the Borgia collection from Velletri, and the cities of Campania.

The main entrance opens into the *Grande Atrio dei Magistrati*, containing statues and tombs of the Imperial Age of Rome. Note N° 6705, *Marble sarcophagus from Pozzuoli*, with Prometheus, the Giant in Greek legend who steals fire from heaven as a gift for man, molding man out of clay in the presence of the gods. The sarcophagus dates from the third century A.D.

In Room I, the Galleria dei Tirannicidi (right), are (N° 153654) a statue of *Aphrodite*, the goddess of love and beauty, from Baiae, the best surviving imitation of the celebrated work by the Greek sculptor Kalamis; and (N° 6009 and 6010) *Harmodius and Aristogeiton*, slayers of the tyrant Hipparchus. From Tivoli, this is a copy of the group made by Kritius and Nesiotes in 477 B.C. for the agora at Athens.

The next five rooms, to the right of this hall, contain sculpture of the Golden Age of Greek art (fifth century B.C.).

Room II. N° 6024 shows *Athena*, the goddess of wisdom and of women's crafts. It is a copy, executed with considerable dignity, of a bronze statue of the school of Phidias. In N° 6727, a bas-relief, we see *Orpheus, Eurydice, and Hermes*, actors in a story that was very popular among the ancients. The legend tells that the musician Orpheus descended to Hades after the death of his wife Eurydice and by his music obtained her release on condition that he not look back at her until reaching the upper world. But he disobeyed, and his wife was once again taken away from him and led back to the underworld by a reluctant Hermes. The story inspired a famous opera by the eighteenth century German composer Christoph Willibald Gluck. The bas-relief is the best of the three known copies of a work by Phidias. Note also N° 5997, *Aphrodite Genetrix*, from Herculaneum; N° 6725, *Votive relief* from Herculaneum, a Greek original from the early Hellenic period, and N° 6322, *Herm of Athena*, also from Herculaneum, with a mild and youthful cast of features, probably copied from a Greek original of 450-425 B.C. N° 5630 is the celebrated statue of *Apollo*, the god of sunlight, prophecy, and music and poetry in Greek mythology, found in the House of the Citharist at Pompeii. The statue, which probably dates from the late first century B.C., is incomplete. The object Apollo grips in his right hand is generally believed to be a plectrum, used for plucking the strings of a cithara or lyre, which he may have held in his left hand. But some scholars maintain the object is an arrow head. In this case he would not be holding a lyre, but a bow. It is a difficult question to settle because his attributes are either the lyre or the bow, depending on whether he is represented as god of song or as an unerring archer.

R III. N° 6011, *Doryphorus* (from Pompeii), is the most complete copy of the famous spear-bearer of Polycleitus (ca. 440 B.C.), which was considered the canon or perfect model of manly proportions.

Room V. The statue of *Diomedes*, a Greek warrior in the Trojan war, was found at Cumae. It is a copy of an Attic original of 450-430 B.C., attributed to Kresilas.

Room VI. N° 145070 and 14080 represent *Nereids*, the sea nymphs held in Greek mythology to be the daughters of the sea-god Nereus. Found in a Roman villa at Formia, they may be Greek originals of the fifth or fourth century B.C.

Returning to the Galleria dei Tirannicidi, we pass through Room VII (which includes several marble works, notably N° 143753, a bronze *Ephebe*, or young man, from Pompeii) to the Galleria di Flora (Room VIII). Here are two colossal statues (N° 5999 and 6409) from the Baths of Caracalla in Rome; N° 6271, *Neptune*, the god of the sea in Roman mythology, a graceful copy of a fourth century original; and N° 6351, *Ganymede*, with the eagle that carried him off to Olympus to be the cupbearer of the gods, and a lifelike dog.

On the right of this the Galleria del Toro Farnese, a long hall of six bays (Rooms XI - XVI) contains Greek sculpture of the fourth to second century B.C., at the far end of which (right), beyond a vestibule, are two small rooms.

Room IX. N° 6012-15, *Four Statues*, are copies of originals commissioned by Attalus, King of Pergamum, to commemorate his victory of 239 B.C.

Room X. N° 6020 is a statue of *Venus*, the Roman goddess

of love and beauty, from the Domus Aurea of Nero. She is shown in the act of undressing to bathe; as her gown falls from her back she looks over her shoulder to admire her figure reflected in the water, in a charming image of femininity.

We return to Room XI. Note N° 124325, *Tomb from Atella* with relief of Achilles, the Greek warrior and hero of Homer's *Iliad*, in a scene drawn from the epic poem.

Room XII. No number, *Aphrodite of Sinuessa*, is probably a fourth century Greek original. N° 6001 is the so-called *Farnese Hercules*, from the Baths of Caracalla in Rome. Although the hero of classical mythology is noted for his great strength and especially for achieving twelve labors imposed on him by Hera, sister and wife of Zeus, he is shown here at rest, his face bearing an expression of melancholy. This is a copy by Glycon of a work by Lysippus; N° 6027, *Mars Resting*, is a very fine replica from a fourth century original. N° 6035, *Aphrodite*, an unusually beautiful torso, is attributed to Praxiteles.

Room XIII. N° 6260, a colossal mask of *Zeus*, chief of the Olympian gods, is similar to the famous Vatican Jupiter. It probably dates from the fourth century B.C. N° 6353 is a copy of a Praxitelean bronze of *Eros*, the god of love in classical mythology. N° 6673, the *Gaeta Vase*, shows the myth of Hermes delivering the young Dionysus to the nymphs of Nysa. It is signed by the Athenian Salpion, an artist of the first century B.C. N° 6282, a relief panel, shows *Paris with Helen and Aphrodite*. The abduction of Helen, the beautiful wife of the king of Sparta, by Paris, son of the king of Troy, led to the Trojan War. Here the goddess attempts to persuade Helen to love her abductor.

Room XIV. N° 6019 may represent *Psyche*, the beautiful priestess of classical mythology loved by Cupid. Some scholars, however, believe it portrays Venus; whereas others see in it Andromeda, an Ethiopian princess rescued from a monster by Zeus's son Perseus, and made his wife. Found at Capua, it is a first century A.D. copy of a fourth century B.C. original. N° 6017, commonly called the *Capua Venus* (after the amphitheater where it was found) is considered by specialists to represent Aphrodite.

Room XV. N° 6022 shows *Dionysus*, the god of wine; and a *satyr*, a woodland deity fond of Dionysian revelry. This is a copy preserving all the liveliness and exuberance of the original Hellenistic bronze. N° 6329 represents *Pan*, the Greek god of forests, pastures, flocks, and shepherds, teaching the young Olympus to play the panpipes. Another woodland deity and companion of Dionysus is portrayed in N° 6333, *Laughing Silenus*.

Room XVI is dominated by (N° 6002) the *Farnese Bull*, the largest known work of antique sculpture. Found at the Baths of Caracalla in Rome, the group represents the vengeance of Zeus and Amphion on Dirce, queen of Thebes. The twins' mother, Antiope, whom the royal family had imprisoned, looks on as the heroes prepare to tie the Persian queen to the horns of a mad bull. Dirce vainly implores their mercy, as the tutelary deity of the place and his barking dog watch. Once again, we are looking at a Roman copy, in marble, of a Hellenistic bronze original.

The Egyptian collection occupies the vestibule prolonging the Gallery of Flora and part of the basement. To our left is a gallery (Room XXIX) devoted to colored marbles, mainly of Eastern deities. Notice particularly N° 6262, *Apollo*, in dark green basalt, a Hellenistic type; N° 6278, *Diana of Ephesus*, a Roman work in alabaster, with face, hands, and feet of bronze; and N° 6281, *Apollo* in porphyry with white marble extremities.

The five rooms (XXIV-XXVIII) leading from this gallery are occupied by a collection of decorative sculpture, and reliefs with interesting details of hunting, etc. Note the fragment (110565 in Room XXVIII) showing two *Fighting Biremes*.

Return to the Grande Atrio, cross to the left wing, and enter the Galleria dei Busti Greci (Room XLV). N° 6023 portrays *Homer;* the straining of the blind poet's eyes to catch the light is admirably rendered. The adjoining corridor (right) contains a display of Roman portrait sculpture.

In the north court is the Sezione Tecnologica, in which are gathered numerous ancient surgical and scientific instruments, many of which have been reconstructed.

Entresol. From the Grande Atrio ascend the main staircase to the mezzanine floor. The right wing (temporarily closed) contains Mural Paintings from Campanian Cities. There are five rooms (LI-LVI), the last two containing the entire pictorial decoration from the Temple of Isis at Pompeii. The finest exhibits in this genre, however, are on the First Floor (Rooms LXVI - LXXVIII, see below). The west wing of the Entresol is occupied by Pompeian Mosaics. Among them are some of the finest known examples of the art; all three types, *opus tessellatum* (formed entirely of square tiles), *opus vermiculatum* (with tiles arranged in lines following the contours of the design), and *opus sectile* (with tiles cut in geometrical shapes) are represented.

Room LIX. N° 9985, entitled *Comic Actors* (but held, by a differing interpretation, to represent begging musicians), is a very fine mosaic from the Villa of Cicero, representing two women, a man, and a dwarf, all masked and playing musical instruments. N° 9987, *Consulting the Sorceress*, is a scene from a comedy. Both of these are signed by Dioscorides of Samos. N° 124545, *The Academy at Athens*, has seven figures (Plato in the center) with the Acropolis as background. N° 120177, a pattern of *Fish, Shellfish, and Marine Creatures*, shows more than twenty species, including an octopus.

Another (9997) may be seen in Room LX; equally realistic are (N° 9990) the panels showing *Nile Scenes*, with crocodiles, hippopotami, ibis, etc., originally the frame of the *Battle of Issus* described below. Also worthy of notice is N° 9991, *Winged Boy Riding a Tiger*.

Room LXI contains mosaics from the House of the Faun, as well as the celebrated *Dancing Faun* from which the house takes its name. The faun, another deity of fields and herds having human shape with pointed ears, small horns, and a goat's tail, was an unrestrained lover of wine, women, and song, an ideal personification of abandonment and pleasure. In the same room are (N° 9994) a *Decorative Band with Festoons and Theater Masks*; (N° 9993) a *Still-Life* in two registers, with a remarkably lifelike cat catching a quail; and (N° 10020) the largest and most intricate of the mosaics found at Pompeii, which probably represents the *Battle of Issus* (333 B.C.), a key encounter in the struggle of Alexander the Great to wrest control of Persia from King Darius. Feder provides a charming description:

> Alexander is the bareheaded horseman at the left, astride his warhorse, Bucephalus. His portraits almost always show him from the side, unhelmeted, with long disheveled hair and a look of wide-eyed intensity, which his admirers

Naples, National Archaeological Museum. The masterpieces of antique art contained in this extraordinary museum include Darius and Alexander at the Battle of Issus (333 B.C.), a finely executed mosaic from the House of the Faun in Pompeii.

associated with genius. His opponent, Darius, stands with outstretched arm at the back of a chariot, right of center. Interestingly, the focus of the composition is on the defeated Darius, not on the victor Alexander, as if by exploring the nobility and psychology of the loser, the artist pays tribute to the man who defeated him.

According to historical accounts, Darius turned his chariot and fled when the tide of battle went against the Persians, and this is the moment shown here. Darius's driver has maneuvered the chariot almost completely around, and we see him furiously whipping the four hourses on. The perspective of the composition is breathtaking. The chariot exists in a pivotal plane; at one end Darius gestures towards a fallen comrade, and at the other end the charioteer drives the horses in the opposite direction. With his upraised arm, he echoes the gesture of the hapless king.

The composition is thought to follow a fourth century Greek painting probably by Philoxenos, and is one of the few ancient works which develops perpendicularly to the picture plane as well as horizontally.

Rooms LXIII - IV are being rearranged.

First Floor. At the top of the stairs, between the left and right wings, is the immense Salone dell'Atlante, now used for temporary exhibitions. The left wing contains the Sale della Villa dei Papiri, in which are displayed artworks and artefacts found in the celebrated villa at Herculaneum, excavated in 1750-61.

Room CXV. Cases 1, 2, and 3: small bronzes from the atrium. Case 4: small bronzes from a room on the west side of the villa. Case 5: small portrait busts, mainly from the third century onwards; dancing and playing satyrs.

In the adjoining room (CXIV) are several murals and carbonized fragments of papyri.

Room CXVI hosts the so-called *Dancers* (N° 5604-5, 5619-21, first century B.C.) and other sculptures, notably (N° 5624) *Sleeping Satyr*, (N° 5628) *Drunken Silenus*, and (N° 5625) *Hermes Resting*.

Room CXVII. N° 5616, *Portrait head* (Seneca? first century B.C.). N° 5610, *Heracles*, copy after Polycleitus. N° 5608, *Bust of a young man*.

The rooms in the right wing are numbered from front to rear of the building. Their contents fall into three groups: the south rooms are devoted to Campanian wall-paintings, the north rooms to bronze objects; while in between are other miscellaneous objects including furniture, household utensils, images, etc., which give a very complete idea of ancient domestic life.

To the left, as we enter, opens the first of six rooms (XC - XCV) containing *Small bronzes from Pompeii and*

Herculaneum. These include numerous *statuettes* (representing mythological subjects, wild animals, hunting scenes, etc.); *household items* (vases, strong boxes, lamps, door handles, locks, various forms of heating apparatus, a colored marble table with bronze feet, mirrors and personal ornaments, writing materials, weights and measures), *theater tickets*; *musical and architectural instruments*; *surgical instruments* (including specula, a forceps, and a catheter); and *Papyri* from Herculaneum, some partly unrolled.

We pass to Room XCVI. In the center is a cork model of Pompeii showing the discoveries made up to 1879. The wall cases contain carbonized food, articles of domestic use (soap, sulphur, etc.), textiles, rope-soled shoes, etc. N° 78614-15 are Triclinia, or couches. Round the walls are Pompeian mural paintings (still life).

Hence we enter Room LXXXIII. Many of the objects in this and the next room have been removed for cleaning and restoration. N° 27611 is the celebrated *Tazza Farnese*, a cup of veined sardonyx, one of the largest known examples of the cameo-maker's art. Here are also gold rings, necklaces, and bracelets.

Room LXXXII contains *Tableware* from the House of the Menander, cups, and other vessels of silver (115 pieces in all), some produced by a late Hellenistic workshop, others by Roman workshops of the Augustan age.

Room LXXXI is devoted to *Glassware*. Notice N° 13521, *Blue glass vase* of fine workmanship, beautifully ornamented.

Room LXXX contains *Lamps, ivories, and enameled terra-cottas*, showing a style of ceramic decoration probably imported from Egypt.

Room LXXIX displays *Arms and armor*, and *trumpets*. Notice N° 5673-4, *Gladiators' helmets*, with delicate reliefs.

From here on the south rooms are devoted to the best of the Mural Paintings from the Campanian cities.

Room LXXVII. N° 9058, a double portrait of convincing realism, is thought to represent the prominent baker and public official *Paquius Proculus and His Wife*. Paquius may be the *Baker Selling Bread* (or, by another interpretation, the civic official distributing loaves as an act of public charity) in N° 9071. We know that there were occasional bread shortages in Pompeii, and that one of the duties of new officials was to undertake at their own expense some civic work. Paquius Proculus, elected to the high office of aedile (whose functions included the supervision of markets and public works), may have spent his money in an official bread distribution, as a means of fixing his name and profession in the eyes of the ever-watchful electorate.

N° 119286, *Bacchus and Mount Vesuvius*, is generally considered an allegory of Pompeii. Bacchus was the god of wine in classical mythology, and wine for Pompeii meant prosperity. The poet Martial, lamenting the destruction of Pompeii, provides a fitting comment for this painting: "This is Vesuvius, shaded yesterday with green vines. Here its far famed grapes filled the dripping vats. These ridges Bacchus loved more than the hills of Nysa, on this Mount of late the Satyrs set afoot their dances . . . Now all lies buried in flames and melancholy ashes". The painting comes from a *lararium* or domestic shrine, and the serpent at the bottom represents the tutelary spirit of the house.

N° 112222, shows the *Brawl In the Amphitheater at Pompeii Between Pompeians and Nucerians* of 59 B.C. To show the interior of the amphitheater, the painter has chosen a birds-eye view, with the tarpaulin that shaded the seats partly rolled back. The brawl is in full swing in the arena; outside the building may be seen the stalls where food and drink were sold.

N° 9514 is a *View of a Campanian port*. It is painted in an illusionistic style reminiscent of that of the Venetian painter Canaletto. Scholars do not know with certainty just what city it represents: some have opted for Puteoli, others for Cumae. Strabo spoke admiringly of the port facilities of the latter town, noting that "They run jetties out into the sea and thus make the wide open shore curve into the form of bays, enabling the greatest merchant ships to moor with safety." The painting was found a Stabiae, which was too small to boast such a developed harbor. It dates from sometime after A.D. 50.

Room LXXIV contains a number of delicately painted works, including N° 9176-9179, and 9215, *Cupids at Work and Play*; and N° 8978, 9546, 9243, and 8834, four small paintings of women, *Medea, Leda and the Swan, Diana*, and a *Girl Gathering Flowers* (so-called Spring), from Stabiae.

In Room LXXIII are two notable mythological scenes: N° 8980, *Meleager and Atalanta*; and N° 111439, *Iphigenia in Tauris*.

Room LXXII is devoted to colored painting on marble. Notice N° 8998, *Perseus and Andromeda*, considered the most faithful copy of the original painted by Nikias; 116085, *Achilles Discovered at Skyros*, by the Greek painter Theon of Samos; 9559, *Nuptials of Jupiter*; 9112, *Sacrifice of Iphigenia* depicted in a manner similar to that of traditional representations of the sacrifice of Isaac; 8976, *Medea*, perhaps copied from a celebrated paining by Timomachus; 9559, *Nuptials of Jupiter and Hera* on Mount Ida; 9562, *Girls Playing with Knuckle-bones* (The Astragal Players), signed by Alexander of Athens and executed in monochrome on marble, in the encaustic technique. The scene may represent the vengeance of Leto, as narrated by Ovid (Metamorphoses, VI).

Room LXX. N° 8992, *Hercules and Omphale*; 9270, Bacchic scene, with a boy of charming vivacity; and 9560,

Battle with a Centaur, are noteworthy.

Room LXVII contains a series of remarkable Italic paintings, including N° 9361-9363, *Tomb Walls with Sacred Vases*, and *Horse and Foot Soldiers*, from Paestum; and 9352-57, *Funeral Dance*, from Ruvo. At the center of the room stands a painted tomb from Afragola (third century B.C.).

The remaining rooms on this floor (beyond Room LXXXIII, see above) contain lesser works. Rooms LXXXIV - LXXXV, common glass objects. Rooms LXXXCVI - LXXX-VII, terra-cotta figures (sixth century B.C. - first century A.D.) from Cumae, Pompeii, Paestum, Metapontum, Capua, etc. Rooms LXXXVII - LXXXIX, small decorative sculptures.

Part of the Second Floor may be reached from Room XCVI (see above). Here, in Rooms XCVII-CV, is the *Collection of Figured Vases*, comprising black and red figured Attic vases of every period, arranged chronologically, and Apulian and early Italian vases arranged according to their place of origin. A parallel gallery houses the Coin Collection, comprising coins, medals, and tokens from the earliest times to the present day. The Greek and Roman coins are especially beautiful and valuable.

II From Rome to the Renaissance

The decline of the Roman Empire is too complicated to go into in detail here. Suffice it to say very simply that the Romans were unprepared-economically, politically, and psychological-ly-for the enormous military effort that three centuries of barbarian invasions required of them. The eastern provinces, with their capital at Constantinople (or Byzantium as it was then called), managed to defend their borders and preserve imperial institutions of law and government. But the weaker provinces of the west were overrun by the Germanic peoples who, driven from their homelands by other invaders, sought a safe refuge on Roman soil.

These historical events found concrete expression in the art and architecture of our area. The Early Christian churches and catacombs that grew up in Naples and its environs in the late Roman period, reflect classical as well as medieval values. They set the spiritual tone of much of the art of later centuries. The finest of these works-the fifth century mosaics in Naples (in the Baptistery of San Giovanni in Fonte and in the Catacomb of San Gennaro) and at San Prisco, near Santa Maria Capua Vetere (in the chapel of Santa Matrona, attached to the parish church)-are distinguished by an explicit naturalism that is rarely seen outside of Rome.

During the fifth century Campania fell prey to the Goths, and for the next five centuries the region lacked both the financial resources and the political stability that are the prerequisites of major artistic undertakings. In 535 the area was conquered by the Byzantine general, Belisarius. Totilla, another Gothic leader, drove the Byzantines from the area in 547; ten years later, it reverted to Byzantine rule. Then, toward the end of the century, the weak hold of the Eastern Emperors relaxed under the pressure of another Germanic people, the Lombards, who in just a few years gained control of the important provinces of Capua, Benevento, Nola, Acerra, and Nocera, reaching the sea at Salerno in 646.

While the Lombards ruled over the interior of Campania, the part of the province remaining under the empire gave its allegiance to the duke of Naples, who was originally a Greek envoy, but after 661 was a native Neapolitan. In 763 Duke Stephen II, while ostensibly maintaining his loyalty to Byzantium, secured for his family the privilege of hereditary power, and gradually detached Naples from the direct domination of the empire. His allies in Sorrento, Amalfi, and Gaeta soon followed suit, their dukes, likewise separated by distance and political interest from their nominal allegiance to

Byzantium, disengaged themselves from the Eastern Empire in 768, 786, 899, respectively. During this period, which historians call the age of the Independent Duchy (763-1139), Latin replaced Greek as the official language in Naples, and the Roman image of St. Januarius substituted the Greek effigy of the emperor on municipal seals and coins. The city developed one of the strongest fleets in Europe, and in the ninth century it joined forces with Gaeta, Sorrento, and Amalfi to rid the Tyrrhenian Sea of the marauding Saracens, who terrorized the coasts and interfered with life-giving maritime trade. By so doing the Campanian cities avenged the Saracens sack of Rome (846); and with a famous victory over the Saracens three years later at Ostia, celebrated by Raphael in the Vatican Stanze, they saved the Eternal City from a new catastrophe.

The Norman conquest (1030-1130) restored political unity to southern Italy. The Norman adventurers who first came to the area in 1016 to seek their fortunes in Apulia and Calabria seem to have had no political ambitions. Lacking organization and experienced leadership, they were prepared to live as mercenaries in the service of the Byzantines or the Lombards.

It was not until 1030 that Sergius of Naples, by awarding the Norman leader Rainulf the country of Aversa in payment for services rendered, gave them the opportunity to begin an organized conquest of the land. In the years that followed, Norman knights, led by the sons of Tancred de Hauteville, intervened in local conflicts and by so doing gradually gained control of Capua (1062), Salerno (1076), and Amalfi (1137). Naples was the last to fall: it maintained its independence until 1139, its citizens resisting even after the submission of its duke. By the middle of the twelfth century Campania was completely in the power of the conquerors, whose dominion extended over all southern Italy and Sicily. This vast territory became the Norman Kingdom of Sicily, with its capital at Palermo. It was administered efficiently, and with great tolerance of the region's Arabic, Jewish, Greek, and Roman traditions. It is a pity that in this scheme of things Naples lost its primacy and was reduced to the status of a provincial town.

The Norman influence is most clearly seen in the maritime cities, which prospered by trade with Sicily and the Orient, and were the chief channels through which the Norman court of Palermo administered its holdings on the mainland.

Siculo-Norman artists, or local artists trained in the Norman schools of Sicily, were active at Salerno, Ravello, Sessa Aurunca, Gaeta, and elsewhere in Campania throughout the eleventh and twelfth centuries. They have left an extraordinary series of sculptures-mainly decorating episcopal thrones, pulpits, paschal candelabra, and altar screens-incorporating colored glass inlay and marble tarsia work that owe their existence ultimately to Saracenic sources. The Normans are also responsible for introducing to the area French architectural forms and styles, which find their most harmonious expression in the Abbey of Fossanova, consecrated in 1208.

Also in the eleventh century, another important event, the rebuilding of the Benedictine abbey of Montecassino under the enlightened direction of the abbot Desiderius, stimulated the renewal of artistic activity in our area. From Montecassino Desiderius masterminded a real revolution of the arts. He brought in architects from Lombardy and artists from Constantinople and trained his monks in their methods, giving rise to a new artistic sensibility which combined the splendor of Oriental mosaic and allied crafts with revived Early Christian narrative methods. Unfortunately Montecassino has lost most of its medieval grandeur. But a reflection of its decorative program may be seen in the marvellous series of contemporary frescoes in the basilica at Sant'Angelo in Formis, near Capua.

Further contacts between Eastern and Western artistic cultures are evident in the bronze doors that appeared on Campanian cathedrals in the eleventh and twelfth centuries. The first of these were installed at Amalfi in 1065. They had been commissioned in Constantinople by the wealthy Amalfitan merchant Pantaleon, who had business interests in the Byzantine capital and must have been impressed by bronze doors on churches there. Desiderius of Montecassino was so moved by these doors when he visited Amalfi that he ordered a pair for the abbey. The fashion spread from there to Salerno, Atrani, Ravello, Benevento, and other southern Italian cities.

In 1194 the crown was claimed by the emperor Henry IV of Hohenstaufen, in the name of his wife, Constance (daughter of Roger II). He was succeeded as emperor and king of Sicily by his son Frederick II (1197-1250), whose splendid court at Palermo drew on Islamic and Jewish, as well as Christian, cultures. Frederick's belief in the principles of just government is reflected in the famous code of laws known as the *Constitutiones Augustales*. His interest in rational science and love of classical sculpture (visible in the remarkable series of classicizing sculptures, now on exhibit in the *Museo Campano* at Capua, that he commissioned to decorate his Porta Romana outside that city) foreshadow the Renaissance. Naples initially challenged his sovereignty, and suffered a humiliating defeat at the hands of an imperial army. In a gesture of calculated magnanimity, Frederick regained the favor of the Neapolitans by making their city, and not Palermo, the intellectual capital of his kingdom: in 1224 he founded the University, where many famous men of letters-including Pier delle Vigne, Andrea d'Isernia, Bartolomeo Prignano, and Cino da Pistoia, were teachers.

Frederick's son Conrad died before he could take posses-sion of his kingdom and Pope Urban IV at once set about finding a rival candidate for the Sicilian crown. He chose Charles of Anjou, the ambitious and ruthless young brother of St. Louis of France. In two fortunate battles, at Benevento (1266) and Tagliacozzo (1268), Charles defeated the last of the Hohenstaufen, establishing himself as the first French king of Sicily. To mark the sharp contrast between his monarchy and that of his predecessors, he transferred his capital from Palermo to Naples, which naturally grew in importance.

The Angevin court of Naples was as sophisticated and cosmopolitan as any contemporary court in Provence. As allies of the pope the French kings employed Florentine bankers and patronized Florentine intellectuals, many of whom, like the famous poet Giovanni Boccaccio, became quite fond of their adopted home. Boccaccio came to Naples as a young man, around 1327, to gain practice as a merchant and banker. He served a long (but fruitless) apprenticeship at the Bardi bank in the lively Portanova neighborhood, an experience which brought him into daily contact with clients from all areas of the Mediterranean. Boccaccio's life could not have been that of an ordinary apprentice-clerk, for he was the son of a partner of the Bardi who in 1328 became a "counsellor and chamberlain" of King Robert. The refined and gay life of the Neapolitan upper classes, divided between the aristocratic opulence of the city and the carefree and voluptuous "idleness" of the gulf-shore resorts (particularly Baia), is delightfully portrayed in his early works. In his Rhymes, for instance, he voices a curious lament:

If I fear the sky and sea of Baia,
the ground and waves and lakes and fountains,
the wild and the domestic places,
no-one should be surprised.
Here one spends all one's time partying
with music and song, and with vain words
seducing wandering minds
or talking about love's victories.

Against this background he chose to set his great love novel, the *Elegia a Madonna Fiammetta*.

The gaiety of the Angevin court unfortunately did not extend to the rest of the kingdom. Indeed, the political life of these years was as turbulent as the social life was exuberant. Charles initially enjoyed the favor of his subjects, but his political ambitions, which necessitated oppressive taxation, soon brought resentment: revolt broke out spontaneously in Palermo on Easter Tuesday, 1282, in the "Sicilian Vespers". Within a month the French garrisons on the island had been either expelled or massacred, and the Sicilian nobles had summoned the Catalonian Peter of Aragon to be their king. Charles died in 1286, and his heir, Charles II, was not crowned until two years later. He was succeeded in 1309 by his second son, Robert, who proved to be a capable ruler and patron of the arts (it was he who financed Boccaccio's literary endeavors), but whose authority was limited by a turbulent and rebellious baronage. He was succeeded (1342) by his granddaughter Joan, whose husband and crown prince, Andrew of Hungary, was assassinated in 1345, probably with the queen's complicity. Joan nominated Louis of Anjou her heir, and he was recognized by the anti-pope Clement VII. Pope Urban VI, however, named Charles of Durazzo, great-grandson of Charles II, king of Naples. Charles conquered the kingdom and took Joan prisoner in 1381, and had her murdered the following year. Louis died in exile three years later. The anarchic reigns of Charles III and his son Ladislas were followed (1414) by the dissolute rule of Joan II, which was torn by the rival claims of Louis III of Anjou and of Alfonso of Aragon to be her heir. Alfonso seized Naples at Joan's death in 1335, and the kingdom passed to the house of Aragon.

During the thirteenth and early fourteenth century the artistic impetus in our area, which came through the Angevin dynasty in Naples, was understandably French-oriented. The Angevins generally imported their architects from France, but they chose their artists from among the representative masters of the major Italian schools: Pietro Cavallini from Rome, Giotto from Florence, Simone Martini and Tino di Camaino from Siena. By so doing they established a pattern of patronage (privileging foreign artists or artists from farther north over local masters) that would continue, with rare exceptions, until the seventeenth century.

During the brief reign of Alfonso of Aragon, nicknamed "the Magnanimous," Naples was again united with Sicily and the kingdom enjoyed a period of renewed splendor, for Alfonso was at once a brilliant ruler, a scholar, and a patron of the arts. When he died (1458) his brother John II succeeded to the throne of Sicily, while Naples adopted his illegitimate son Ferdinand I (Ferrante) as king. Like his father, Ferrante surrounded himself with artists and humanists and was a typical Renaissance prince, though he often showed a vein of cruelty (it was his policy to imprison his enemies in the Castel Nuovo until they died; they would then be mumified and exhibited to his guests, dressed in the clothes they had worn when living). Ferrante was succeeded by Alfonso II, who in September 1491 surrendered the kingdom to Charles VII of France. Many months later Alfonso's son Ferdinand II (Ferrandino), with the help of Spain, returned to his capital where he died in 1496. During the reign of his successor, Frederick, the country was torn by civil war and brigandage as both the French and the Spanish continued to press their claims. A series of victories of the Spanish forces under Gonzalo de Cordoba secured the kingdom for Spain in 1503. Naples was not united with Sicily, but governed by a separate viceroy, Gonzalo being the first.

While Renaissance painters in Florence, Rome, and Venice produced works of art that are known the world over, very little of note was done in fifteenth century Naples. Like the Angevins, the Aragonese entrusted their most important commissions to famous names of the north (notably the Florentines Donatello, Michelozzo, Antonio Rossellino, and Benedetto da Maiano). This was only to be expected, as they could afford the best works and considered themselves to be on a level with the great families of northern cities. The major Neapolitan painter of the fifteenth century is Colantonio, whose style shows debt to Flemish painting. Andrea da Salerno has left many fine works throughout Campania. Despite the fine sculpted works by northern Italian artists in the major churches of Naples, there was still no local school of any merit. The most successful architects were Tommaso and Giovanni Tommaso Malvito, and Giovanni Francesco Mormanno, who are responsible for several churches and chapels.

Site Visits

a Early Christian Naples

Walking tour, about 8 km (5 miles), with buses.
Some very old legends tell that St. Peter visited Naples on his way to Rome, interrupting his journey to establish a diocese in the city and name St. Asprenus as its first bishop; numerous chronicles describe the martyrdom, near Pozzuoli, of the bishop Januarius; and unsubstantiated legends attribute the foundation of the city's first Christian churches to the time of Constantine (A.D. 306-337). But recent studies show that St. Peter did not visit Naples, the birth date of the Neapolitan Episcopate is still uncertain, and although there is evidence that followers of the new religion existed in the city shortly after the time of Christ, we now know that Naples' first Christian churches were erected only at the end of the fourth century.

This route takes us to the **Catacombs of San Gennaro and San Gaudioso** (the only Early Christian cemeteries of southern Italy that have a certain artistic importance); the **Baptistery of San Giovanni al Fonte** (built by the bishop Soterus in the late fifth century and later incorporated in the Cathedral); and the church of **San Giorgio Maggiore** (the interior of which contains part of the first Christian religious building erected in Naples).

From the Castel Nuovo (Map 2, 14) the via San Carlo leads

past the San Carlo Theater to the piazza Trento e Trieste (see Route 1A). Here it is best to take a bus (No. 24) or taxi up the busy via Roma and its continuations to the Tondo di Capodimonte, a wooded traffic circle near the top of the Capodimonte hill. Continue on foot along the via di Capodimonte to reach (left) the Madre del Buon Consiglio, a large, modern church built in imitation of St. Peter's in Rome. Hence follow the lane on the left side of the building to the entrance to the **Catacomb of San Gennaro** (Map 4, 2).

This catacomb dates from the second century A.D., and seems to have developed around the family tomb of an early member of the Christian community. It probably became the official cemetery of Christian Naples after the burial here, in the third century, of the bishop-saint Agrippinus, over whose tomb a basilica was built. Later, when the fifth century martyr and patron saint of the city, St. Januarius, was entombed here, the catacomb became a place of pilgrimage. Here also are buried the first dukes of Naples, notably Stephen I (d. A.D. 800) and Stephen III (d. 832). In 831 Sicone, prince of Benevento, carried the relics of St. Januarius off to his city; and around the mid-ninth century the bishop-saint John IV transferred the remains his illustrious predecessors to the Cathedral. But he, like his successor St. Athanasius (d. 877), was buried here, and the catacomb remained in use throughout the tenth and probably the eleventh century.

From the entrance, steps descend to the first of two levels. We emerge into a large room, on the right of which is a smaller chamber containing a tomb adorned with the oldest known representation of St. Januarius: it dates from the fifth century. Just around the corner, in another small room, are tombs frescoed with the images of St. Peter and St. Paul (left), and the deceased, Bitalia, praying (right). We return to the larger room. The tomb (left) showing the deceased, Eleusinius, in a tondo surrounded by foliage, also dates from the fifth century.

We retrace our steps and turn right at the foot of the stairs to enter the main hall. Beside the stairs, on the left, is another small chamber with two tombs adorned with delicate paintings perhaps the finest in the catacomb. The first represents Theotecnus with his wife and daughter between four lighted candles symbolizing Christ and eternal beatitude. The second shows the deceased, Proculus, praying between two candles and four palms. Next door is another chamber frescoed with the images of St. Peter and a figure bearing a crown (left); and St. Paul and the deceased Lawrence, who also holds a crown, symbol of his canonization (right).

Pass beneath a triple archway with fragmentary remains of frescoes, and enter a large hall. Beyond a second triple archway, with columns carved out of the tufa, on the right, are tombs frescoed with birds and the monogrammed cross, respectively symbolizing the faithful and the Resurrection. Further along, in a deep chamber on the right, is a tomb with carved architectural elements reflecting the high social standing of the deceased. Across the main hall is a rectangular room formerly used as a basilica. In the vaulted ceiling are fragments of the original, sixth century decoration, with portraits of the first fourteen bishops of Naples. Here is the recently excavated **Crypt of the Bishops**, containing the tombs of eight fifth century Neapolitan bishops. Four of these still bear a fine contemporary mosaic decoration representing the bishops surrounded by foliate motifs. The portrait on the tomb to the right is believed, on the basis of the subject's north African facial features, to represent St. Quodvultdeus, bishop of Carthage.

A corridor at the end of the main room leads to a vestibule, the ceiling of which contains poorly preserved fragments of second and third century frescoes of Adam and Eve, David and Goliath, and other subjects. From here three arches in the tufa bring us out into a lane flanking the **basilica of San Gennaro Extra Moenia**.

The church, a plain basilica probably of the eighth century, but rebuilt several times in later epochs, stands on fifth century foundations; the fresco in the south aisle, representing Christ and two Apostles, is from the earlier building.

On the left side of the church is the entrance to the lower level of the catacomb. The first room is the Basilica-Tomb of St. Januarius, once lighted by a skylight with a colossal fresco of Christ and Angels (poorly preserved). Notice, in the altar, the small aperture through which one could touch the sepulcher of the saint. Behind the altar stand an urn that contained the relics of the saint, and, against the end wall, the bishop's throne, carved out of the tufa. The south wall bears traces of a cross and the letters VIN (*Jesus Christus VINce*, or "Jesus Christ Triumphs"). The north wall contains two tombs with ninth century frescoes of bishops; and a crypt with traces of a mosaic and two painted figures with haloes. Below are remains of an inscription, and, further down, a Greek cross.

Cross the Basilica and enter the Vestibule of the lower catacomb, in which part of the foundation of the fifth century church of San Gennaro can be seen. This, the most beautiful room of the catacomb, was almost certainly once a patrician burial place. On the side walls are fifth century tombs carved out of the tufa; the tombs in the floor are of a much later date. Notice the fresco fragments on the ceiling, painted in the second century in a vaguely Pompeian manner. The baptismal font dates from the eighth century. At the far end of the room, between the entrances to the main halls of the catacomb, is a nich containing tenth century frescoes: Christ in the half-dome, St Agatha between St. Catherine of Alexandria and St. Eugenia below, and St. Juliana (left) and St. Margaret (right) on the side walls. On the adjoining wall are a tondo with a jumping goat and, above, a thirteenth century representation of the Baptism of Christ. The first chamber on the left is the Crypt of St. Januarius, a ninth century structure with frescoes of various epochs representing the saint (end wall) and other early Christians who were martyred with him. On the arch of the entrance are a Byzantine inscription (Jesus Christ Shall Be Victorious) and a Greek cross.

Return to the Vestibule and enter, on the left, the Large Hall. The first chamber on the left contains fragmentary frescoes of a beardless Christ and a Saint (?); the second, a fresco of Moses making water spring from the rock. The next chamber on the same side contains an important fresco cycle showing the Good Shepherd, Jonah, and, in the ceiling, a beardless Christ. Across the way in the lunette of another chamber is a peacock between two vases surmounted by birds, with flowers and more birds above. In the next chamber is a vase containing a vine laden with grapes. A passageway brings us to the small hall, where there is a room with a Hebrew inscription, used by the ancient Jews of Naples as meeting place.

Returning to the Tondo di Capodimonte, we retrace our steps to the via San Vincenzo, which is followed to join the via della Sanità at the point where this is crossed by the road to Capodimonte. On the far side of the bridge, to the left, is Santa Maria della Sanità (Map 5, 3), a Domenican church of 1602-13 with a fine majolica dome, designed by Giuseppe Nuvolo. The **Catacomb of San Gaudioso** lies beneath the church (apply to the Sacristan for admittance).

According to a very old legend, the African bishop Gaudiosus was deposed by the Vandal king Genseric and set adrift in a small boat, along with Quodvultdeus and several followers. After many vicissitudes the ecclesiastics landed at Naples, where they founded a monastery. Gaudioso died in 451 or 452, and was venerated as a saint. Around his tomb there developed an extensive catacomb, only a small part of which remains today.

Opposite the entrance is the tomb of St. Gaudiosus, once decorated with mosaics, some traces of which remain. In front of the tomb is a more recent altar; on the walls of the room frescoes depict (left) St. Agnello (abbot of the monastery founded by St. Gaudiosus) and (right) a bishop, possibly St. Gaudiosus. Both paintings are of a late epoch. Retracing our steps we enter a room containing a tomb with an incised cross. The ceiling is decorated with two portraits of Christ, the lower one dating from before the sixth century. In the corners are fifth century Evangelist Symbols. A passage on the right leads to other areas of the catacombs, of lesser interest. In the rooms and corridors nearby can be seen a mosaic with a Grape Vine and Peacocks (fifth century); a Dead Christ carved in the tufa; a painting of St. Peter and other figures; two Lambs and a Cross; and a portrait of St. Sossio, deacon of Pozzuoli.

The catacomb also contains some seventeenth century tombs of unusual construction. According to custom, the body of the deceased were placed on a sort of seat carved out of the rock until the flesh had rotted away. It was then walled up, leaving only the skull exposed. The rest of the skeleton was then painted in, and a conventional sign or attribute was added to identify the occupation or social standing of the deceased: notice the sword of soldier Scipione Brancaccio, the robes of magistrate Marco Antonio De Ponte, the sumptuous gown of princess Giovanna Gesualdo, and the brushes and palette of painter Giovanni Balcucci.

From the church of Santa Maria della Santità follow the via della Santità and its continuation, the via Arena della Santità, to the via Vergini. This ends at the porta San Gennaro, opposite which the via del Duomo leads to the **Cathedral** (Map 3, 3).

In the north aisle is the entrance to the chapel of Santa Restituta, the oldest surviving church in Naples. Founded in the fourth century on the site of a temple of Apollo, it was rebuilt after an earthquake in 1688. Recent restorations have revealed the bases of various columns and fragments of the Early Christian mosaic floor.

At the end of the right aisle is the Baptistery, or chapel of San Giovanni in Fonte. It is square in plan, with a small dome, and is believed to be the earliest (fifth century) example of this form of building in Italy. It preserves fragmentary fifth century mosaics. In the center of the dome is a gold Cross on a blue background with white and gold stars, flanked by the Greek letters Alpha and Omega (signifying that Christ represents both the beginning and the end), and surmounted by the hand of God holding a gold crown (a sort of warning that those who aspire to the crown must first bear the cross). Around this runs a band of flowers, fruit, and birds (including a phoenix with a halo, symbol of the Resurrection). Eight radial bands containing flowers, fruit, festoons, and birds divide the cupola into eight wedges, four of which are well preserved. The mosaics depict a turquoise drapery with gilded detail, a vase with two birds, the Women at the Sepulcher (extensively ruined), Christ Saving Peter from the Waters, the Miracle of the Fish, the *Tradito legis* (a bearded and haloed Christ giving the book of laws to St. Peter), and St. Paul (ruined).

From the Cathedral it is a short walk to **San Giorgio Maggiore** (Map 3, 7), founded by St. Severus in the late fourth century, destroyed by fire in 1640, and rebuilt by the baroque architect Cosimo Fanzago, who reversed its orientation. Just inside the entrance are the extensive remains of the apse of the Early Christian basilica. These include a half-dome resting on three arches that spring from two columns. The Corinthian capitals were taken from ancient Roman buildings. The walls are made of alternating courses of brick and tufa, in the Roman manner.

b Anjou and Aragon

Walking tour, about 5 km (3 miles), with buses along much of the way.

This route takes us to the magnificent churches and palaces of the thirteenth, fourteenth, and fifteenth centuries.

Above Naples harbor rises the royal residence of the Angevin kings, the **Castel Nuovo** (Map 2, 14), commonly, but less correctly, called the *Maschio Angioino*. Built for Charles I by Pierre de Chaulnes (1279-82), it was largely reconstructed under Alfonso of Aragon, and rearranged by Ferdinand IV for use as the royal and viceregal residence. Now beautifully restored, it houses the offices and library of the *Società Napoletana di Storia Patria*, the *Biblioteca Comunale Cuomo*, and the meeting rooms of the City Council of Naples and the Regional Council of Campania. Among the events that took place within the castle walls are the abdication of Pope Celestin V and the mock-marriage of Ferdinand I's niece to a son of Count Sarno, when the king arrested Sarno and other barons who were conspiring against him. The emperor Charles V stayed at the castle on his return from Tunis, and the revolt of Masaniello (see Chapter III) was formally ended here in the pacts signed by the viceroy and the Prince of Massa. Fronting the square across the dry moat is the long north wall between two massive fifteenth century towers, the *Torre del Beverello* at the seaward end and the *Torre di San Giorgio*. Beyond this is the impressive main façade, entered between two further towers by the famous Triumphal Arch, erected (1454-67) to commemorate the entry of Alfonso I into Naples (1443). This masterpiece of the Italian Renaissance was most likely inspired by the celebrated Capua Gate of Frederick II. However, it differs from that monument in that it is not free-standing, but adapted to serve as the entrance to the castle. In this sense it is unique among the architectural inventions of its day, having no parallel in Tuscany or Lombardy. Many prominent sculptors, including Domenico Gagini, Isaia da Pisa and Francesco Lurana, were brought to Naples to assist in its decoration. The large bas-relief shows the Triumph of Alfonso. Above the second arch stand the four Cardinal Virtues, followed by two large river gods and, atop the whole, St. Michael.

The castle is best seen in the morning, and may be visited without charge; apply to the custodian. Pass through the arch into a vestibule, then enter the polygonal courtyard. Straight ahead is the façade of the *Cappella Palatina* or church of santa Barbara, with a delicate Renaissance door surmounted by a Madonna by Laurana. The fourteenth century chapel (now a store room) is lighted by a large rose window of Catalan design and by tall Gothic lancet windows, the splays of which contain frescoes attributed to Giotto's illustrious follower, Maso di Banco. Adjoining the chapel is the *Sala dei Baroni*, reached by an external staircase. The large hall was damaged by fire in 1919; it is now the meeting place of the City Council. The door next to the entrance communicates with the Viceregal Apartments, which occupy the north side of the castle, on the wall opposite are a monumental fireplace and two choir lofts, of Catalan workmanship.

The seaward side affords an impressive view of the huge bastions with the *Torre del Beverello* on the right and the *Torre dell'Oro* set back to the left; between them rises the restored east end of the chapel, flanked by two polygonal turrets.

From the piazza del Municipio we take the via Medina and soon reach (left) the Gothic doorway of **Santa Maria Incoronata**, a church built and named by Joan I (1352) to commemorate her coronation of 1351 and embodying the chapel of the old Vicaria, where, in 1345, she had married Louis of Taranto, her second husband. The interior has kept its original form (somewhat restored after bomb damage to the roof). In the vault are remarkable frescoes of the Seven Sacraments and the Triumph of the Church by Roberto Oderisi (ca. 1370); the *Cappella del Crocifisso* contains others of like date. The street rises gently amid huge new buildings of varying merit to an important intersection of the reconstructed Carità quarter. The via Sanfelice leads (right) to the piazza Bovio; the via Diaz, realigned since 1945, leads left toward the via Roma, opening immediately into the piazza Matteotti (Map 2, 10), focal point of the quarter. Its north side is dominated by the obtrusive Post Office, a vast edifice in marble and glass (1936), leaving which on the left we enter the via Santa Maria la Nova. **Santa Maria la Nova** (Map 2, 10), built by Charles I for Franciscans expelled from the site of the Castel Nuovo (1279) and redesigned by Agnolo Franco in the sixteenth century, escaped damage in the war. The façade is a fine work of the Renaissance. The aisleless nave has a richly painted ceiling incorporating works by Fabrizio Santafede, Francesco Curia, and other sixteenth century artists. The first chapel on the south side contains a St. Michael by Marco Pino (1525-87). The angels on the dome are by Battistello Caracciolo (1570-1637). The second chapel on the north side (San Giacomo della Marca), built by Gonzalo de Cordoba (1504), contains the tomb of Marshal Lautrec (d. 1528 of plague while besieging Naples) by Annibale Caccavello, and statues by Giovanni

Domenico D'Auria (sixteenth century); in the transept is wooden Crucifixion by Giovanni da Nola (1488-1558). The high altar, which combines complex and unusual architectural members with fine floral inlay, is one of the more important works of the seventeenth century artist Cosimo Fanzago. The two cloisters contain fifteenth century tombs and later frescoes.

Behind the Post Office is the **Cloister of Monteoliveto** (Map 2, 6). The double order of arcades, built to compensate for the slope of the land (monks entering the cloister from the church emerged on the upper level) open directly onto the street, a reminder that the convent was initially surrounded by gardens. On the opposite side of the via Monteoliveto, farther on, is the **Palazzo Gravina** (Map 2, 6), a beautiful Renaissance building in the purest Tuscan style, by Gabriele d'Agnolo and Mormanno (1513-49), spoilt by the addition of a storey in 1839. Once the Post Office, it now houses the University Faculty of Architecture.

In the piazza Monteoliveto, with its baroque fountain, stands the church of Monteoliveto (Map 2, 6) or **Sant'Anna dei Lombardi.** Begun in 1411, it contains a wealth of Renaissance sculpture, mostly undamaged when the church received a direct bomb hit in March 1944. The façade, shorn of its eighteenth century additions, has been reconstructed in its original style; in the vestibule is the tomb (1627) of Domenico Fontana, architect to pope Sixtus V. On either side of the entrance are marble altars, that on the right by Giovanni da Nola, the other by Girolamo Santacroce. Above them is the huge baroque organ. On the south side, the Mastrogiudice Chapel (near the door) contains an Annunciation and other sculptures by Benedetto da Maiano (1489), and the tomb of Marino Curiale (1490), in a similar style. The third chapel has a tomb attributed to Giovanni da Nola. Beyond the fifth chapel a passage leads to the Chapel of the Holy Sepulchre, with a terracotta Pietà by Guido Mazzoni (1492; the eight life-size figures are said to be portraits of the artist's contemporaries). A corridor on the right leads to the Old Sacristy which is frescoed by Vasari and contains fine tarsia stalls by Giovanni da Verona (1510). The apse contains sixteenth century stalls and the tombs of Alfonso II (d. 1495) by Giovanni da Nola, and of Guerello Origlia, founder of the church. The sixth chapel on the north side was designed by Giuliano da Maiano, and contains repainted sixteenth century frescoes. In the fifth chapel are a St. John the Baptist by Giovanni da Nola, and a Pietà by Santacroce. The third chapel contains a marble relief of the Flagellation (1576); and the first chapel, an Ascension on wood (ca. 1492). From here we pass to the Piccolomini Chapel (restored after bomb damage) with a Nativity, a charming composition by Antonio Rossellino (1475). The beautiful tomb of Mary of Aragon (d. 1470), daughter of Ferdinand I, was begun by Rossellino and finished by Benedetto da Maiano. It was in the former Olivetan monastery here that Tasso in 1588 took refuge from the persecution of Alfonso d'Este.

Cross the via Monteoliveto and follow the Calata Trinità Maggiore to the piazza del Gesù Nuovo. In the center stands the **Guglia dell'Immacolata**, a curious baroque column (1747 - 50) typical of Neapolitan taste, its ornate marble emphasized by the severe west front of the **church of the Gesù Nuovo** (Map2, 6; also called Trinità *Maggiore*), built between 1584 and 1601. The embossed stone façade, once a wall of the Palace of Roberto Sanseverino (by Novello da San Lucano, 1470) is pierced by a sixteenth century sculptured doorway. The church is discussed at length in Chapter III, a.

Almost opposite is the great church and Franciscan convent of **Santa Chiara**, built in 1310-28 for Sancia, queen of Robert the Wise, who here died a nun. The church was completely burnt out by incendiary bombs on August 4, 1943, when the magnificent baroque interior of 1742-57 was destroyed and most of the large monuments wrecked. The reconstruction has preserved the original Provençal-Gothic austerity, a quality so foreign to Naples as to be all the more striking. The Gothic west porch was undamaged. The aisleless interior, the largest in Naples, has a new open roof nearly 150 ft high, and tasteful modern glass in the lancet windows. Of the glorious series of Angevin royal monuments, the principal survivals are the lower portions of the tombs of Robert the Wise (d. 1343), the work of the Florentine brothers Giovanni and Pacio Bertini (behind the high altar) and of Charles, Duke of Calabria, by Tino di Camaino (on the south side); the undamaged tomb of Mary of Valois (d. 1331), wife of Charles of Calabria, by Tino di Camaino and followers (to the right); and, also undamaged, the monument (1399) to their daughter, Mary of Durazzo (to the left). But every chapel has some tomb or Gothic sculpture which merits inspection. Off the Chiostro dei Minori (reached from the sacristy) in the refectory is a huge fresco by a follower of Pietro Cavallini.

Free access (contributions to conventual funds) is allowed to the conventual buildings of the ground floor; the entrance is reached by passing between the north side of the church and the detached bell-tower (not finished until 1647), passing through the first court, and turning right. The parts seen include the huge fourteenth century cloister, transformed (1742) by Domenico Antonio Vaccaro into a rustic garden, adorned with majolica tiles and terracottas. The austere *Refectory of the friars*, with a charming fountain in the center, adjoins the east side of the cloister.

We are now in the **Spaccanapoli** (the *decumanus inferior* of ancient Neapolis), which changes its modern name several times during its length, but never its straight and narrow course.

Its decayed medieval and Renaissance palaces make it the most characteristic of old Neapolitan streets.

Beyond the house (tablet) where Benedetto Croce spent his last years, is the piazza San Domenico, with the baroque Guglia di San Domenico (1737), enclosed by sixteenth century mansions. On the left is the apse of **San Domenico Maggiore**, a noble Gothic church, built in 1289-1324, rebuilt after damage by earthquake and fire (1465 and 1506), and much altered since. The church of the Aragonese nobility, its chief interest is in its Renaissance sculpture and monuments, which include some of the finest expressions of the Tuscan manner in Naples.

A small court off the vico San Domenico gives on to the façade, by which we enter. The interior with aisles and transepts, is more than 120 ft long. Photography is forbidden.

South Aisle. On the right of the entrance is the Cappella Saluzzo with decorated Renaissance arches (1512-16) and containing the monument of Galeotto Carafa (1507-15), all the work of Romoli di Antonio da Settignano. The tomb of Archbishop Brancaccio (died 1341) in the second chapel is by a Tuscan follower of Tino di Camaino. The seventh chapel leads to the Cappellone del Crocifisso. Here is the little painting (covered) of the Crucifixion which spoke to St. Thomas Aquinas when he was living in the adjacent monastery. To the left stands the fine tomb of Francesco Carafa (d. 1470), by Tommaso Malvito and behind is a side-chapel (1511) with other family tombs and frescoes by Bramantino. From the eighth chapel, we enter the Sacristy. On the ceiling is a brilliant fresco by Francesco Solimena (1657-1747), above the presses are the coffins of then princes of Aragon and thirty five other illustrious persons. The Sacristan can be persuaded to show these.

South Transept. Tomb of Galeazzo Pandonee (1514), a fine work probably by a Tuscan artist; above, tomb slab of John of Durazzo (d. 1335), by Tino di Camaino. Perhaps the best of the tombs in the Old Church (Sant'Angelo *a Morfisa*) is that of Tommaso Brancaccio by Jacopo della Pila (1492); note also that of Porzia, wife of Bernardo Roa, by Annibale Caccavelo and Giovan Domenico D'Auria (1559), in the vestibule.

Choir. The altar and recessed seats at either side are adorned with marble mosaic by Cosimo Fanzago (1646); the paschal candelabrum (1585) is supported by nine sculptured figures from a tomb by Tino di Camaino.

North Transept. First chapel: Contemporary copy of the Flagellation by Caravaggio (1607); the original, formerly on the opposite wall, is now at Capodimonte. Second Chapel: Spineli monument (1546) by Bernardino Del Moro. Fourth chapel: Annunciation (much damaged) by Titian (Tiziano Vecèllio, 1488-1576).

The **North Aisle** chapels have many good fifteenth to

seventeenth century tombs, including that of Giovan Battista Marino (d. 1625), the poet, in the eighth, where the altar bears a lovely group by Giovanni da Nola. Fourth chapel, St. John the Baptist by the same artist with two paintings by Mattia Preti (1613-99) above. In the end chapel Luca Giordano (1632-1705), Crowning of St. Joseph.

On the right of the via Nilo, just beyond the square, is the little church of **Sant'Angelo a Nilo** (Map 2, 6), with a fine Renaissance doorway. Within (apply to the caretaker of the Palazzo Brancaccio, 15 vico di Donnaromita) is the tomb of Cardinal Rinaldo Brancaccio, the first work of Renaissance sculpture to be brought to Naples (1428). The architectural framework, the classical detail of which represented a clean break with the formal and aesthetic canons of the Angevin Gothic, is designed by Michelozzo. The relief of the Assumption is by Donatello. The tomb was executed in Pisa and sent by ship to Naples.

Keeping straight on, we pass (left) an antique statue of the Nile at the beginning of the via San Biagio ai Librai, in which are the former Palazzo Carafa, birthplace of pope Paul IV, and (right; N° 121) the Palazzo Santangelo (1466) in the Tuscan style.

A little to the north, on the site of the Roman basilica is the **Franciscan church of San Lorenzo Maggiore**, begun by Charles I to commemorate the victory of Benevento and completed by his son. There is a fine door and doorway of 1325 in the eighteenth century façade. Here on Easter Eve 1334 Boccaccio first saw Maria, natural daughter of Robert of Anjou, whom he immortalized as Fiammetta. Inside, the nave has been patiently restored to that Gothic simplicity retained unaltered by the transepts and the apse. The latter has nine radiating chapels: the high altar is by Giovanni da Nola. Among a number of good medieval tombs note that of Catherine of Austria (d. 1323), first wife of Charles the Illustrious, by a pupil of Giovanni Pisano. In the chapels are two large canvases by Mattia Preti; a Crucifixion with St. Francis and Franciscan saints, and a Madonna and Child with St. Clare and Franciscan saints. The Cloister is entered from outside by a fifteenth century doorway to the left of the Bell-Tower (1507). The Chapter House is supported on Roman columns.

We join the via del Duomo and turn right to the Palazzo Cuomo, a severely elegant Florentine building of 1464-90, that now houses the attractive **Filangieri Museum** (archaeological finds, oriental arms, sculpture, paintings, porcelain). A little farther on, beyond San Giorgio Maggiore (see Route 2a) we regain the line of the Spaccanapoli, turning right into the via della Vicaria Vecchia.

The **church of Sant'Agrippino** (right) has a beautiful fifteenth century façade.

Bear left and follow the via Pietro Colletta to the Castel Capuano, begun by William I and finished by Frederick II. It was the residence of the Hohenstaufen and of some of the Angevin kings. Here in 1432 Ser Gianni Caracciolo, lover of Joan II, was murdered. Much altered, the castle has been used as the court of Justice since 1540.

Beyond the Castel Capuano lies the beautiful **Porta Capuana**, between two mighty Aragonese towers. The graceful exterior decoration is by Giuliano da Maiano. It was completed after his death in 1490 by Luca Fancelli. Smaller and more delicate than the triumphal arch of Alfonso at the Castel Nuovo, it is a rare and particularly fine application of the late fifteenth century Florentine style in sculpture to a town gate. The only other project of the kind undertaken during the Renaissance was Agostino di Duccio's gate at Perugia, built around 1475. The open space in front of the gate is used as a market place, and is always an animated and colorful scene. Adjoining the porta Capuana is the Renaissance church of Santa Caterina a Formiello.

We turn northwest along the broad via San Giovanni a Carbonara. At the end of the street a long flight of steps (right) curves in two stages to the Gothic doorway of the **chapel of Santa Monica**, which has a fine tomb by Andrea da Firenze (1432). Adjoining (reached through a court to the north) is **San Giovanni a Carbonara** (Map 3, 3), built in 1343 and enlarged by King Ladislas at the beginning of the fifteenth century. The structure of the church was gravely damaged in 1943, but the fine monuments escaped unharmed. Facing the entrance is the **Cappella Miroballo**, a richly decorated Renaissance monument with fifteenth century statues. Behind the high altar towers the Tomb of Ladislas (d. 1414), master-piece of Marco and Andrea da Firenze, a three-storied composition of trefoil arches, statues, and pinnacles. Beneath this we pass into the Cappella Caracciolo del Sole (1427) with Andrea da Firenze's unfinished tomb of Ser Gianni Caracciolo, steward of Joan II, stabbed at the Castel Capuano in 1432. On the walls are fifteenth century frescoes; the tiled floor dates from 1440. To the north of the sanctuary is the marble-lined Cappella Caracciolo di Vico (1517), attributed to Tommaso Malvita, one of the most remarkable early sixteenth century designs in Naples, containing tombs and statues by Giovanni da Nola. In the Sacristy is the tomb of Scipione Somma (died 1533).

A short walk to the west and south brings us to the **church of Santa Maria Donnaregina**. A convent has existed on this site since the eighth century. Following an earthquake in 1293, the church was reconstructed by Mary of Hungary, queen of Charles II of Anjou, after whom it is named. A second church, in the baroque manner, was added when the nuns were incorporated in the Theatine Order. The beautiful fourteenth century church is reached from the vico Donnaregina. Enter from the southwest corner and pass below a stone vault supporting the nuns' choir. The presbytery, stripped in 1928-36 of later accretions, ends in a plain polygonal apse. To the right is the Cappella Loffredo, to the left the Tomb of Queen Mary by Tino di Camaino and Gagliardo Primario (1326). Ascend to the nuns' choir, a rectangular gallery built over the west end of the church, open to the presbytery but having a sixteenth century wooden roof. Here, on the walls are the celebrated frescoes, by Pietro Cavallini and his pupils (begun 1308), representing the Passion the legends of saints Elizabeth of Hungary, Catherine, and Agnes, and the Last Judgment. Here external stairs can be climbed to see another Cavallini fresco above the choir roof.

The seventeenth century church, elaborate but in good taste, has colored marbles, majolica pavements, and paintings by Luca Giordano.

From the largo Donnaregina the **Archbishop's Palace** extends south to the Cathedral, begun in the French Gothic style by Charles I in 1294 and finished by Robert the Wise in 1323. The façade, shattered by an earthquake, was rebuilt by Baboccio in 1407. Only his portal remains, however, the rest being mainly from a design by Enrico Alvino (1877-1905). The remainder of the building was rebuilt after the earthquake of 1456.

Inside, **the nave** has an elaborate painted ceiling by Fabrizio Santafede (1621), supported on sixteen piers in which are incorporated over 100 antique columns. On the walls above the arches are forty six saints, painted by Luca Giordano and his pupils. Above the central doorway are (left to right) the tombs of Charles I of Anjou (died 1285); Clementina of Hapsburg; and her husband Charles Martel (died 1296), king of Hungary and son of Charles II, all moved from the choir in 1599, when the monuments were executed by Domenico Fontana.

South Aisle. The third chapel is the Cappella di San Gennaro, or Treasury, built by Francesco Grimaldi in 1608-29. It is closed by an immense grille of gilded bronze by the baroque artist Cosimo Fanzago. The luminous interior, faced with marble, has seven ornate altars, four of which have paintings by Domenichino (Domenico Zampieri, 1581-1641), who began the frescoes; these were completed by Giovanni Lanfranco (1582-1647) after Domenichino had been hounded from the city. Above the altar on the right side is a large oil by Giuseppe Ribera (1588-1652). The balustrade of the main altar is by Cosimo Fanzago, with small doors by Onofrio d'Alessio, and the sumptuous silver altarfront is by Francesco Solimena.

In a tabernacle behind the altar are preserved the head of St. Januarius (martyred at Pozzuoli, compare Chapter I, e) in a silver-gilt bust (1305), and two phials of his congealed blood, which tradition states first liquefied in the hands of the sainted bishop Severus, when the saint's body was translated to Naples from Pozzuoli. The miracle is documented from 1389 and repeats itself three times yearly on the first Saturday in May at Santa Chiara, and in the cathedral on September 19 and December 16. On the speed of the liquefaction the prosperity of the city is believed to depend. The ceremony attracts an enormous crowd and travelers who wish to be present should secure in advance a place near the altar by applying to the sacristan.

The fifth chapel contains the tomb of Cardinal Carbone (died 1504) under a Gothic canopy.

Choir Chapels. The outer chapel on the right (Cappella Minutolo; apply to the sacristan), paved with majolica, contains the tomb of Cardinal Arrigo Minutolo, by Roman marble workers who came to Naples with Baboccio (1402-5), other tombs by a follower of the Florentine sculptor and architect Arnolfo di Cambio, and repainted fourteenth century frescoes. The polyptych on the side altar is by Paolo di Giovanni Fei. The Cappella Tocco, adjoining, also Gothic, has frescoes (1312; restored). Below the high altar is the Crypt of St. Januarius or Cappella Carafa (apply to the Sacristan), by Tommaso Malvito (1497-1506), perhaps the masterpiece of Renaissance art in Naples. We enter through two fine bronze doors. Within, the delicate ornamental carving should be noticed; likewise the statue of the founder, Cardinal Oliviero Carafa, near the altar which covers the remains of the patron saint.

In the **North Transept** (right to left) are the tomb of Innocent IV (died 1254), the opponent of Frederick II, an inlaid work (1315) partially reconstructed in the sixteenth century; the tomb of Andrew of Hungary, murdered in 1345 by his wife Joan I; and a cenotaph of Innocent XII (1703; buried in St. Peter's Rome).

In the **North Aisle** is the entrance to the basilica of Santa Restituta, founded in the fourth century on the site of a temple of Apollo, rebuilt in the fourteenth century and poorly restored in the seventeenth century. The ceiling painting, showing the Arrival of St. Restituta at Ischia, is by Luca Giordano. At the end of the right aisle is the Baptistery (see route 2A), square with a small dome, the earliest example (late fifth century) of this form of building in Italy; it preserves fragmentary fifth century mosaics. The fifth and seventh chapels on the left contain beautiful thirteenth century bas-reliefs in marble; in the sixth is a fine mosaic (1322) of the Virgin enthroned, by Lello da Roma, showing Byzantine influence.

c South of Naples

Road, 210 km (131 miles) round trip. Autostrada A3 to Castellamare di stabia; Highway 145 to Meta and Sorrento; Highway 163 to Amalfi and Salerno. Return to Naples via Nocera by Highway 18 or Autostrada A3. Bus service throughout the route (see your travel agent).

Railway from Naples to Sorrento (Circumvesuviana Railway) in about 1 hour; from Naples to Salerno (FS) in about 1 hour 15 min.

Beyond Castellammare the road hugs the shore, passing the pleasant beaches of Pozzano and Scraiò, both with sulphur springs.

Vico Equense is the ancient Aequana, destroyed by the Goths and restored by Charles II of Anjou. The fourteenth century ex-**cathedral church** of **San Salvatore** contains the tomb of Gaetano Filangieri (died 1788), the jurist. Adjoining the offices of the Azienda di Soggiorno (corso Umberto) is a small Antiquarium containing material from a necropolis of the seventh to fifth century B.C. discovered beneath the present town. The Angevin Castello Giusso, rebuilt in 1604, is now a convent. Below the sheer cliff is a pleasant beach.

We round the head of the pretty valley behind Seiano, beyond which we turn the promontory of Punta di Scùtolo and gain a first view of the magical **Plain of Sorrento**. The famous plain with a general level of 80-100 m above sealevel, is a huge garden of perennial spring, covered with orange, lemon, and olive groves, interspersed with figtrees, pomegranates, and aloes. The villages are rather closely crowded, but an indefinable spirit of peach broods over them all.

Meta, a pretty village, is connected by an elevator with its two small harbors. We pass Santa Maria del Lauro, believed to occupy the site of a temple of Minerva. The road to Positano, Amalfi, and Salerno here diverges to the south. The road winds across the plain, crosses some deepset torrents, and touches the villages of Carotto and Pozzoppiano which, together with Meta, make up the commune of Piano di Sorrento.

Sant'Agnello is now almost an extension of Sorrento which we enter by the corso Italia; the views are restricted by the walls of the gardens and orange groves.

Sorrento, Surriento in the Neapolitan dialect, is the ancient *Surrentum*, frequented by the Romans for the sake of its breathtaking scenery and mild climate. In the Middle Ages it was an important maritime republic. Situated in a district of singular beauty, on the north side of the famous peninsula that bears its name, it is an enchanting place at all seasons. Its most illustrious son is Torquato Tasso (1544-95), the poet. In the nineteenth century Sorrento was a favorite winter residence of foreigners; here in 1867 Ibsen finished Peer Gynt and here some ten years later occurred the famous quarrel between Wagner and Neitzsche. The district is noted for oranges, lemons, and nuts, and the town for tarsia work, lace, and straw plaiting.

The town stands on a tufa rock, rising more than 150 ft. above the sea and surrounded on three sides by deep ravines. The central piazza Tasso, with a monument to Torquato Tasso by Gennaro Calì (1870), commands a view of the Marina Piccola, many feet below. The corso Italia stretches to the west, passing the **Bell Tower** with its four columns and antique ornamentation. The vault space beneath the Archbishop's Palace, leading to the neglected palaces of the via Pietà, was once the scene of council meetings. The **Cathedral** has a marble side portal of 1479; the façade was rebuilt in 1913-24. Inside, the first chapel on the right has reliefs of the fourteenth or fifteenth century. In the nave are the Archbishop's Throne (1573) with a marble canopy, and a pulpit of the same year, below which is a Virgin with Saints John the Baptist and John the Evangelist, a painting on panel by Silvestro Buono of Naples (1582). The stalls show typical local tarsia work.

Behind the cathedral is the south *wall* of the town, rebuilt in 1558-61, after a sack by pirates, on the line of the Greek or Roman wall; an arch of the Roman gate survives in the via Parsano.

Sorrento, surnamed La Gentile, is perched on a tufa rock, rising 150 above the sea and bounded on three sides by steep ravines. This stone stairway is one of several which link the town to the harbor, below.

The via Tasso, opposite, leads toward the sea. In the via San Nicola (left, N° 29) is the **Casa Fasulo** (formerly Sersale), marked by a tablet as the house of Cornelia Tasso, who here received her illustrious but fugitive brother in 1577. In the via San Cesario (right) is the **Sedile Dominova**, a covered porch of the fifteenth century with capitals in an archaic style. It was the meeting place of the town government. Beyond the baroque church of San Paolo, is the piazza della Vittoria, overlooking the sea. Below, on the shore, are remains of a ***Roman Nymphaeum.*** To the left a road descends, latterly in steps, through an arch to the Marina Grande. Turning right we pass the Tramontano Hotel, which incorporates the remaining room of the house in which Tasso was born, and come to the ***church of* San Francesco d'Assisi**. The annexed convent, now a School of Art, preserves a fourteenth century cloister, where concerts and exhibitions are often held. Behind the church is the little Villa Comunale (view). Continue to the piazza Sant'Antonino with the church and statue of Sant'Antonino Abate (died 830), the patron-saint of Sorrento, where he found refuge from the Lombards. In the little streets near the church of the Grazie are some attractive fifteenth century doorways. At the piazza join the winding strada Luigi De Maio on its way from the Marina Piccola to the piazza Tasso.

From the east side of the piazza Tasso the via Correale leads

The former convent of San Francesco has a charming cloister with round arches on two of the sides, and pointed Saracenic arches on the others. The capitals are particularly noteworthy, for each design is different from the others.

to the **Museo Correale di Terranova**, a villa containing an important collection of Campanian decorative art of the fifteenth to eighteenth century, including furniture, tarsia and intaglio work, and porcelain; sculpture, and a small library of Tasso's works. Among the pictures is a unique collection of works of the Posillipo School (a school of landscape painting that flourished in our area in the nineteenth century), in particular by Giacinto Gigante. The scenic overlook commands a superb view. On the coast 1,5 km farther east, near the Capuchin Convent, is the Villa Crawford, the residence of the novelist F. Marion Crawford, who died here in 1909. The villa stands above Sant'Agnello beach.

The neighborhood of Sorrento affords opportunity for many excursions.

The **Piccolo Sant'Agnello**, a hill 1.30 hour southeast of the piazza Tasso, commands wide views of the plain of Sorrento and the bays of Naples and Salerno.

The Deserto (1.30 hours) is a suppressed convent commanding a wonderful view of Capri and the Gulfs of Naples and Salerno. Follow the Strada di Capodimonte, diverging to the left from the road to Massa Lubrense. At the second fork keep to the left (to the right is Capodimonte, a fine point of view). Beyond *Priora* ascend to the left and then turn right. The return to Sorrento may be made via Sant'Agata sui Due Golfi (15 minutes southeast), a favorite summer resort and an excellent center for excursions. The church has a Florentine altar of inlaid marble (sixteenth century) moved here in 1845 from the Gerolomini in Naples).

Massa Lubrense is reached by a road running at some distance from the sea but so high up as to afford a uninter- rupted series of delightful views. On leaving Sorrento cross the gorge of the Conca. A little farther on the Strada di Capodimonte diverges on the left (see above). At Capo Sorrento a track on the right descends (7 minutes) to the seaward extremity of the cape, with the ruins of the **Roman Villa of Pollio Felix**, worth visiting for the view if not for themselves. Next is Villazzano, at the landward end of the Punta di Massa; the view of the Capo di Sorrento with its dense groves of olives is more extensive from the Telègrafo (239 m), a hill 25 minutes to the left. On rounding the point Capri and the Faraglioni can be seen. The road turns inland and reaches Massa Lubrense, a village in an exquisite frame. From the Villa Rossi here Murat watched the French assault on Capri in 1808. The lovely descent to the little harbor follows the via Palma, the via Roma (right) and the via Marina, passing the church of the Madonna della Lobra (1528), near the supposed site of the legendary temple of the Sirens. The fishing hamlet of Marina di Massa possesses remains of a Roman villa.

Beyond Massa Lubrense the road passes below the

Annunziata and the remains of a Castle of 1389, leaves the attractive road to Términi on the right, and ascends to Sant'Agata (see above). The by road to Termini continues as a steep path (well preserved sections of Roman paving) to **Punta della Campanella** (153 ft; 1.30 / 2 hours from Massa Lubrense), the Promontorium Minervae of the Romans, which takes its modern name from the warning bell of a tower built in 1335 by Robert of Anjou. The lighthouse commands an enchanting view of Capri.

Pleasant trips by small boat also may be made to the **Grotte delle Sirene**, the **Grotta Bagno della Regina Giovanna** (at the Villa Pollio Felix), and other points, many showing vestiges of classical buildings.

Return to Meta. Leave the coast road on the left and climb abruptly over the spine of the Sorrentine Peninsula to Colli di San Pietro, with incomparable views in both directions, then drop steeply to the Costiera Amalfitana, along which the road still remains high above the sea.

Positano is a favorite resort, where the characteristic square white houses and luxuriant gardens descend in steep steps to the sea. The second Sunday in August is the festival of the *Sbarco dei Saraceni*, when a mock landing from the sea is defeated amid fireworks, etc. The road traverses the upper part of the town. Farther on, the terrace behind the solitary little

The remains of a Roman nymphaeum may be seen on the shore near the Marina Grande.

church of San Pietro offers an admirable view-point.

Beyond Vettica Maggiore the road passes through Capo Sottile by the first of a series of short tunnels. Praiano, on the hillside above, has a good church. Delightfully situated on the shore is Marina di Praia, a fishing village with a fine sandy beach.

On the steep slopes above the road lie the scattered hamlets of Penna and Furore, and between two tunnels a viaduct crosses the Vallone di Furore, one of the most picturesque gorges in Italy, which, narrow and fjord-like, runs inland between imposing rocky walls until almost vertically below the plateau of Agerola.

The road passes close above the **Grotta di Smeraldo**, which may be reached by steps or by elevator; a visit occupies about 1 hour. The name of the cavern derives from the apparent color of the interior, which glows with a remarkable green light. It was once dry before the sea eroded the coast.

Stalagmites may now be seen under the water, also columns formed by others which have joined to stalactites.

Amalfi, though known in the fourth century, did not attain any degree of prosperity until the middle of the sixth century, in the time of the Byzantine empire. It was able to defy the Saracens and developed an important Oriental trade, its ships visiting the most remote seas. Governed by its own *Doges*, it

View of the Amalfi Coast. The drive from Colli San Pietro to Vietri, along the rugged, lofty Costiera Amalfitana, is one of the most beautiful in Italy.

attained great wealth and a population of 70,000, but it was subdued by King Roger of Naples in 1131 and soon after twice captured by the Pisans (1135 and 1137). Since then its decline has been continuous. Much of the ancient town was destroyed by the sea in 1343. Its maritime laws, the so-called *Tavole Amalfitane*, remained effective till 1570. Merchants from Amalfi maintained in Jerusalem the hospital of St. John the Almoner, the nuclueus on which the Crusader Knights built the Order of St. John after 1099. Webster's *Duchess of Malfi* is based on the life of the hapless Joanna of Aragon (about 1478-1513), consort of Alfonso Piccolomini, Duke of Amalfi.

The town nestles in the ravine of the Valle dei Molini. Its churches, towers, and arcaded houses, grouped together with attractive irregularity, rise above a small harbor, and are backed by precipices of wild magnificence. From the piazza Flavio Gioia, on the waterfront, near which are the remains of the thirteenth century republican *Arsenal*, the via del Duomo leads to the piazza del Duomo, with a fountain of 1760. On the east side of the piazza stands the ninth century *Cathedral* (Sant Andrea), the highly colored façade of which (1203) is approached by a lofty flight of steps. Both façade and steps were restored in their original Lombard-Norman style by Enrico Alvano, Luigi Della Corte and Guglielmo Raimondi in 1875-94. The mosaic at the top is by the nineteenth century

View of Amalfi, from the north. The arcaded houses typical of Amalfi rise above the small harbor, and are backed by precipices of wild magnificence.

artist Domenico Morelli. The Bell Tower, built in 276 and restored in 1768, is partly Romanesque and partly Saracenic in form.

The imposing porch is divided by columns into two. The magnificent bronze doors, with cross and saints in inlaid silver, were commissioned by the head of the Amalfitan colony in Constantinople, and made there before 1066 by Simeon of Syria. The frescoes at either side of the entrance, executed in 1929 to a design by Domenico Morelli, add little to the decorative integrity of the porch. The interior, thoroughly restored, consists of nave (fine ceiling), aisles, and chapels. From the fourth chapel on the right a flight of steps descends to the Crypt, constructed in 1253 and restored in 1719 (visitors must knock on the door at the left of the gate for entrance). It contains an altar by Domenico Fontana and a statue of St. Andrew by Michelangelo Naccherino. Below the altar rests the body of St.. Andrew the Apostle, brought here from Costantinople in 1208. At the entrance to the choir are two large columns from Paestum and two candelabra adorned with mosaic. Flanking the high altar are ancient pulpits, also with mosaics.

The thirteenth century cloister (*Chiostro del Paradiso*; entered from the portico; fee), with interlaced arches of marked Saracenic appearance, once the burial place of famous citizens,

Chiostro del Paradiso. This thirteenth-century cloister, with its interlaced Saracenic arches, was once the burial-place of eminent citizens. It is now a museum.

is now a museum of architectural fragments.

To seaward of the Duomo lies the **Municipio**, where the Tavole Amalfitane (see above) may be seen. From the main road west of the town (see above) we may ascend the long flight of steps on the right mounting to the old **Capuchin Convent**, now a hotel. It was founded in 1212 and was at first a Cistercian house. The cloisters are picturesque and the beautiful flower screened verandah commands a justly famous view.

A pleasant walk may be taken in the cool Valle dei Molini, with its water-run paper mills and tall rocky sides. The favorite point is the Molino Rovinato, about 1 hour from the piazza.

The Salerno road leaves Amalfi along the shore, passing between the Albergo Luna, and another convent with a good twelfth century cloister, and a sixteenth century tower.

Atrani rises in an amphitheater at the end of the valley of the Dragone. The road bridges the gorge between the village and the sea. From the bridge we descend, passing under the arches, to the little piazza, with **San Salvatore del Bireto**, a church of 940, restored in 1810. Its name refers to the cappings of the Doges of the Republic of Amalfi. The handsome bronze doors, executed at Costantinople in 1086, resemble those of Amalfi. The church of **La Maddalena**, beyond the bridge, has an elegant Bell Tower and a painting of the Incredulity of St. Thomas by Andrea da Salerno.

From Amalfi to Ravello by road (bus), 5 km (3 miles), a walk of about 1.30 hours.

The road diverges to the left beyond Atrani and ascends in windings, affording beautiful views of the Dragone valley. Walkers may shorten the distance a little by taking a mountain path from Atrani, but this is much less open than the road. They ascend the steps to the right of the church of La Maddalena, turn to the right, pass another church, follow a vaulted land, and ascend a long flight of steps. They then enter the Dragone valley and join the road, profiting, however, by various short cuts. At a fork they turn to the right round the small church of Santa Maria a Gradillo, and obtain the first characteristic view of Ravello. Passing below the ruined castle, they then reach the square.

Ravello is an isolated and markedly individual little town in a situation of extreme charm. It is the see of a bishop and one of the most famous beauty spots in Italy. The contrast between its bold situation and its seductive and richly colored setting, between the rusticity of its hilly streets and the delicate perfection of its works of art, between the gaiety of its gardens and the melancholy of its Norman Saracenic architecture, is extraordinarily impressive.

Built in the ninth century under the rule of Amalfi, Ravello became independent in 1086 and maintained its liberty down to 1813. It enjoyed great prosperity in the thirteenth century, and its wealthy citizens, forming relations with Sicily and the East, introduced the Norman Saracenic style of architecture to their native town. Characteristic of the doorways of Ravello are the antique colonnettes, at the side, which give them the appearance of the Graeco-Roman prothyrum.

The **Cathedral** (san Pantaleone), built in 1086, was remodeled in 1786. The façade has three portals and four ancient columns. The fine bronze doors in the middle, executed (1179) by the Italian artist Barisano da Trani in imitation of the Byzantine doors of Amalfi and Atrani, are divided into fifty four panels with saints, scenes of the Passion, and inscriptions. They are protected on the inside as well as the outside by a double set of wooden doors, and are shown on request by the Sacristan. In the nave (right) is a magnificent marble pulpit, borne by six spiral columns and adorned with mosaics. It was executed in 1272 by Nicola da Foggia at the order of Nicola Rufolo, husband of Sigilgaita della Marra. The beautiful bust, above the door of the stairs, is not, however, a portrait of that woman. A smaller pulpit on the left, of earlier date (about 1133), has a mosaic of Jonah and the whale. In the south aisle are two sarcophagi; in the choir are the bishop's throne (mosaic) and two old paschal candlesticks. On the left is the largest chapel, that of San Pantaleone, whose blood (preserved here) liquefies on 19 May and 27 August. In the sacristy are a

Ravello, Cathedral. Built in the ninth century under the rule of Amalfi, Ravello became independent in 1086 and maintained its liberty down to 1813. The Cathedral was begun in the year of independence, but it was remodeled in the eighteenth century.

Byzantine Madonna and two pictures by Andrea da Salerno.

We pass to the south side of the cathedral, noting its fine thirteenth century Bell Tower, and arrive at the entrance to the *Palazzo Rufolo*, begun in the eleventh century and occupied in turn by Pope Adrian IV (1156; Nicholas Breakspeare), Charles of Anjou, and Robert the Wise. An ensemble of Norman-Saracenic buildings, partly in ruins, the palace is enhanced by tropical gardens; here Wagner found his inspiration for the magic garden of Klingsor in *Parsifal*. The arcading of the tiny cloister court is striking. The terrace (1100 ft above the sea) commands an extensive panorama.

Ascend to the right by the street behind the cathedral and walk past old Bishops Palace to the **Palazzo D'Afflitto** with its bizarre portal (both these buildings are now hotels). Opposite is **San Giovanni del Toro**, a twelfth century church, with a low and characteristic Bell Tower. Inside (if closed apply to the custodian at the house across the square; gratuity), the nave is borne by ancient columns. The pulpit, resembling those in the cathedral, has mosaics, tiles of Persian majolica (1175), and ancient frescoes. A chapel off the south aisle contains a statue of St. Catherine, in stucco (thirteenth century).

A little farther on is a small square, with a Norman **Fountain**, from which there is a view of Scala (see below). From here return by the long Strada Vescovado, which passes the twelfth century church of **Santa Maria a Gradillo** and continues south from the cathedral, passing between the Palazzo Rufolo and the Post Office. Beyond the churches of

Bronze Doors of Ravello Cathedral (detail). These doors, by a local artisan named Barisano da Trani (1179), are directly inspired by the doors of Amalfi Cathedral, which were made in Costantinople by Byzantine craftsmen.

Sant'Antonio, with a Romanesque cloister, and Santa Chiara, we reach the **Palazzo Cimbrone** with an open vaulted terrace-room (reconstructed). At the end of a straight avenue through the lush gardens is the **Belvedere Cimbrone**, the most advanced point of the ridge on which Ravello lies. The open view of Atrani and the bay is unrivalled.

A short walk (1,5 km, or 1 mile) may be taken round the head of the valley to Scala (374 m), once a populous and flourishing town, but ruined by pestilence and the rivalry of Ravello. The **Cathedral** has a handsome Romanesque portal and contains a mosaic pulpit, a mitre with enamels of the thirteenth century, and a spacious crypt. The nearby villages of Santa Caterina, Campidoglio, and Minuto all have interesting churches. From Minuto walkers may cross the via Pontone into the Valle dei Mulini (see above) to reach Amalfi (paths rather steep and rough).

From Atrani the road skirts the shore to Minori, a delightful village. To the left of the road lie the remains of a first century Roman villa, including a large *peristyle*, a *nymphaeum*, and some vaulted rooms with frescoes. The **Antiquarium** houses paintings found amid the ruins of other Roman villas destroyed by the eruption of Vesuvius in A.D. 79, assorted pottery, and architectural fragments.

Maiori is a fortified village with a sandy beach at the mouth of the Tramonti valley.

Beyond Cetara, a colorful fishing village, the road runs at so high a level that it commands the whole Gulf of Salerno as far

Pulpit of Ravello Cathedral (detail). Borne by six spiral columns and adorned with mosaics, this excellent example of the marble-worker's art was executed in 1272 by Nicola da Foggia.

112

as the Punta Licosa, with a glorious prospect of Vietri sul Mare and Salerno.

Salerno is beautifully situated on the Gulf of the same name (the Roman *Paestanus Sinus*). The old quarter inland has narrow streets, while along the shore a modern quarter extends behind an excellent beach. The town succeeds the ancient *Salernum*, which became a Roman colony in 194 B.C. In the early Middle Ages it was subject to Benevento, but between the ninth and eleventh centuries it was ruled by its own princes. Then it fell to the Normans in 1076. It was famous for its school of medicine, which reached its zenith in the twelfth century, and which St. Thomas Aquinas considered as the most important in Europe. Salerno was a key beach-head in the allied invasion of Italy in September 1943. Much of the town was destroyed in the heavy fighting which followed the landing.

We enter the town above the small harbor. The road divides into two long streets that run parallel with the sea, passing left and right of the Teatro Verdi and the Villa Comunale. A quarter mile farther on, the via del Duomo leads into the old town, between the **churches of Sant'Agostino** (right) and **San Giorgio** (left), both of which contain paintings by Andrea da Salerno (1480-1545), and to the via dei Mercanti (see below). Farther on is the **Cathedral** (San Matteo), founded in 845, and rebuilt by Robert Guiscard in 1076-85. The **Porta dei Leoni**, a fine Romanesque doorway, admits to the atrium, the twenty eight columns of which were brought from Paestum. To the right the detached twelfth century bell tower rises above the colonnade. The central doorway, decorated in 1077, has a bronze door with crosses and figures of niello work, made in Costantinople in 1099. In the Nave are two spendid pulpits (1173-81) and a paschal candelabrum, in a mixture of Saracen and Byzantine styles. The north aisle contains the tombs of Margaret of Anjou (died 1412), wife of Charles III of Durazzo, by Baboccio da Piperno, and of Bishop Nic. Piscicelli (died 1471), by Iacopo della Pila. Off the Sacristy, on the left, is the **Museo del Duomo**, containing a large *Paliotto*, or altar frontal, of fifty four ivory panels decorated with twelfth century mosaic. The east end of the church terminates in three apsidal chapels; in that to the left is a Pietà by Andrea da Salerno; that on the right contains, beneath a mosaic vault, the tomb of Gregory VI, the great Hildebrand , who died in exile in 1085 while the guest of the Norman king Robert Guiscard. To the left Archbishop Carafa is buried in a pagan sarcophagus showing a relief of the Rape of Prosperine. Other interesting tombs should be noticed at the end of the south aisle. The little door, beside a curious relief of a ship unloading, leads to the crypt, in which is preserved the body of St. Matthew, brought here in 954.

Behind the cathedral the via san Benedetto leads past the

modest **Museo Provinciale**.

The via dei Mercanti, typical of the old quarter, leads west from the via del Duomo to the **Arco Arechi**, part of an eighth century building, beneath which the road continues to the **Fontana dei Delfini**. Hence a street to the right leads to the church of **Sant'Andrea**, with a small twelfth century belfry. It is worthwhile, for the sake of the view, to ascend behind the town to the old **Castle** (296 ft), the ruined stronghold of the Lombard princes.

The return to Naples may be made by Highway 18 or Autostrada A3, which pass north of the Monti Latari, bypassing the Costiera Amalfitana and Sorrento to regain the coast beneath Vesuvius. This route touches two interesting towns.

Cava de' Tirreni is a pleasant town frequented by Neapolitans in the summer. The cylindrical towers on the surroundinng hills were used for netting wild pigeons by a curious local method now rarely seen. The main street, the corso Italia, is arcaded like the streets of Bologna. The principal object of interest is the Benedictine abbey of **La Trinità della Cava**, 4 km (2 miles) southwest, romantically situated near the hamlet of Corpo di Cava beneath a crag on the Bonea torrent. The abbey (served by buses from Naples), founded by the Cluniac St. Alferius, was built in 1011-25 and consecrated in 1092 by pope Urban II in the presence of king Roger of Sicily, whose second wife Sibylla is buried here. So also are the founder and the antipope Theodoric (d. 1102). The structure was radically altered in 1796; the bell tower dates from 1622. The *Church* contains a fine mosaic pulpit and a candlestick from the original building, as well as the eleventh century altar frontal. The crypt has fourteenth century frescoes. The Chapter House has carved and inlaid stalls, perhaps designed by Andrea da Salerno. An earlier **Chapter House** is reached from the beautiful thirteenth century **Cloister**. The **Guest Hall** houses a museum with archaeological material, pictures and items from the archives, which, with about 15, 000 Lombard and Norman documents, are among the most important centers for the study of the medieval history of Southern Italy.

Nocera Inferiore, the Nuceria Alfaterna destroyed by Hannibal in 216 B.C., is now a flourishing agricultural center. Here Queen Beatrice, first wife of Charles of Anjou, died in 1267. In captivity in the **Castle**, Helena, the queen of Manfred of Hohenstaufen, died in 1271; and here Urban VI put six cardinals to the torture and was himself kept a prisoner by Charles of Durazzo (1384). The **Museo dell'Agro Nocerino** occupies the fourteenth century **Church of sant'Antonio**. Opened in 1965, it houses the Pisani collection of prehistoric material from the Sarno valley and material from recent local excavations.

In the nearby village of santa Maria Maggiore is a round **Church** of the fourth or fifth century, probably built as a baptistery. The double cupola, resting on thirty two monolithic columns, covers a large octagonal font.

d North of Naples

Road, 410 km (246 miles) round trip. Highways 7 quarter, 7 dir, and 213 (all built along the ancient Appian Way) to Terracina; Highway 7 and local roads to Fossano- va; Highway 156 to Frosinone; Highways 214, 82, and 6 to Cassino; Highways 6 and 7 or Autostrada A2 to Capua; local roads to Caserta Vecchia, then Highway 87 or Auto- strada A2 to Naples.

This is a circular route that takes us to the northern border of the medieval kingdom of Naples and back again, calling on towns and monasteries founded during the Lombar and Norman periods. Two days are recommended for a leisurely visit.

From Naples to Pozzuoli, see Route 1e. Pass the southwestern spur of Monte Massico, then turn northeast toward the extinct volcano of Rocamonfina.

At the foot of the latter stands **Sessa Aurunca**, the ancient *Suessa*, in the Middle Ages the seat of an important duchy. The town is famous for its **Cathedral**, built in the twelfth century in

Sessa Aurunca is the ancient Suessa, capital of the Aurunci, an Italic people who inhabited the wooded hills northwest of Naples. Today the town is visited for its ancient and medieval monuments.

the Lombard Romanesque manner, utilizing fragments from antique buildings. (The town preserves some remains of these, including a theater and baths.) The façade is preceded by a magnificent thirteenth century portico of a characteristically Campanian type with three arches (notice the carvings illustrating the life of St. Peter in the central arch supported by compound piers and surmounted by zoomorphic carvings). The upper part of the façade ends in a triangular pediment carried by arched corbels. It contains a fine window in a frame borne by animals and adorned with fragments of antique sculpture.

Beneath the portico are the three main doors to the church, all richly carved. The main portal, the largest and most profusely decorated, has two lions at the sides; an architrave with panthers, theater masks, and foliate motifs (taken from the Roman theater); and, in the lunette, a relief of the Blessing Christ between St. Peter and St. Paul on a mosaic background. On the left of the portico is the ceremonial Bishop's Door, which also has an architrave borrowed from the Roman theater. Above is a fine molded arch on zoomorphic corbels.

The basilican interior preserves the simple majesty of Romanesque churches despite its eighteenth century stucco work. It is divided into a nave and two aisles by eighteen monolithic columns of various size, shape, and material, all with interesting Roman capitals. On the floor of the nave is an

Many charming fifteenth-century houses may be seen in Sessa Aurunca and neighboring towns. These architectural details, both of which show a Catalan influence in the form and decoration of the arches, were photographed at Carinola.

intricate mosaic of geometric designs, dating from the twelfth century. More mosaics, dating from the thirteenth century, decorate the candelabrum, pulpit (with the story of Jonah), and choir screen. Steps at the end of the south aisle lead to the raised Presbytery. On the right is the baroque *Cappella del Sacramento*, with fine marble tarsia work and a painting of the Communion of the Apostles by Luca Giordano. Beneath the Presbitery is the Crypt, with twenty antique columns and some mosaic fragments possibly from a second pulpit.

Sessa Aurunca is known also for its majolica church-domes and its many charming fifteenth century houses.

Return to the coast by Highway 7, crossing the Garigliano River near Minturno British Military Cemetery. The road now follows the Appian Way, which in ancient times linked Rome with Brundusium (Brindisi). On the west bank of the river are the ruins of *Minturnae*, once an important town built amid marshes formed by the overflowing of the river. A clue to its decline may be found in the *Metamorphoses* of Ovid (XV, 716), where allusion is made to its malaria infested waters.

Formia is the ancient Fo*rmiae*, the fabled abode of Lamus, king of the savage Laestrygones, and the scene of the death of the Roman statesman Cicero (43 B.C.). Today, as in ancient times, it is a favorite bathing resort. The Appian Way turns inland and begins to climb into the Auruncian Hills, once notorious as a haunt of brigands. We continue along Highway 7 dir, which follows the shoreline to the south.

Gaeta is a pleasant little town on a headland at the southern extreme of the gulf of the same name. According to legend, it is the burial place of Caieta, the nurse of Aeneas, from whom it receives its name. Once an important fortress, it preserved its freedom throughout the Gothic and Saracenic invasions, and it reached a high level of importance under the Normans. The **Cathedral** (Sant'Erasmo), consecrated in 1106, but rebuilt in the seventeenth and eighteenth centuries, has a fine Bell Tower (1148-1279) incorporating architectural fragments from antique buildings. In the archway beneath the tower are steps leading to the interior. The passageway contains Roman sarcophagi and fragmentary reliefs from a thirteenth century pulpit. Inside the church are the marble shaft of a candelabrum with thirteenth century reliefs depicting the lives of Christ and St. Erasmus, a small Lapidary Museum, and paintings by Southern Italian artists.

Farther west is the little tenth century church of **San Giovanni a Mare**, commonly called San Giuseppe, surrounded by the most picturesque (or melancholy, depending on the season) of the medieval quarter's narrow streets, vaulted passageways, and winding steps. The interior (keys at the rectory of the Cathedral) has a nave and aisles divided by Romanesque columns with interesting capitals. On the walls are fresco fragments, some perhaps dating from the tenth century. The altar-frontal is taken from an Early Christian sarcophagus.

Above the town rises the **Castle**. First built in the eighth century, it was enlarged and fortified by Frederic II (1227), Charles II of Anjou (1289), Alfonso I of Aragon (1436), and Charles V of Spain (1536). The lower part dates from the Angevin period, the upper from the Aragonese. During the Risorgimento this was the last stronghold of the Bourbon king Francis II, who surrendered to the Piemontese in 1861, bringing Naples under the dominion of King Victor Emanuel II of Savoy (see Chapter IV).

Having time, one may also visit the **Roman tomb of Munatius Plancus**, founder of Lyons, on the summit of the promontory; and the **Montagna Spaccata**, a fantastic triple rift in the rock with an eleventh century sanctuary dedicated to the Holy Trinity. The adjacent convent, founded by the Benedictines, is now a seminary.

Beyond Gaeta the road continues along the coast, offering an uninterrupted series of magnificent views.

Sperlonga is a select resort consisting of an old quarter on a rocky headland and a new quarter behind. Before reaching the town we pass a **Museum** housing an extraordinary collection of antique sculpture found in the nearby **Grotto of Tiberius**.

Fondi, 10 km (6 miles) inland is the *Fundi* of Horace's satires and produced the famous Caecuban wine of antiquity. Although the town was sacked and burned by the Saracens in 866 and again destroyed by fire in 1222, its street plan still follows the traditional lines of the Roman battle camp. The medieval quarter is rectangular in plan, each side measuring about 400 m (1300 ft). At the center of the grid, on the site now occupied by the church of Santa Maria, stood the ancient Forum. The **Castle** was once the seat of two influential families, the Caetani and the Colonna. It was the scene of the conclave of 1378, when the dissident cardinals, outraged by the savage and erratic Urban VI, elected Clement VII as antipope, an act which marked the beginning of the Great Schism. In 1534 the corsair Barbarossa, fired by the fame of the beauty of Giulia Colonna, attempted to abduct her from the palace here. But Giulia was warned in time, and fled inland. The baffled pirate sacked the town and massacred many of its people.

The church of **San Pietro** contains an early fourteenth century Caetani tomb, and a thirteenth century pulpit and throne. **Santa Maria Assunta** and **San Domenico** (where St. Thomas Aquinas taught) are also interesting.

Terracina was an important stage on the Appian Way from Rome to Capua and Brundusium, and a favorite seaside resort of the Roman aristocracy.

The piazza del Municipio, picturesque center of the

medieval quarter, occupies the site of the ancient Forum. The **Cathedral,** at the far end of the square, was built (1074) amid the ruins of a Temple of Roma and Augustus, of whose pavement considerable traces remain. In the portico, antique columns on medieval bases (notice the carvings of lions and monkeys) support a white marble architrave decorated with twelfth century mosaics. These were probably done by Norman artists from Sicily. To the left of the façade the thirteenth century Bell Tower rises from an open arcade. Above, blind colonnades frame elegant mullioned windows. The interior, although remodeled in the eighteenth century, follows the general lines of the Romanesque basilica seen at Sessa Aurunca: it has a nave and three aisles separated by antique columns, a raised presbytery, and a fine mosaic pavement. Mosaics also adorn the pulpit and candelabrum. The two ciboria and the high altar are made up of antique fragments. The carved chest in the sacristy has been assigned to the eighth or ninth century.

Along the right side and the rear of the church are vestiges of the ancient *cella* walls, which provided the foundation of the Christian building. The stones on the right flank are carved with a running acanthus-leaf pattern. Opposite is a small square containing ruins of the first century B.C. **Capitoline Temple**, brought to light accidentally by fighting in 1944. Beside and behind the temple are well-preserved tracts of Roman street pavement. The curved segments of Roman masonry just north of this site suggest the presence of a theater.

The ascent to the right of the cathedral leads in 30-45 minutes to the summit of the hill dominating the town. Here are ruins of the walls of the Italic town of Anxur and of the **Temple of Jupiter Anxurus** (possibly dedicated to Venus Obsequens, the bringer of good fortune). The powerful arches of the foundation dominate the surrounding landscape. The view is superb.

At Terracina we rejoin the Appian Way and turn inland across the Pontine Marshes. After roughly 16 km (10 miles) a secondary road leads right to the spendid Cistercian **Abbey of Fossanova**, where St. Thomas Aquinas died in 1274 while on his way from Naples to Lyons.

The monastery is mentioned for the first time under the name of santo Stefano in documents dating from the eleventh century. It passed in 1134-35 to the Cistercians, who built the present complex, in the late twelfth century, along the lines of the Cistercian convents in France. The **Church**, consecrated in 1208, has a plain façade (originally intended to be preceded by a three-bayed portico) with a rose window and a monumental door adorned with roll and fillet molding and staggered shafts with beautifully carved capitals. The lintel bears a delicate interlace relief that is echoed in the tracery of the tympanum.

The majestic interior consists of a nave and aisles separated by
compound piers; shallow transepts; and a rectangular
presbytery flanked by four chapels, two on each side; The
ceiling is cross-vaulted, with pronounced transverse arches.
The shafts attached to the piers are continued to the springing
of the arches; and the crossing is surmounted by an octagonal
tower with mullioned windows, terminating in a lantern.

To the right of the church is the **Cloister**, striking in its
harmony of proportion and detail. The older, Romanesque
sections are distinguished by sequences of five arches carried
by coupled columns. The side opposite the church,
rebuilt in 1280-1300 in the Burgundian Gothic style, is articulated into groups of four arches, with a small aedicule projecting
into the garden midway along. The Sacristy, Chapter House,
Refectory, and Kitchen occupy the ground floor, the Monks
Cells, the floor above. Detached from the cloister are the **Lay
Brothers Quarters**, the **Guest House**, and the **Infirmary**.
The room where St. Thomas died, later made into a chapel,
has an eighteenth century relief of the saint's death.

Priverno, 5 km (3 miles) north, has a beautiful **Cathedral**
of 1283 and a Gothic **Town Hall.** The town preserves the name
of the *Volscian Privernum*, whose ruins lie in the valley to the
northeast.

Beyond Priverno our route winds through the Monti Lepini
to the broad, fertile valley of the Sacco River.

Frosinone is a hilltop town, the capital of the province of
the same name and the chief place in the *Ciociaria*, a district

*Abbey of Fossano-
va. The Church,
consecrated in
1208, is built in the
Burgundian Gothic
style brought from
France by the
Cistercians.*

noted for the picturesque costumes of the peasantry. Of the ancient *Frusino*, a town of the Hernici, only fragmentary walls and traces of an amphitheater remain. Leaving the town on our right, we proceed northeast.

The **Abbey of Casamari**, beautifully situated in a wooded valley, was founded by the Benedictines in the eleventh century. It passed to the Cistercians in 1151, and to the Trappists in 1717. In 1864 it was returned to the Cistercians, who still hold it. The plan of the original abbey has been remarkably well preserved. The church, fine cloister, aisled chapter house, and guest house, all dating from the thirteenth century, adhere to the Burgundian Gothic types imported to Italy by the Cistercians, and admirably embodied at Fossanova. The convent was visited by the Emperor Frederick II, when he was admitted to the brotherhood, an event that may be celebrated in the capital carvings of the cloister.

A large archway in the Abbot's Residence brings us to the courtyard. On the left are the remains of a Roman colonnade and opposite the entrance the simple façade of the church, preceded by a rather heavy Gothic portico with a fine portal. On the right, flanked by the **Pharmacy** (where liqueurs made by the monks may be bought), is the monastery proper. Steps ascend to the **Museum,** with archaeological finds from the area and numerous paintings of little interest. From here entrance is gained to the beautiful rectangular **Cloister**, surrounded by a portico on small double columns with richly varied capitals. On one side a fine doorway flanked by lancet windows opens onto the aisled *Chapter House*, with a fine ribbed vault. From the cloister we enter the **Church**, consecrated in 1217, with nave and aisles separated by compound piers and pointed arches and cross-vaulted ceiling. Next to the entrance to the church is the **Refectory**, a long hall divided into two aisles by piers.

At **Isola del Liri** the old town is built around two beautiful waterfalls, the *Cascata Valcatoio*, and the *Cascata Grande*. We turn south. The River Liri and its continuation, the Garigliano, formed the ancient boundary between the Kingdom of Sicily and the states the Church. Dating from Norman times, this remained until 1860 the oldest surviving border in Europe.

The village of Roccasecca is dominated by its castle, the birthplace of St. Thomas Aquinas (1226-74), son of Count Landolfo d'Aquino. Ahead we glimpse the **Abbey of Montecassino** on its hilltop.

Montecassino, perhaps the most famous monastery in the world, was founded in 529 by St. Benedict of Norcia, who according to the legend was led to the site by three tame ravens. Reorganized several times since then, it became a beacon of civilization throughout the Middle Ages. Here in 790 Paulus Diaconus wrote his history of the Lombards, and here the torch of learning was kept burning by the devoted labors of the

Benedictines. The present abbey is a reconstruction: its predecessor, dating chiefly from the seventeenth century, was destroyed in the Second World War.

Access to the abbey is through the ceremonial entrance in the southwest corner. A brief ascent brings us to three communicating **Cloisters**, rebuilt along the lines of those constructed in the sixteenth and eighteenth century. The cloister nearest the entrance contains a bronze Death of St. Benedict by the modern sculptor, Attilio Selva. The lines of the destroyed church of San Martino, where the saint is reputed to have died, are marked in the pavement.

In the central cloister is a well-head of good design and, at the foot of the staircase, a statue of St. Benedict (1736) which survived the bombing unharmed. The staircase, of monumental proportions, leads to an elegant atrium and, beyond, the *Chiostro dei Benefattori*, fronting the basilica, with statues of saints, popes, and sovereigns, built to a design by Antonio da Sangallo the Younger.

The rebuilt **Church** has entrance doors by Canonica, with four bronze reliefs illustrating the four destructions of the abbey. Its predecessor was itself a rebuilding in 1649-1717 from designs by Cosimo Fanzago. As richly baroque as it was before, the interior is faced with marble intarsia which faithfully repeats the earlier design. Among the several paintings are works by Cavalier d'Arpino, Francesco de Mura, and Francesco Solimena. Beneath the high altar, in a silver and bronze casket, are the remains of St. Benedict and of his twin sister St. Scholastica. In the choir of the old church were the tombs of Pietro de' Medici (d. 1503) by Antonio and Francesco da Sangallo, and of Guido Fieramosca by Giovanni da Nola (1535-48). Beneath the church is the interesting **Crypt**, only the central vault of which was seriously damaged. It is built in brightly colored granite, with traces of old frescoes and decorations by the monks of Beuron in Germany (ca. 1900), executed with great severity of style.

The **Library** has 500 incunabula. Among the precious documents are the Paulus Diaconus collection (eighth century), the eleventh century Biblia Hebraica of St. Gregory the Great and the Liber Moralium with notes in the handwriting of St. Thomas Aquinas. Also preserved is the old main door of the church, a wonderful piece of bronze work, cast at Costantinople in 1066, and found damaged in the debris.

From the *Loggia del Paradiso* above the portico visitors can enjoy a panorama famous throughout Italy.

Beyond Cassino Highway 6 runs parallel to the railway and to Autostrada A2.

Teano, at the foot of Monte Roccamonfina, occupies the site of the ancient *Teanum*, capital of the Sidicini. An **Amphi-**

theater, near the road to the station, is the most important Roman relic. Beyond is the Romanesque church of **San Paride**. The medieval **Cathedral** has been restored.

Capua, situated within a narrow bend of the Volturno River, was founded in 856 by refugees from the ancient city of the same name (see Route f). The medieval Capua was the center of a fertile agricultural region known as the *Terra di Lavoro* and an important border town of the realm of Sicily. Its famous gate, designed by Frederick II in 1247, was destroyed in 1557. Because of its strategic position Capua was attacked many times during the Middle Ages, but it rarely capitulated. In 1501 it was taken by treachery by the French and their ally Caesar Borgia, who massacred 5000 of its inhabitants, an event which is still commemorated every year.

The center of town life is the piazza dei Giudici. This stands midway along the corso Appio, the main street of the present town, which follows the path of the ancient Appian Way. The sixteenth century **Town Hall**, on the south side of the square, incorporates seven marble busts from the Amphitheater at Santa Maria Capua Vetere. To the right of this is the church of Sant'Eligio, founded in 1286-96 but rebuilt in its present form in 1747. The adjacent **Arco di Sant'Eligio** dates from the thirteenth century.

The via del Duomo, opposite, leads to the *Cathedral*, founded in 835 and almost completely rebuilt. Of the twenty four columns in the Atrium, sixteen are original; the beautiful Bell Tower dates from 861. The Crypt, with fourteen antique columns, contains mosaics.

The via del Duomo ends at the former palace of the Dukes of San Cipriano, which now houses the **Museo Campano**. The museum contains ancient, medieval, and Renaissance sculpture (including fragments of Frederick's Capua Gate), and a small picture gallery.

We leave Capua by the via Roma, which takes us along the Volturno River and across the Autostrada to **Sant'Angelo in Formis**, a sleepy farming community famous for its eleventh century church. Climb to the top of the town and pass (quickly) beneath a crumbling arch. The caretaker, whose house is on the right, accompanies visitors from this point on.

The basilica of Sant'Angelo in Formis is a splendid Lombard Romanesque church preceded by a picturesque portico with pointed arches, and flanked by a fine bell tower. It was built, probably in the tenth century, over the ruins of a Temple of Diana. In the eleventh century it came into the hands of the Benedictine monks of Monte Cassino. The famous abbot Desiderius (1058-87) rebuilt the church in its present form in 1073 and rebuilt the convent, which soon became quite powerful.

The church is preceded by a portico with five arches carried by four columns with Corinthian capitals (two of granite and two of *cipollino*). The first column on the right incorporates an antique fragment believed to come from the Temple of Diana. Beneath the central arch is a white marble doorway of classical design flanked by two Corinthian columns. An inscription in the architrave recalls the abbot Desiderius. In the lunette is an eleventh century fresco of St. Michael; above the doorway is a twelfth century Madonna in a tondo held by two angels. The lunettes of the other arches bear ruined frescoes of Saints (thirteenth century).

The interior is a three-aisled basilica with fourteen columns, some in granite and others in *cipollino* (notice the fine capitals) and three semicircular apses. The present floor of the church is the original pavement of the Temple of Diana. Adjoining the first column on the south side of the church is a holy-water stoup made from a Roman altar; that in the other aisle was carved out of a medieval capital. The Baptismal Font is made of two fragments of antique fluted columns. On the left of the high altar is a simple marble pulpit of the thirteenth century, with the eagle of St. John and traces of mosaics. Remains of a mosaic pavement may be seen at the end of the south aisle.

St. Angelo in Formis. The frescoes in the basilica of Sant'Angelo in Formis, near Capua, were carried out a few years after the scheme at Montecassino, which they are believed to reflect. Although they were carried out by local artists, there paintings are clearly inspired by Byzantine values of line and color. The painting reproduced here shows the Kiss of Judas.

The most striking feature of the church is the beautiful cycle of frescoes that cover the walls. These were executed in the eleventh century, presumably by the same artists who worked at Montecassino, and show a strong Byzantine influence. Between the arches of the nave are Prophets, Sibyls, and Kings of Isreael; Old and New Testament scenes are arranged above in three tiers. The small apse at the end of the south aisle contains a Madonna and Child with Angels, and a seventeenth century fresco. The large, central apse is adorned with a huge seated Christ flanked by the evangelist symbols, below which are three archangels and Desiderius (holding a model of the church) and St. Benedict (the founder of the order). Desiderius's square nimbus indicates that he was still alive when the frescoes were painted. On the west wall is a great Last Judgment, with a phony Christ added in the nineteenth century.

On leaving Sant'Angelo in Formis, turn left at the bottom to the hill to Santa Maria Capua Vetere (cf. Route f). A turning (left) just outside of town on the Caserta road brings us to the village of San Prisco, where the parish church contains, in the Chapel of Santa Matrona, sixth century mosaics like those in the Naples Baptistery. The chapel is all that remains of a basilica built by Matrona, princess of Lusitania. It was probably intended as her tomb. Although the mosaics are damaged, the most important parts remain intact. These are the two lunettes under the dome, one (left) showing an empty throne (the hetimasia) flanked by two of the evangelist symbols, the bull and the eagle (signifying Luke and John); the other (above the entrance) showing a bust of Christ blessing, holding a book in one hand and flanked by the letters Alpha and Omega (signifying that He represents both the beginning and the end). The richly colored dome is filled with a luxurious foliate design and inhabited by doves.

No tour of medieval Campania is complete without a visit to **Caserta Vecchia**, set in the hills above the new town and reached by a series of country roads (unfortunately, poorly marked). The town, founded in the eighth century, is built entirely of black volcanic rock. The Cathedral, a fine example of Southern Norman architecture, dates from 1123-53; the central cupola and campanile (the latter with a roadway through it) were added about 100 years later. The exterior sculptures are interesting, while within may be noted the eighteen antique columns, the paschal candelabrum, and (in the transepts) the tombs of Count Francies II (d. 1359) and Bishop Giacomo (d. 1460), as well as many mosaic details. The ruins of the Castle (thirteenth century) lie in a lovely park to the east. The view over the plain of Capua, with the Royal Palace of Caserta in the foreground, is magnificent.

A short drive (30 km, 18 miles) to the east brings us to

Benevento, an important place under the Roman Empire (cf. Route 1,f) which rose again to fame in 571 as the first independent Lombard duchy, and preserved its autonomy until 1053, when it passed to the Church. On February 26, 1266 the chivalrous and accomplished Manfred of Hohenstaufen was defeated here by Charles of Anjou and sought a voluntary death in the battle after the treacherous defection of his allies. The city was damaged in the Second World War, the lower town and the cathedral having been almost completely destroyed.

The corso Garibaldi traverses the town from east to west. At its east end stands the **Castle** (*Rocca dei Rettori*), built in 1321 by John XXII; here Attendolo, first of the Sforza, was once imprisoned. The adjoining public garden affords a good view. On the right of the corso is a little piazza in which stands Santa Sofia, a church of 760, rebuilt in 1668, with a dome borne by antique Corinthian columns and a twelfth century cloister. Adjoining the cloister is the Museo del Sannio with a collection of antiquities, paintings, prints, and drawings. The **Cathedral**, a thirteenth century Romanesque building, was shattered by bombardment. Its richly sculptured façade, badly damaged, and its campanile of 1279, still standing, incorporate fragments of Roman and Lombard architecture. The famous bronze doors, possibly of Byzantine workmanship, were seriously injured; two thirds of their plaques were saved and placed in the Seminary. The contents of the Treasury, notable for a golden rose and a bronze coffer of the eleventh or twelfth century, and of the Chapter Library, including interesting Lombard manuscripts, illuminated choir-books and the thirteenth century Necrologio di Santo Spirito, had been removed to safety.

From Caserta the return to Naples is most conveniently made by Autostrada A2.

III Viceregal Rule

During the period of the Spanish viceroys, and during that of the Austrian viceroys that followed them after 1707, Naples was oppressed by excessive taxation and the graft of delegated rule. Brigands terrorized the countryside, and pirates roamed the seas discouraging trade and endangering travelers. Thomas Hoby, an English writer of the sixteenth century, reports that he was compelled to sail from Rome to Naples by night in order to avoid being captured and sold into slavery by the Barbary pirates who controlled the coast:

"We sayled all that night after and passed Monte Circello . . . . In a little port under the hill lye many times Moores and Turks with their foistes and other vesselles to take the passinger vesselles that go betwixt Roome and Naples . . . yf we had cum bye yt by daye . . . we had bine all taken slaves."

The scarse attention that the Spanish governors dedicated to the provinces brought increasing numbers of immigrants to the capital, giving rise to a phenomenon of overcrowding that several viceroys, and especially don Pedro de Toledo (1532-1553) tried to attenuate by constructing new roads and new buildings. Nevertheless the population increase outran these measures and the city became a human anthill, until a terrible plague of 1656 killed or dispersed half the population.

In the provinces, as in the capital, life was dominated by the nightmare of high taxes. Despite reduced profits, country-dwellers devoted themselves as always to the cultivation of fields and orchards, and the sale of agricultural products remained their principal source of income. In the cities an educated and ambitious middle class climbed steadily to wealth and political power, the successful buying titles and estates (it is estimated that seventeenth century Naples had at least 119 princes, 156 dukes, 173 marquesses, and several hundred counts). In contrast to these, and to the virtual army of clergy (which came to represent one fortieth of the population), stood the hoards of ragged beggars known as *lazzeroni*. On one hand, they were considered as thieving, treacherous, seditious, lazy, and corrupt ("There is not such another race of rogues as the common people of Naples", Henry Swinburne commented); but on the other their "way of being satisfied with so little, of living on the air of time," was idealized, especially by Northern Europeans, like Goethe, who attributed to them a peculiarly Mediterranean sense of freedom.

The French never quite got over the idea that they had lost the kingdom of Naples to the Spanish (a French army under Lautrex de Foix, viscount of Lautrec, laid siege to the capital in

1528), and the Neapolitans themselves considered the foreigners tyrants whose unjust rule was to be cast off at the earliest possible opportunity. When Viceroy Pedro de Toledo levied a new round of taxes in 1535 the people appealed in vain to the Spanish emperor Charles V, who passed through Naples on his way back from his Tunisian campaign. With more success the city rose up in 1547, when Toledo tried to revive an old project to introduce the Inquisition, in full swing at that time in Spain. Naples is nevertheless deeply indebted to this energetic viceroy, for it was he who undertook the most ambitious (and successful) urban development program in the city's history.

Toledo curbed ecclesiastical building (a sticky political problem throughout the viceregal period) by acquiring property in the city center so that tenement houses would not be torn down and convents built in their place. He alleviated day-to-day "commuter" traffic by moving administrative offices out of the downtown area (it was by his order that the law courts were moved to their present seat at the *Castel Capuano*).

Most importantly, he doubled the area available for building within the city walls by constructing a new set of fortifications that ran from the Castel Capuano, on the east side of town, to the Castel Sant'Elmo (rebuilt in the form of a six-pointed star) on the Vomero hill , and from the latter the Castel dell'Ovo, on the sea to the west.

In place of the now obsolete Aragonese walls he built the great thoroughfare known officially as via Roma, but popularly called via Toledo in his honor. To the west of this road he constructed a whole new quarter to house the Spanish garrison at Naples (the mazes of lanes and steep staircases that chara-cterize this area have changed little since then, and repay a visit).

The via Toledo became the fashionable residential street of the aristocracy. At the southern end of the street don Pedro himself erected a new viceregal palace, which became known as the "Palazzo Vecchio" when, at the beginning of the follo-wing century, Viceroy Ferrante di Castro, in expectation of a visit that never took place by King Philip III, commissioned Domenico Fontana to build the magnificent Royal Palace.

At the end of the sixteenth century Naples had 240,000 inhabitants, which became 300, 000 if one counted the suburbs that extended outward from the town gates. And it was a city that bristled with churches and convents: at least 400 of the former, not counting private chapels, and about 200 of the latter. At the beginning of the eighteenth century a petition was sent to the viceroy, urging him to prevent the clergy from acquiring more property-which suggests that don Pedro de Toledo's nightmare remained a major political concern of his successors. Yet the construction of churches and convents

Tower of Palazzo Rufolo. This elegant palace was begun in the eleventh century and was occupied in turn by Pope Adrian IV, Charles of Anjou, and Robert the Wise. An ensemble of Norman-Saracenic buildings, partly in ruins, the palace is enhanced by tropical gardens; here Wagner found his inspiration for the magic garden of Klingsor in Parsifal.

Belvedere Cimbrone. A straight avenue leads through the lush garden of the Palazzo Cimbrone to the Belvedere, the most advanced point of the ridge on which Rafaello lies. The open view of Atrani and the Gulf of Salerno is unrivalled.

Palazzo Cimbrone and its beatiful terrace.

Scala, once a populous and flourishing town, was ruined by pestilence and the rivalry of nearby Ravello. The Cathedral has a handsome Romanesque portal and contains a mosaic pulpit, a mitre with enamels of the thirteenth century, and a spacious crypt.

The Ponte degli Aurunci, or Auruncian Bridge, stands just outside of town. Its 21 arches (now largely walled up) span the Rio Travata and its ravine.

The Cathedral of Sessa Aurunca, built in the twelfth century utilizing fragments from antique buildings, is a treasure-house of medieval art. This photo shows the mosaic pavement, candelstick, and pulpit, all executed by local craftsmen in the thirteenth century.

The Cloister, in which Gothic architectural motifs combine with Romanesque, is striking in tits harmony of proportion and detail. In the infirmery here St. Thomas Aquinas died in 1274 while on his way from Naples to Lyons.

The National Gallery of Capodimonte, in a way, may be considered a double legacy of Bourbon dynasty: it occupies the sumptuous hunting lodge built by Charles I, and contains the magnificent Farnese collection of painting and sculpture, which the king inherited from his mother, Elisabetta Farnese. Among the masterpieces may be seen Caravaggio's Flagellation.

National Gallery of Capodimonte. Masolino's Foundation of Santa Maria Maggiore in Rome.

formed the basis of the great artistic flowering of the seventeenth and eighteenth centuries, characterized by the presence of architects, sculptors, and painters who were famous throughout Europe-Cosimo Fanzago, Caravaggio, Giuseppe Ribera, Domenichino, Giovanni Lanfranco, Giovan Battista Caracciolo, Massimo Stanzione, Bernardo Cavallino, Salvator Rosa, Mattia Preti, Luca Giordano, and others. "That which seemed to us most extraordinary at Naples," wrote one seventeenth century observer "was the number and magnificence of the churches. It may be justly said, that in this respect it surpasses imagination... If you would look upon rare pictures, sculptures, and the rarity of vessels of gold and silver, you need but go to the churches: the roofs, the wainscots, the walls are all covered with pieces of precious marble, most artificially laid together, or with compartments of *basso rilievo*, or of joiner's work gilded, and enriched with the works of the most famous painters. There is nothing to be seen but jasper, porphyry, mosaic of all fashions, all masterpieces of art."

Another connoisseur of the Neapolitan baroque, the eminent British art historian, Anthony Blunt, warns that "the architecture of Naples is like its inhabitants: lively, colourful, and with a tendency not to keep the rules," adding that "if you go to Naples expecting its architecture to behave like that of Rome, you will be as surprised as if you expected its traffic to behave like Roman traffic, though you will be in less physical danger." Many of the architects who worked in Naples at this time came from outside the city (Cosimo Fanzago, the most imaginative architect and sculptor of the period, was a native of Bergamo), yet they all seem to have become acclimatized; to a remarkable degree they ignored, and in some cases they anticipated, the accomplishments of their contemporaries in Rome and elsewhere in Europe. In ecclesiastical architecture, the most characteristic examples of the Neapolitan baroque style are those which combine simple ground plans with rich and varied decoration; for it was in carrying out elaborate decorative schemes without bringing confusion to the overall form of their buildings that Neapolitan architects were most accomplished. As a consequence, the great churches of the sixteenth and seventeenth centuries lack the interest in new spatial forms that distinguishes ecclesiastical architecture in Rome during the same period.

It was not until the eighteenth century and the rococo creations of Domenico Antonio Vaccaro and Ferdinando Sanfelice that Neapolitan church architects displayed inventiveness in planning. As for domestic architecture, the pressure of overcrowding caused Neapolitans to build higher than their counterparts in other Italian cities. This permitted them to move the *piano nobile* of lordly palaces from the first to the second

floor and to introduce the vast,
monumental doorways or *portes cochères* which, together with
the magnificent external staircases, are the most striking and
individual features of Neapolitan palaces.

In painting, the seventeenth century was dominated by the
dark, dramatic styles of the Spaniard Ribera and of Caravaggio
(the latter, exiled from Rome where he had killed a man in a
moment of rage, and from Malta where he had insulted the
Grand Master of the Order of St. John, took refuge in Naples
until his involvement in a brawl in a waterfront tavern got him
expelled from this city, too). Ribera and another foreigner, the
Greek Corenzio, leagued together with the native Caracciolo in
the "Cabal of Naples" to exclude Northern competition. Using
Southern methods of intimidation, sabotage, and the hired
assassin, they hounded Annibale Carracci, the Cavaliere
d'Arpino, and Guido Reni from Naples, and Domenichino to
his death (1641). After Caracciolo's death in the same year, and
Ribera's in 1652, the soul of Naples found its most perfect
expression in the exuberant compositions of Luca Giordano,
who also frescoed the rooms the Medici-Riccardi palace in
Florence.

The first native school of sculpture in Naples arose in the
sixteenth century with Girolamo Santacroce and Giovanni da
Nola and their pupils, alongside whom worked the Florentines
Michelangelo Naccherino and Pietro Bernini, the father of Gian
Lorenzo Bernini, of Vatican fame. In the seventeenth century
the fanciful Cosimo Fanzago was prominent, followed in the
eighteenth century by the disciples of Gian Lorenzo Bernini
and the technicians of the Cappella Sansevero.

The last years of Spanish rule were undistinguished. The
usual burdensome taxation aroused the Neapolitans to
insurrection (1647) under Masaniello (an Amalfi fisherman
who was used as a figurehead by liberal reformers who sought
to undermine the power of the nobility, more than the authority
of the viceroy), but the ensuing "Parthenopean Republic"
endured only a few months. In 1707, after the War of the
Spanish Succession, Naples passed to the Archduke Charles of
Austria (Charles VI), but the succession of viceroys was
continued. In 1734, however, the Infant Charles of Bourbon
(Charles VII, known as Charles III) seized Sicily and
subsequently Naples, and in 1744 defeated the Austrians at
Velletri, near Rome, thus founding the Neapolitan Bourbon
dynasty. One of the first acts of the new king was to tax
ecclesiastical assets, which tripled the revenue of the realm.

Site Visits

d Spanish Naples

Walking tour, about 10 km (6,2 miles), with buses.
Many of the churches and palaces built by the Spanish viceroys, members of their courts, and contemporary religious orders were taken over and rebuilt or redecorated by the Bourbons and their followers. Nevertheless, several of the more interesting monuments have survived in reasonably good shape. This circular route takes us all around the old city center, from the Palazzo Reale, near the harbor, to the church of the Girolamini, near the cathedral, to the former Carthusian monastery of San Martino, now a National Museum, on the Sant'Elmo hill. The climb up the hill, by the way, is long and steep, and is best made by bus (No 49 from the Museo Nazionale) or by funicular railway (see below).

From the Castel Nuovo it is a short walk to the **Palazzo Reale** (Map 2, 14), built in 1600-02 by Domenico Fontana for the viceroy Ferrante di Castro, in anticipation of a visit by Philip II of Spain. Under the Spanish the palace was occupied only by viceroys, but under the Bourbons it became the official residence of the king. Today the royal apartments on the first floor are a museum; the second floor houses the National Library (*Biblioteca Nazionale*, see below). The only remaining parts of the original construction are the façade facing the piazza del Plebiscito and the cortile d'onore. Renewed in part inside and enlarged toward the east in 1743-48, it was enriched by Joachim Murat and Carolina Bonaparte with neoclassical decorations and furniture, in part from the Tuileries. Damaged by a fire in 1837, it was restored by Gaetano Genovese under Ferdinand II. Genovese is responsible for the decorations of the monumental staircase and the stepped form of the southern façade with its elegant hanging garden, to a plan first conceived by Antonio Niccolini.

The magnificent façade, with its ground floor portico and two orders of windows above, is 550 ft long. It preserves its original classical forms, except in the portico, where in the second half of the eighteenth century, the architect Vanvitelli closed up alternate arches to make the building sturdier. In the walled-up arches Vanvitelli made niches, which today contain statues representing the eight dynasties of Naples: Roger the Norman, Frederick II of Swabia, Charles I of Anjou, Alfonso of Aragon, Charles V of Austria, Charles III of Bourbon, Joachim Murat, and Victor Emmanuel II of Savoy.

From the square we cross the immense courtyard to the entrance to the *Appartamento Storico*. In the atrium, the

Chapel, attributed to Cosimo Fanzago (1668), is at the foot of the *Grand Staircase* (1651, restored 1837). Here also are the original bronze doors of the Castel Nuovo, by Guillaume le Moine and Pietro di Martino, on which six reliefs depict Ferdinand of Aragon's struggle with the rebel barons. The cannonball lodged in the lower relief on the left door is a relic from the naval battle between the French and the Genoese (1495), in which the doors and other loot en route to France from Naples were recovered and returned to the city.

The first floor contains various fine halls with period furniture, tapestries, paintings, and porcelain, preceded by the small *Teatro di Corte*, built by Ferdinando Fuga in 1768 and restored after war damage in 1950. From here we enter the *Salone Centrale* (Room I), with a ceiling painting (an allegory of the virtues of Charles of Bourbon and his wife Maria Amalia) by Francesco De Mura; and perspective paintings by Vincenzo Re. On the walls are two large Gobelins tapestries representing Air and Fire; around the room are French porcelain vases decorated in Naples, Chinese porcelain vases presented to Ferdinand II by Czar Nicholas I; and assorted furniture, many pieces of which are in the heavy baroque style. Room II has a ceiling painted with a military display of Alfonso of Aragon, by Belisario Corenzio. On the walls are paintings of Orpheus charming the animals, by Gerrit van Honthorst; and St. Ignatius Loyola taking the habit, by Massimo Stanzione; a Madonna and Child with St. Bruno, by Giuseppe Ribera; and a St. John the Baptist, by the Roman artist Guido Reni. In Room III the ceiling painting of Minerva rewarding the Virtues is by Giuseppe Cammarano. On the walls are Christ among the Doctors, by Giovanni Antonio Galli; St. Joseph in Ecstasy, by Guercino (Giovanni Francesco Barbieri, from Ferrara; 1591-1666); Fire, an eighteenth century tapestry of Neapolitan manufacture. Room IV is the Throne Room of the Neapolitan Bourbons. The ceiling is adorned with stuccoes by Camillo Beccalli; at the top of the walls are represented the twelve provinces of the kingdom of Naples. The throne and its baldachin are relatively recent: they date from after 1850. Room V was the waiting room of the ambassadors to court. The ceiling shows military displays of the Spanish Kings, by Belisario Corenzio. On the walls are tapestries representing historical events (wounding of the duke of Sully, death of admiral Coligny, by P. F. Cozette); Elements (Earth and Water, by the Gobelins workshop; these form a set with the tapestries of Air and Fire in Room I), a female portrait (by Laniée); and the Flautist, by Alexis Grimou. The furniture is in the Empire style. Room VI was the bedroom of queen Maria Amalia and, later, a part of the apartment of queen Maria Cristina, first wife of Ferdinando II. On the walls are paintings of the Circumcision, by Belisario Corenzio; a portrait of a cardinal, attributed to Baciccia; a copy of Marinus Claesz van Roymerswaele's Ursurers; a Madonna and Child by Francesco Ruviale, and a copy of a Holy Family by the Florentine artist Filippino Lippi. In front of the windows are two large vases of Sevres porcelain. Notice the Empire style clocks and gilt bronze vases, by Fil Thomire. Adjoining the room, on the left of the entrance, is the private chapel of Maria Cristina, with a fine tabernacle, frescoed ceiling, and paintings of the Adoration of the Magi, Flight into Egypt, and Visitation by Francesco Liani. The ceiling painting of Room VII, representing Gonzalo de Cordoba's defeat of the French (the first of a series of victories that would bring Naples under the dominion of the kings of Spain) and his Triumphal entrance into Naples, is attributed to Belisario Corenzio. On the walls are more tapestries, and twelve Proverbs painted by Federico Zuccari. In Room VII the ceiling shows an obscure historical scene (Tancred returning Constance to Henry IV) concerning the passage of power from the Normans to the Swabians. It is by Gennaro Maldarelli. On the walls are a Female portrait, by Sofonisba Anguissola; Crucifixion by Francesco Curia; and minor works by anonymous sixteenth century artists. In the center of the room is a flower pot adorned with views of Fontainebleau and St. Petersburg, presented by Czar Nicholas I to Ferdinand II. Notice also the bronze cage with Sèvres porcelain details. Room IX was the apartment of the king's body guard. On the walls hang eighteenth century Neapolitan tapestries of the Four Elements. The furniture is all in the Empire style. Room X has a ceiling painting showing the Norman king Roger landing at Palermo, by Gennaro Maldarelli. The cabinets and bookcases are in the Empire style. On the walls, Lucretia, by Massimo Stanzione; two neoclassical paintings of the Rape of Europa and Andromeda, in octagonal frames; and Galatea, by E. H. Montagny. Room XI is adorned with paintings of an Apostle, by Cesare Fracanzano; the Return of the Prodigal son, by Mattia Preti; Orpheus and Baccantes and Rachel and Jacob, by Andrea Vaccaro; and Lot and his daughters, by Massimo Stanzione; and David and Goliath by Giovanni Lys. Room XII contains two paintings representing the ambassadors of Turkey and Tripoli, by Giuseppe Bonito; and cartoons for a series of tapestries narrating the legend of Don Quixote, by Antonio Dominici, Giuseppe Bonito, Antonio Guastaferro and Benedetto Della Torre. Room XIII is hung with landscape paintings, and Room XIV with portraits of historical figures, all by minor artists. Room XV contains numerous paintings, chiefly of religious subjects (notably Holy Family, Charity, Sts. Peter, Paul, Sebastian, and Giovanni Battista, by Bartolomeo Schedoni; and Madonna and Child with St. Augustine, by Giovanni Lanfranco). Room XVI contains seventeenth and

eighteenth century still lifes. Room XIX has some fine baroque
furniture and paintings by minor artists. Room XX contains
more cartoons for the Don Quixote tapestries, and Room XXIV
a San Gennaro by Fedele Fischetti.

The **National Library** (entrance in the via Vittorio Emanuele III), founded in 1734, grew out of the Farnese library
brought to Naples by Charles III. It includes 1, 500, 000 volumes and over 17, 000 incunabula and manuscripts. Annexed are
the Lucchesi-Palli Library of Music and Dramatic Literature,
and the J. F. Kennedy Library of American studies. The library
also hosts the famous Herculaneum Papyrus found (1752) at
the so-called *Villa dei Papiri*.

From the north side of the piazza Trento e Trieste
(Map2, 13), the via Roma begins its long, steady ascent to the
piazza Dante, after which it changes its name. It is the favorite
shopping street of the Neapolitans, and all day is filled by a
noisy and lively throng, especially in the afternoon. It is still
commonly called via Toledo after its founder Don Pedro de
Toledo, who built the 1,5 km long thoroughfare in 1536 to
relieve the city's chronic (!) traffic problems. The streets on the
right (broad and modern to the south of the piazza Carità)
descend through the business quarter of the town toward the
harbor; those on the left (narrow and often squalid) ascend
steeply, sometimes in steps, toward the corso Vittorio
Emanuele. The tenements in this densely populated
neighborhood were originally built to house the Spanish troops
stationed in Naples.

Beyond the Galleria Umberto I (Map 2, 13-14), in the tiny
piazza Duca d'Aosta, is the station of a funicular to the hilltop
Vomero quarter, described below (another funicular leaves
from Santa Teresa a Chiaia and from the corso Vittorio
Emanuele, and a third from the Cumana Railway Station off via
Montesanto). In the next turning to the right is the church of
Santa Brigida, built in 1612 in honor of St. Brigid of Sweden.
Here is buried Luca Giordano, whose clever perspective
paintings add apparent height to the dome. The St. Francis
receiving the stigmata, in the transept, is by Massimo
Stanzione.

Where the via Roma crosses the Spaccanapoli (Route IIb)
stands the baroque Palazzo Maddaloni (right), rebuilt in the
mid-seventeenth century by Cosimo Fanzago and decorated
with paintings by prominent contemporary artists. We turn
right to piazza del Gesù Nuovo.

The **church of Gesù Nuovo** (also called *Trinità Maggiore*)
was built in 1584-1601 for the Jesuit Order on the site of a
fifteenth century palace. The façade of the church is a
readaptation of the former palace façade, made of diamond-
shaped blocks of the black volcanic stone known as *piperno*.
The lateral doorways date from the sixteenth century, the

central doorway from 1685. After a fire in 1639 the church was restored and embellished under the direction of Cosimo Fanzago, who is responsible for the present character of the interior. The original dome was damaged by earthquake in 1688 and replaced by the present structure in 1744.

The interior follows a modified Greek cross plan, the nave and choir being only slightly longer that the transept. The original design (by the distinguished Jesuit architect, Giuseppe Valeriano) called for white plaster walls and a discreet use of colored marble and black piperno. A highly original plan, it differed considerably from the Roman Gesù, which served as the model for all Jesuit churches of the day. Its symmetrical layout, and the flat, continuous wall surface that defines the space with maximum clarity, can still be discerned beneath the rich colored marbles of Fanzago, who seems to have gone to great lengths to respect the intrinsic qualities of the spatial design. The nave contains frescoes by Francesco Solimena (Expulsion of Heliodorus, on the west wall above the door) and Paolo De Matteis and Belisario Corenzio (Conception and Presentation of the Virgin, in the ceiling). The Evangelists under the dome are by Giovanni Lanfranco. The first chapel of the south aisle has a rich marble decoration, carved doors, paintings, and sculptures of Saints by Cosimo Fanzago (right) and Michelangelo Naccherino (left). The second chapel, also with a fine marble decoration, hosts a Visitation by Massimo Stanzione and fragmentary remains of frescoes by Luca Giordano and Francesco Solimena. In the south transept are ceiling frescoes by Belisario Corenzio and Paolo De Matteis. The elaborate altar is the work of Donato Vanvitelli, Cosimo Fanzago, and Michelangelo Naccherino. The episodes from the story of St. Francis Saverio are by Luca Giordano. The chapels on this side of the choir are decorated by Sebastiano Conca (right) and Corenzio.

The choir itself has ceiling paintings representing the Story of Mary, and the Prophets and Angels on the walls, by Massimo Stanzione. The High Altar is a magnificent agglomerate of rare stones and bronze (1854). The chapel adjoining the choir contains frescoes of Angels and Putti by Francesco Solimena. The ceiling of the north transept is adorned with paintings illustrating the Life of St. Ignatius Loyola, by Belisario Corenzio and Paolo De Matteis. The altar, the work of Cosimo Fanzago and assistants, is surmounted by paintings by Paolo De Matteis (Sts. Ignatius and Francis Saverio) and Giuseppe Ribera (St. Ignatius in glory and Pope Paul III approving the Rule). Against the piers are a Madonna of the Rosary (right) by Fabrizio Santafede, and a Trinity and Saints, attributed to Guercino. In the chapel adjoining the transept, the statues of St. Andrew and St. Mattew are by Michelangelo Naccherino and Pietro Bernini, respectively.

Leave the piazza del Gesù Nuovo by the via Benedetto Croce. At N° 12 is the **Palazzo Filomarino**, built in the fourteenth century by a branch of the Brancaccio family, and bought and remodeled in the sixteenth century by the Sanseverino. The palace was virtually rebuilt following damage in the revolt of Masaniello, and again in the early years of the eighteenth century, when Ferdinando Sanfelice added the magnificent baroque doorway. Benedetto Croce died in this building in 1952. N° 45 is the beautiful palazzo **Carafa della Spina**, built in the late sixteenth century and reconstructed with a tall baroque doorway in the early eighteenth century.

The **piazza San Domenico Maggiore** (Map 2, 6) is enclosed on three sides by more fine old mansions. At N° 3 is the Palazzo Del Balzo, built in the early fifteenth century and renovated after the earthquake of 1688; the marble doorway and the courtyard, with its low arches and elegant first-floor portico (elements typical of the Catalan architectural style brought to Naples by the Aragonese) belong to the original building. To the right, at N° 17, is the eighteenth century palace for the Sangro family by Mario Gioffredo and remodeled by Luigi Vanvitelli. The impressive portico is carried by Greek columns unearthed during construction of the building. Across the square, at N° 12, is the palace of Giovanni di Sangro, with a fine eighteenth century doorway. N° 9 is the Palazzo Sangro (the Neapolitan residence of the first-born of this illustrious noble family, the princes of Sansevero). It was built in the early sixteenth century and later enlarged. The magnificent doorway was added by Vitale Finelli to a design by Bartolomeo Picchiatti (1621). The stucco reliefs of the entrance way were executed by Giuseppe Sammartino for Raimondo di Sangro (1711-71).

The baroque Guglia di San Domenico, a neighborhood ex voto for deliverance from the plague of 1656, was completed two years after the tragedy by Domenico Antonio Vaccaro.

Around the corner is the **Cappella Sansevero** (Map 2, 6), also called *Santa Maria della Pietà dei Sangro* or *Pietatella*, the burial chapel of the princes of Sansevero. Founded in 1590 by Giovanni Francesco, it was renovated in 1608-13 by his son Alessandro and decorated in 1749-66 by Raimondo. It was joined to the palace by a raised walkway which collapsed in the nineteenth century. The interior is an intense medley of painting, sculpture, and marble work designed to commemorate the deceased and celebrate their virtues. Most notable are the allegorical figures, particularly Modesty (completely veiled), by Andrea Corradini, and Disillusion (a man struggling in the net of vice), by Francesco Queirolo. The Dead Christ, a veiled statue in alabaster, by Giuseppe Sammartino (1753), is a work of astonishing realism.

The church of **Santi Severino e Sossio** (Map 3, 7), together with the adjoining monastery (now the State Archives), was founded in 902 when Benedictines fearing a Saracen incursion abandoned their convent on the site of the Castel dell'Ovo and moved into a small church on this site. This was enlarged in 1494-1561 and decorated in the seventeenth century. The interior has ceiling paintings by Corenzio, who fell to his death while retouching them and is buried near the entrance to the sacristy. In the fourth chapel on the south side is an interesting sixteenth century polyptych. On the north side is the sacristy vestibule, in which are two fine Cicaro tombs of the sixteenth century, both with inscriptions by Sannazaro. The *Cappella Sanseverino* (right of the choir) contains the tombs by Giovanni da Nola of three Sanseverino brothers, all of whom were poisoned on the same day (1516) by their uncle. The choir stalls (1560-75) are beautifully carved.

The Benedictine convent has four cloisters, the most interesting of which is the *Chiostro del Platano*, named after a plane-tree said to have been planted by St. Benedict, and frescoed by Andrea Solario. It is reached by a door at the left of the vestibule.

At the top of a scenographic staircase stands the church of **San Paolo Maggiore** (Map 2, 2), formerly part of a convent founded by Saint Gaetano da Thiene (1538). It was built in 1583-1603 on a design by Francesco Grimaldi, over the ruins of a ninth century church which in turn arose on the site of a Roman temple of the Dioscuri. The portico of the latter remained until the earthquake of 1688 overthrew all the columns but two. The church is famous for its spacious interior, where the alternating large and small bays of the nave arcade create an unprecedented sense of movement. The transept and apse are less ingenious. The church is decorated with paintings by Massimo Stanzione (in the nave ceiling and fourth south chapel), and by Francesco Solimena (in the sacristy).

We return to the Spaccanapoli, here called **San Biagio ai Librai**. A little to the north lies **San Gregorio Armeno** (Map 3, 7), a convent of Benedictine nuns, whose charming cloister (an oasis of tranquility in contrast with the noise of the streets outside it) is overlooked by the seventeenth century Bell Tower and a tiled cupola. At the center of the garden is a baroque glorification of the well of Samaria, with figures of Jesus and the Samaritan woman (carved by Matteo Bottiglieri in 1730) which from a distance appear to be walking among the orange trees. The church has a fine gilded ceiling of 1582, a gilded bronze *comunichino* (1610), and frescoes by Luca Giordano of the life of the saint. The nuns here were trad-itionally the daughters of noble families, accustomed to a life of luxury which they could hardly be expected to renounce. An English traveler of the eighteenth century, who visited San Gregorio Armeno in the royal suite, provides us with a charming account of the famous conventual cuisine:

The company was surprised, on being led into a large parlour, to find a table covered, and every appearance of a most plentiful cold repast, consisting of several joints of meat, hams, fowl, fish, and various other dishes. It seemed rather ill-judged to have prepared a feast of such a solid nature immediately after dinner; for those royal visits were made in the afternoon. The Lady Abbess, however, earnestly pressed their Majesties to sit down; with which they complied... The nuns stood behind, to serve their royal guests. The Queen chose a slice of cold turkey, which, on being cut up, turned out a large piece of lemon ice, of the shape and appearance of a roasted turkey. All the other dishes were ices of various kinds, disguised under the forms of joints of meat, fish, and fowl, as above mentioned. The gaiety and good humour of the King, the affable and engaging behaviour of the royal sisters (Queen Maria Carolina and the Princess of Saxe-Teschen), and the satisfaction which beamed from the plump countenance of the Lady Abbess, threw an air of cheerfulness on this scene; which was interrupted, however, by gleams of melancholy reflection, which failed not to dart to mind, at sight of so many victims to the pride of family, to avarice, and superstition. Many of those victims were in the full bloom of health and youth, and some of them were remarkably handsome.

The nearby **church of the Monte della Misericordia**, a charitable foundation of 1601; (entrance in via dei Tribunali Map 2, 2) contains the celebrated painting by Caravaggio of the Seven Acts of Mercy (1607). The recently reordered Pinacoteca has paintings by Fabrizio Santafede, Francesco De Mura, Luca Giordano, and others.

The **church of the Girolamini** (or *San Filippo Neri,*) was begun in 1592 by Giovanni Antonio Dosio and completed after his death (1619) by Dionisio di Bartolomeo. The façade, designed by Ferdinando Fuga (about 1780) is now blocked up. Entrance is gained from the side facing the cathedral.

The interior is well and richly decorated and has twelve monolithic granite columns. The fine wooden ceiling was damaged in 1943. Over the principal entrance is a famous fresco by Luca Giordano, Christ driving the Moneylenders from the Temple (1684). The chapels of the south aisle are adorned with paintings by Pietro da Cortona (first chapel, Death of St. Alessio), Fabrizio Santafede (second chapel, Holy Family), Belisario Corenzio (fourth chapel, Epiphany), and Luca Giordano (sixth chapel, St. Maria Maddalena de' Pazzi). The transept hosts frescoes of Moses, David, Abraham, and Melchisedech by Francesco Solimena. In the Choir is Crucifixion by Corenzio, and in the chapel of St. Philip Neri (left) frescoes illustrating the life of the saint by Solimena. The adjacent sacristy contains a St. John the Baptist by Guido Reni. The statues of Saints on the large altar of the north transept were carved by Pietro Bernini (1606); the Annunciation to the Shepherds is by Fabrizio Santafede. The chapels of the north aisle contain paintings by Paolo De Matteis and Francesco De Mura (chapel adjoining the transept, St. Francis de Sales), Guido Reni (fifth chapel, St. Francis of Assisi), and Luca Giordano (fourth chapel, St. Januarius, St. Nicholas, and Angel; third chapel, Meeting between Sts. Philip and Charles). Near the last column on this side is the tomb of Giovanni Battista Vico (1668-1744), founder of the philosophy of history.

Adjoining the church is the Casa dei Padri dell'Oratorio, built around two fine cloisters, both built by Dionisio di Bartolomeo and Dionisio Lazzari. A staircase at the end of the second cloister leads to the Library, with a beautiful eighteenth century reading room decorated by contemporary painters and wood cutters. Adjoining the cloister is the celebrated Pinacoteca, with paintings by Andrea da Salerno, Guido Reni, Federico Zuccari, Cavalier d'Arpino, Pomarancio, Fabrizio Santafede, Battistello, Andrea Vaccaro, Massimo Stanzione, Domenichino, Sebastiano Conca, Paolo De Matteis, Francesco Solimena, and others.

From the **National Museum** (Map 2, 2) the via Salvator Rosa diverges left to climb to the piazza Mazzini, whence the corso Vittorio Emanuele starts its winding course round the slopes of Sant'Elmo. Just west of the piazza stands **the church of Santa Maria della Pazienza** (or L*a Cesarea*; 1636) with the tomb of the founder, Annibale Cesareo, by Michelangelo Naccherino (1613). The via Santacroce leads to the piazza (Leonardo), whence the via Michelangelo runs to the huge quarter of Vomero, which is built on a regular plan around the central piazza Vanvitelli. From here the via Alessandro Scarlatti mounts to the upper station of the Montesanto Funicular Railway (visitors following the route by car may reach the same point by turning left in the via Raffaele Morghen). The bus terminates in the via Tito Angelini, beyond which the road ends at the Castel Sant'Elmo, on the summit of the hill. Built in 1329-43 and altered to its present form in the sixteenth century by Pier Luigi Scriva of Valencia, the fortress was long used for political prisoners. It commands an extensive and magnificent view.

Adjoining is the former **Carthusian monastery of San Martino** (Map 2, 0), founded in the fourteenth century but transformed in the late sixteenth and early seventeenth century. Architecturally beautiful in themselves, the conventual buildings now also provide and admirable setting for the treasures of the **Museo Nazionale di San Martino**. The Museum, occupying 90 rooms, illustrates the history, life, and art of Naples.

The monastery was begun in 1325 by order of Charles of Anjou, son of King Robert, and completed in 1368 under Queen Joan I. In the late sixteenth and early seventeenth century the medieval buildings were added to and redecorated in the Neapolitan baroque manner by the architects Giovanni Antonio Dosio, Giovanni Giacomo Conforto, and Cosimo Fanzago. Credit is due chiefly to the latter for the convent's present appearance.

The main entrance brings us into a long, narrow courtyard designed by Dosio, dominated by the southeast bastion of the Castel Sant'Elmo. On the left is the **Church**, preceded by a fourteenth century porch remodeled by Dosio (who closed up two of the five arches to make two new chapels within), and by Fanzago. The fine seventeenth century wooden doors are surrounded by frescoes by Micco Spadaro (Persecution of the English Carthusians, 1651-56), Giovanni Baglione (Angels, St. Martin) and Belisario Corenzio.

The interior is entered by the main door in summer, and from the **Great Cloister**, at the rear of the church, in winter. It consists of a single broad nave flanked by chapels. It is one of the few instances in which a modern decorative scheme has been satisfactorily applied to a Gothic building (the original ribs of the nave vault can still be discerned), and it is certainly the most beautiful expression of the baroque aesthetic in Naples. The nave, begun by Dosio and finished by Fanzago, is rich in marble tarsia work, notably the floor by Bonaventura Presti. The Ascension on the ceiling is by Lanfranco; the twelve magnificent Prophets are by Ribera; and the Descent from the Cross, over the principal door is Stanzione's masterpiece. The chapels on both sides (not always accessible) contain many notable works of art. Their marble balustrades and bronze grilles are by Cosimo Fanzago. The first south chapel (A) dedicated to St. Hugh has an altarpiece showing the Madonna and Child with Sts. Hugh and Anselm by Stanzione, wall paintings (St. Hugh Raising a Dead Child and Founding Lincoln Cathedral) by Andrea Vaccaro, and ceiling frescoes (Life of the Saint) by Corenzio. The adjoining Cappella del Rosario (B), made by closing up an arch of the porch, was decorated around 1700 by Domenico Antonio Vaccaro, who painted the altarpiece (Madonna of the Rosary) and designed the floor and stucco ornaments; and by Battistello, who did the paintings on the walls (St. Januarius, St. Martin, and other saints). The second Chapel (C) St. John the Baptist contains the fine inlaid marble designs by Fanzago. The statues of Grace and Providence are works of Lorenzo and Domenico Antonio Vaccaro. The altarpiece (Baptism of Christ) is by Carlo Maratta (1710); the paintings of Christ and the Baptist (left wall) and the Baptist preaching (right wall) are by Paolo De Matteis; the others, showing the Feast of Herod (left) and Beheading of the Baptist (right) are by Stanzione, who also did the ceiling frescoes (Descent into Limbo and Cardinal Virtues). The third chapel (D) St. Martin, has statues and medalions by Giuseppe Sammartino and paintings by Battistello (altarpiece with St. Martin), Francesco Solimena (St. Martin and the beggar), and Paolo D. Finoglia (ceiling frescoes illustrating the Legend of the Saint).

Returning to the west end of the nave, the first north chapel (E) St. Januarius has ceiling frescoes by Battistello (Story of the Saint) in contemporary frames by Fanzago; more paintings by Battistello (Torture and Decapitation) on the walls, and a series of fine sculptures by Domenico Antonio Vaccaro (notably the relief with the Virgin Mary presenting the keys of the city to St. Januarius, on the altar). The adjacent Cappella di San Giuseppe (F), reached by a door in the left wall, is adorned with gilded stuccoes by Domenico Antonio Vaccaro and canvases by Paolo De Matteis. The central chapel (G) St. Bruno is decorated with a series of extraordinary paintings by Stanzione, illustrating the Legend of St. Bruno and (in the ceiling vault) St. Bruno in glory. The statues of Solitude and Penance are by Domenico Antonio and Lorenzo Vaccaro. Lorenzo is also responsible for the floor and the marble Cupids. The bust of St. Bruno on the altar is the work of Biase Monte. The third chapel (H) dedicated to the Assumption contains three paintings by Francesco De Mura (Assumption, Annunciation, Visitation) on the walls and altar; and beautiful ceiling frescoes illustrating the Life of the Virgin, by Battistello. The statues are by Giuseppe Sammartino. A doorway on the right gives access to the Chapel of St. Nicholas (I), also called the Sacristiola, with frescoes of the Martyrdom of St. Agatha and St. Catherine by Belisario Corenzio, and an altarpiece with St. Nicholas by Pacecco De Rosa.

The Choir (J) is decorated with frescoes of Old and New Testament subjects by the Cavalier d'Arpino; at the back are a Crucifixion by Lanfranco and a Nativity by Guido Reni, who died before completing it; on the left, Institution of the Eucharist by Ribera, and Washing of the Disciples' feet by Battistello (his masterpiece); on the right, Last Supper by Stanzione, and Institution of the Eucharist by a son and pupils of Paolo Veronese. The statue of Meekness (*Mansuetudine*) is by Pietro Bernini; the other, Obedience, is by an unknown mannerist. The beautiful seventeenth century choir stalls are the work of Orazio De Orio and G. Mazzuoli.

Leading off the choir is the Sacristy (K) with ceiling paintings (Passion, Virtues, and Biblical figures) by the Cavalier d'Arpino, from which an antechamber, with frescoes by Stanzione and Giordano, leads into the Treasury (L). Above the altar, Descent from the Cross, Ribera's masterpiece; the vault fresco of Judith was Luca Giordano's last work (1704).

From the choir we pass by the side of the high altar (a gilded wooden model by Francesco Solimena for a final design which was to be executed in marble and semi-precious stones) into the Lay Brothers Choir (M), with inlaid stalls of the fifteenth century. Hence a passage leads to the Cappella della Maddalena (N), adorned by Fanzago and Andrea Vaccaro, the Chiostrino (O), and the Refectory (P). Returning to the Choir, we take the door opposite the Sacristy to the Chapter House (Q), with frescoes by Corenzio, whence we pass to the frescoed Parlour (R) and, from here, exit to the Great Cloister.

The latter, with its white and grey marble ornamentation and beautifully kept gardens, is one of the more striking achievements of Italian baroque architecture. The original conception of the cloister, its general layout, and the form of the arcade, are due to Andrea Dosio (sixteenth century); but its present character is largely a result of the sculptural program developed by Cosimo Fanzago in the seventeenth century. His design, conceived in 1623, is strongly conditioned by the style of the Florentine architect Buontalenti (note especially the curved and twisted framework of the niches above the doors), introduced to Naples in the first quarter of the century by Michelangelo Naccherino and other Florentine artists. Five of the six busts (St. Martin of Tours, Bishop Nicola Albergati, St. Bruno, St. Hugh, and St. Dionysius) are by Fanzago's hand, whereas the sixth (St. Januarius) is an early work of Domenico Antonio Vaccaro. Fanzago is also partly or wholly responsible for the eight statues at the corners and center of the arcade (that of the Resurrected Christ was begun by Naccherino).

A door on our immediate right leads past the refectory to the little seventeenth century *Chiostro dei Procuratori*, on the far side of which the **Museum** is entered. The Entrance Hall, with two fine carriages, opens onto the Convent Gardens, originally laid out on three levels. The upper level was given over to medicinal herbs, the middle level was the Prior's Garden (it preserves its lovely pergola), and the lower level was planted as a vineyard. The view from the gardens is superb.

Our visit to the Museum begins with the Maritime Section. Rooms 2-3 contain models of ships of the seventeenth, eighteenth, and nineteenth centuries; in the ceiling, fresco by Paolo De Matteis. Rooms 4-6. Maria Teresa Orilia bequest; ecclesiastical furniture from Sant'Agostino degli Scalzi. Rooms 7-23. Historical Section, containing records of the kingdom of Naples with paintings, prints, proclamations, costumes, coins, etc., down to the time of the Risorgimento. Note, in Rooms 14-15 (the former Priors Apartment) ceilings frescoed by Micco Spadaro. Beyond Room 24, with interesting documentation of the eruptions of Vesuvius, we enter the Belvedere, a little room with two balconies, commanding a magnificent view of the whole Gulf of Naples and the Campanian plain, backed by the Apennines. Room 26 contains baroque furniture from the Certosa, including tarsia-work lecterns. Rooms 27-30. Topographical Section. Historical (seventeenth and eighteenth century) views of Naples; maps. Hence return through rooms 16-19, past (left) Room 31, the profusely decorated Prior's Chapel, to reach Rooms 32-33, dedicated to popular feasts and costumes. In Room 32 is a frescoed ceiling by Crescenzio la Gamba (eighteenth century); Room 33 has a majolica pavement representing a sundial. Rooms 34-37. Sezione Presepiale. These rooms house the celebrated collection of Presepi, or representations of the Nativity, elaborate compositions with hundreds of statuettes, some by prominent Neapolitan sculptors, (eighteenth and nineteenth centuries). Rooms 38-40. Records and stage setting of the Teatro San Carlino (1770-1884).

From Room 40, the Great Cloister is crossed to reach the Art Collections. Rooms 42-61. Paintings by various artists, including early Neapolitan and Campanian masters, and painters of the sixteenth to the nineteenth century (Battistello, Micco, Spadaro, Luca Giordano, Francesco de Mura, Francesco Solimena, Giuseppe Rivera, Angelica Kauffman, Domenico Morelli, Gaetano Gigante, Francesco Paolo Micchetti, Vincenzo Gemito, Giuseppe Palizzi, Marco De Gregorio, and others). Rooms 62-70. Works from the fourteenth to the eighteenth century by Tino di Camaino, Girolamo Santacroce, Pietro Bernini, as well as by minor and anonymous sculptors. Rooms 72-76. Ceramics, glass, and other objects of applied art; records of the monastery.

The return to the Castel Nuovo area may be made by funicular railway, from the via Cimarosa (Map 4, 9).

IV The Bourbons

Charles III (1734-59) was the first of the Bourbon kings who ruled Naples until the unification of Italy in the nineteenth century. Although he was not without his faults, he was certainly the most generous and enlightened member of this controversial dynasty, whose name was later to become a byword for misrule. He restored order to public finance; curtailed ecclesiastical jurisdiction and immunities; and taxed clerical property, then about one third of the whole kingdom. He modernized the university and gave it a new home in the Palazzo degli Studi (now the National Museum); began the excavations at Pompeii and Herculaneum; and published the finds in nine splendidly illustrated volumes. Sir James Gray, resident English minister at Naples, described him thus:

> The King of Naples . . . is of a very reserved temper, a great master of dissimulation, and has an habitual smile on his face, contracted by a constant attention to conceal his thoughts; has a good understanding and a surprising memory, as his father had, is unread and unlearned, but retains an exact knowledge of all that has passed within his own observation, and is capable of entering into the most minute detail. He is in many things his own Minister, passing several hours every day alone in his cabinet.

Charles was an absolute ruler, and he behaved like one. "He has too good an opinion of his own judgement, and is so positive and obstinate, that he is seldom induced to alter his resolutions," says Gray. "He has very high notions of his prerogative and his independency, and thinks himself the most absolute monarch in Europe." Yet the king chose his servants wisely, in spite of his autocratic character. Beginning with Bernardo Tanucci, the Tuscan law professor whom he made his Prime Minister, and the architect Vanvitelli who designed the magnificent palace and gardens of Caserta, he appointed to high office men of competence and unquestioned personal integrity. As a patron of the arts, Charles was uncommonly generous. His ambition to make Naples the most brilliant center of musical culture in Italy (a position it would maintain throughout the eighteenth century) culminated in the construction of the famous San Carlo Theater, so named because it was inaugurated on his Saint's Day, November 4, 1738. These and many other improvements made in public and private life bear witness to this sovereign's acute mental vision, especially if one considers the briefness of his reign (twenty five years, compared to Frederick the Great's forty six and Louis XV's fifty nine) and the sound political and economic position in which he left the kingdom at the end of it.

Charles's son and heir Ferdinand IV (1759-1825), or Ferdinand I as he called himself after the Congress of Vienna, unfortunately possessed few of his father's virtues. He reigned with the enthusiastic approval of the Neapolitan mob, which fondly called him Nasone on account of his bulbous nose. To his peers he was known as the *Lazzarone* King, "beloved by the vulgar Neapolitans . . . from his having been born amongst them," and inclined "rather to seek the company of menial servants and people of the very lowest class than those of a better education." Ferdinand was famous for his indolent bonhomie, his love of the hunt, his inclination for crude practical jokes, and his indifference to anything not directly related to his physical well-being. Sir William Hamilton, who succeeded Gray as resident English minister in 1764, called him insensitive, choleric, and obstinate, commenting that at the end of his regency "the young King . . . seems to have been more desirous of becoming his own master to follow his caprices, than to govern his kingdoms." When Ferdinand married Maria Carolina of Austria (daughter of Maria Theresa and sister of Marie Antoinette), Sir William described the young husband as follows:

> On the morning after his nuptials, which took place in the beginning of May 1768, when the weather was very warm, he rose at an early hour and went out as usual to the chase, leaving his young wife in bed. Those courtiers who accompanied him, having inquired of his majesty and how he liked her: "Dorme come un'ammazzata," replied he, "e suda come un porco" [She sleeps as if she had been killed, and sweats like a pig]. Such an answer would be esteemed, anywhere except at Naples, most indecorous; but here we are familiarized to far greater violations of propriety and decency . . . When the King has made a hearty meal and feels an inclination to retire, he commonly communicates that intention to the noblemen around him in waiting, and selects the favoured individuals, whom, as a mark of predilection, he chooses shall attend him. "Sono ben pranzato", says he, laying his hand on his belly, "adesso bisogna una buona panciata"
>
> I've eaten well, now I need to move my bowels. The persons thus preferred then accompany his majesty, stand respectfully round him, and amused him by their conversation during the performance.

On the outbreak of the French Revolution Ferdinand was not at first hostile to the new movement; but in the months that followed he was compelled to move against republicanism at home and abroad. Every tremor that emanated from Paris was registered with particular anxiety in Naples, where the opposing forces had polarized more sharply than elsewhere in Italy. Rightly or wrongly, the Neapolitan liberals believed that they had suffered more under the Bourbons than inhabitants of other regions of Italy had under their sovereigns; and they saw in the cause of revolutionary France the glimmer of hope for a free and united Italy. The royalists, on the other hand, rallied in defense not only of their beloved Nasone, but also of their queen, the sister of the martyred Marie Antoinette. Sir John Acton, the French-born English baronet who became Ferdinand's Prime Minister, counselled prudence; but Maria Carolina, who exercised considerable influence over the king, maintained that the best defense was a strong offence. In 1793 Naples joined the first coalition against republican France, instituting severe persecutions against all those who were remotely suspected of French sympathies. The eruption of Vesuvius in May 1794, widely regarded as an expression of divine wrath over the execution of Louis XVI and Marie Antoinette, won popular approval for the initiative.

In 1798, during Napoleon's absence in Egypt and after Nelson's destruction of the French fleet at the Nile, Maria Carolina persuaded Ferdinand to go to war with France. The king promptly sent an army against French-held Rome, which fell without resistance. For a few ecstatic days that December the Neapolitans occupied the Eternal City; but the French under Championnet quickly counter-attacked, retook Rome, and entered Naples so swiftly that the royal family had to be evacuated by Nelson himself, with the aid of Emma Hamilton, the lovely young bride of Sir William, who had her servants carry the crown jewels of Naples aboard the British flagship before it set sail for Sicily. On January 23, 1799 the second Parthenopean Republic was proclaimed, but like its predecessor (which, it will be recalled, was instituted during the revolt of 1647), it was short lived. Governed by local liberals and precariously supported by the French army, it claimed dominion over the peninsular portion of the former kingdom while Ferdinand and Maria Carolina ruled Sicily from Palermo, protected by the British navy patrolling the Strait of Messina. Although the republicans had noble aims, they were doctrinaire and impractical, and they knew very little of the lower classes of their own country. A violent anti-French feeling in Southern Italy coincided with French defeats by Austro-Russian forces in the North. The following year the king and queen, with the aid of Nelson and of Cardinal Ruffo, who swept up from Calabria with a band of peasants, brigands, convicts, and a few soldiers, managed to reconquer the mainland provinces of the kingdom. The French and their republican allies found the themselves confined to Naples proper, and before long surrendered to a promise of amnesty. The foreigners were allowed to evacuate thanks to the implicit blessing of St. Januarius, the liquefaction of whose blood was supposedly helped along in that year by the President of the Parthenopean Republic, who held the archbishop at gunpoint during the ceremony. Had the miracle not taken place the French might well have been seized and lynched by the angry mob, whose sympathies were, as always, with their king.

There followed a period of severe repression in which Nelson, prompted by Emma Hamilton (lately become his mistress) and Maria Carolina, set out to eradicate all trace of the Parthenopean Republic, while the two husbands left him *carte blanche*. Sir William was lamenting the loss of much of his precious collection of antiquities, which had gone down with the ship that was transporting them to England, and Ferdinand had grown so fond of his Sicilian hunting grounds that he could barely be persuaded to return to the throne in Naples. While the *lazzeroni* plundered the republicans' property to cries of "*Chi tien pan' e vino ha da esser giaccobino*" [He who has bread and wine is surely a Jacobin], Nelson unabashedly violated the terms of surrender, summarily executing the liberal leaders-among them the Admiral Francesco Caracciolo, the philosopher Mario Pagano, the scientist Domenico Cirillo, and other prominent Neapolitan intellectuals. After Napoleon's successful second Italian campaign the king was forced to grant an amnesty to the surviving republicans, to close all the ports of his kingdom to the British fleet, and to allow a French garrison to be stationed deep within his territory, at Taranto. Even so, the Neapolitans could consider themselves lucky, for Napoleon had treated them more leniently than his other and more powerful enemies. Only when he found out that they had been negotiating with Austria with a view to joining the third coalition, his patience gave out: after the Austerlitz campaign (1805), he issued the famous proclamation, "the Bourbon dynasty has ceased to reign," and sent his brother Joseph to dethrone Ferdinand, who again fled to Sicily under the protection of a British fleet.

Joseph Bonaparte, though certainly no genius, was a cultivated and well-meaning man. He abolished the privileges of the nobility and the clergy, and introduced several important reforms. But his taxes and forced contributions were resented, and royalist risings undermined his authority in much of the kingdom. In 1808 Napoleon gave Joseph the crown of Spain and appointed his colorful and flamboyant brother-in-law, Joachim Murat, king of Naples. Murat continued Joseph's reforms, put down the Bourbon guerilla bands in the provinces, and instituted a program of public works that included new roads to Posillipo and Capodimonte. Meanwhile, in Sicily, where the king's extravagance and methods of police espionage rendered the royal presence a burden instead of a blessing, a bitter conflict broke out between the court and the parliament. In 1812 Sir William Bentinck, the British minister, obliged Ferdinand to grant a liberal constitution. But the wind changed as a consequence of Napoleon's defeat at Waterloo, and the king dissolved parliament in May 1815, after concluding a treaty with Austria for the recovery of his mainland dominions. A month later Ferdinand re-entered Naples amid some discontent, while Murat fled to Corsica. At first the king abstained from persecution and received many of the usurper's officers into his own army. Murat, believing he still had a strong following in the kingdom, landed with a few companions at Pizzo in Calabria, but was immediately captured, court-martialled, and shot.

Ferdinand proclaimed himself king of the Two Sicilies at the congress of Vienna, incorporating Naples and Sicily into one state, and abolishing the Sicilian constitution of 1812. In 1818 he signed a Concordat with the Church, reinstating ecclesiastical jurisdiction over education and censorship. But ideas of national unity and personal continued to make progress throughout the country. In 1820 a spontaneous insurrection which began in the army at Nola, quickly took fire under the leadership of General Guglielmo Pepe, the mutineers demanding a new constitution while assuring their continued loyalty to the king. Ferdinand, feeling himself helpless to resist, acceded to the demand. These events seriously alarmed the powers responsible for the preservation of the peace in Europe, who at the Congress of Troppau (October 1820) issued the famous protocol affirming the right of collective "Europe" to interfere to crush dangerous internal revolutions. The following year Ferdinand repudiated his engagements and the powers authorized Austria to march an army into Naples to restore the autocratic monarchy. General Pepe was sent to the frontier at the head of 8,000 men, but was defeated by the Austrians at Rieti on March 7. There followed a period of severe repression, the inevitable State trials resulting in the usual harvest of executions and imprisonment.

The conditions of the country continued to worsen under Ferdinand's worthless successors, Francis I (1825-30) and Ferdinand II (1838-59). At the same time, the desire for a constitution became ever more fervent. Revolution broke out in Sicily on January 12, 1848, under the leadership of Ruggiero Settimo; while demonstrations shook Naples, too. On January 28 the king granted the constitution; but the following Spring he refused to open the parliament, and sent an army under Carlo Filangieri against the revolutionary government of Palermo, which fell on April 14. Open despotism followed during which liberal sympathizers were condemned to prison or the galleys for life. Thousands of respectable citizens were thrown into prison, such as Luigi Settembrini, Carlo Poerio, and Silvio Spavento. The kingdom, reduced by indolence to squalor and by corruption, persecution, and fear to moral decay, provoked Gladstone's famous denunciation of it as "the negation of God erected into a system of government."

Francis I refused several opportunities to strike an alliance with Victor Emmanuel, king of Sardinia, for the division of Italy. On May 5, 1860, Garibaldi embarked at Quarto, near Genoa, with 1,000 picked followers on board two steamers, and sailed for Sicily. On the 11th the expedition reached Marsala and landed without opposition. Garibaldi was somewhat coldly received by the astonished population, but he set forth at once for Salemi, where he issued a proclamation assuming the dictatorship of Sicily in the name of Victor Emmanuel, with Francesco Crispi as secretary of state. On the 15th he attacked and defeated 3,000 of the enemy under General Landi at Calatafimi; the news of this brilliant victory revived the revolutionary agitation throughout the island. By a cleverly devised ruse he avoided General Colonna's force, which expected him on the Monreale road, and entering Palermo from Misilmeri received an enthusiastic welcome. After three days' street fighting the Bourbonist commander, General Lanza, not knowing that the Garibaldians had scarcely a cartridge left, asked for and obtained a 24 hours' armistice (May 3). Garibaldi went on board the British flagship to confer with the Neapolitan generals Letizia and Chrétien; then he informed the citizens by means of a proclamation of what he had done, and declared that he would renew hostilities on the expiration of the armistice. Lanza became so alarmed that he asked for an unconditional extension of the armistice, which Garibaldi granted; 15,000 Bourbon troops embarked for Naples on June 7, leaving the revolutionaries masters of the situation.

The news of Garibaldi's astonishing successes entirely changed the situation in the capital, and on June 25, 1860 the king granted a constitution. The king appealed to Great Britain and France to prevent Garibaldi crossing the Strait of Messina, and only just failed. On August 19 Garibaldi crossed with 4,500 men and took Reggio by storm. He was soon joined by the rest of his troops, 15,000 in all, the Neapolitan army collapsed before Garibaldi's advance, and the people rose in his favor almost everywhere. Resistance dissolved as the march became a race for Naples, which Garibaldi entered with a small staff forty eight hours ahead of the vanguard of his troops, although the city was still full of troops, and was received with delirious enthusiasm. Francis II fled to Gaeta, to take the field with his still loyal army. Two months later a successful campaign on the Volturno opened the way to Garibaldi's meeting with Victor Emmanuel which sealed the unity of Italy.

The numerous building projects undertaken during the reigns of Charles III and his successors changed the face of Naples. The architects who were most involved in these initiatives (which to a large extent gave the city the appearance that it still retains today) were Ferdinando Sanfelice, Domenico Antonio Vaccaro, Ferdinando Fuga, and Luigi Vanvitelli. The other art forms also played a major role in making Naples a truly European capital: Francesco Solimena was the last and perhaps the greatest of the Neapolitan baroque painters; Giuseppe Sammartino made hundreds of statuettes for the *presepi* that filled the churches and palaces of the city; and the Capodimonte Porcelain Works turned out some of the finest porcelain in Europe.

Site Visits

a From the San Carlo Theater to the Quarter of Santa Lucia

Walking tour, 10 km (6 miles), no buses.

This route is for music lovers. It takes us to the fabulous **San Carlo Theater**, once the largest opera house in Italy: and to the far-famed quarter of Santa Lucia, birthplace of the Neapolitan song. In between the ascent is made to the charming quarter of Pizzofalcone (site of the anciente *Parthenope*), where many members of the Bourbon aristocracy had their palaces.

On the west side of the piazza del Municipio (Map 2, 10) stands the Palazzo del Municipio (or di *San Giacomo*;1819-25), the Palace of the Ministers under the Bourbons. It incorporates the church of San Giacomo degli Spagnoli, described in Route 00.

We take the via Vittorio Emanuele III (popularly San Carlo) past the Castel Nuovo to the entrance (left) to the Royal Garden and the National Library. Adjoining the gate are groups of Horse Trainers, by Baron Clodt, presented to Ferdinand II by Czar Nicholas I. Farther on, on the left, we reach the San Carlo Theater (Map 2, 14), built for Charles of Bourbon by the contractor and impresario Angelo Carasale on a plan by court architect Giovanni Antonio Medrano. Begun in March 1737, it was finished in the following October and opened to the public on November 4, the King's Saint's Day. In the decades that followed it was remodeled several times, notably in 1762 by

Giovanni Maria Bibiena, in 1768 by Ferdinando Fuga, in 1797 by Domenico Chelli, and in 1812 by Antonio Niccolini (who added the courtyard and loggia). Destroyed by a fire on the night of February 12, 1816, the old theater was rebuilt in its present form by Niccolini (who, it is said, inserted hundreds of clay pitchers in the walls in order to improve the acoustics). The foyer on the garden side was added in 1938.

The huge Concert Hall (88 x 70 ft) seats 3, 000. It is famous for its perfect acoustics. The 185 boxes are arranged in six tiers; above the centrally situated Royal Box, the fifth and sixth tiers open up in the manner of an amphitheater. Throughout the theater red upholstery and gold trim combine to create a rich and festive atmosphere. The ceiling is adorned with a painting of Apollo introducing the Greek, Latin, and Italian poets to Minerva, by Giuseppe Cammarino; while the curtain bears a representation of Homer and the Muses with poets and musicians, the work of Giuseppe Mancinelli. On the stage (measuring 101 x 105 ft) were performed the prémiers of Rossini's *Lady of the Lake* and *Moses*, Bellini's *Sonambula*, and Donizetti's *Lucia di Lammermoor*.

At the time the San Carlo was built, Italy was the center of European musical culture, and Naples was the leading center of music in Italy, thanks to Charles III 's generous patronage of composers and performers. Rousseau, in his famous essay on *Genius*, advised the aspiring musician to go to Naples to study; his eminent contemporary Lalande declared that in Naples music could be discerned in the gestures, the inflection of the voice, and even the cadence of everyday conversation. "Music is the triumph of the Neapolitans," he wrote. "Everything there expresses and exhales music." In the light of these considerations, it is hardly surprising that Charles should have desired to provide his capital with a large and splendid opera house, even though he had no personal passion for this particular art form. Indeed, the king often talked during one half of a performance and slept during the other, a habit that scandalized the prudish French President de Brosses during a visit of 1739. De Brosses heard Domenico Sarro's *Parthenope* in the royal company, and has left us a written account of his experience which is all the more valuable as Neapolitan opera of the time depended largely on a type of vocalization now extinct: the *castrato* or male soprano, who "combined the high range and sweetness of the female with the power of the male voice." Such *castrati* as Senesino, mentioned in de Brosses's account, and Caffarello, his arch-rival, were the rage in every European capital. De Brosses writes:

> The performance was perfect. The famous Senesino took the first role, I was enchanted by the taste of his singing and dramatic action. However, I perceived with astonishment

that the people of the country were not at all satisfied with it. They complained that he sang in an antiquated style. For the musical fashion here changes at least every decade. All the applause was reserved for the Baratti, a new actress both pretty and self-assured, who recited in male disguise…The structure of the libretto in Italian operas is very different from ours …They pander much to the taste of the lower orders. An opera would not please at all unless it contained, amongst other things, a mimic battle. Two hundred urchins on either side take part in this, but they are careful to put in the foreground a number of bravos skilled in the use of weapons. This cannot fail to be amusing; at least it is less absurd than our combats between Cadmus and Thesus, who kill each other while dancing. In this opera of Parthenope there was an effective cavalry charge which gave me infinite pleasure. Before coming to blows the two regimental commanders on horseback sang a contradictory duo in perfect harmony.

Some twenty four years after de Brosses, an English traveler named Samuel Sharp attended a performance at the San Carlo. He provides us with an interesting insight into the original appearance of the theater, which today is lost to us. He also offers a description of the Neapolitan manner of listening to opera from which we may conclude that the king's behavior was in perfect keeping with local etiquette:

The King's Theater, upon the first view, is, perhaps, almost as remarkable an object as any man sees in his travels. The amazing extent of the stage, with the prodigious circumference of the boxes and the height of the ceiling, produce a marvellous effect on the mind …Notwithstanding the amazing noisiness of the audience during the whole performance of the opera, the moment the dances begin there is a universal dead silence, which continues so long as the dances continue. Witty people, therefore, never fail to tell me, the Neapolitans go to *see* not to *hear* an opera . . . . It must be confessed that their scenery is extremely fine; their dresses are new and rich; and the music is well adapted, but, above all, the stage is so large and noble, as to set off the performance to an inexpressible advantage . . . . It is customary for gentlemen to run about from box to box between the acts, and even in the midst of the performance; but the ladies, after they are seated, never quit their box the whole evening. It is the fashion to make appointments for such and such nights. A lady receives visitors in her box one night, and they remain with her the whole opera; another night she returns the visit in the same manner. In the intervals between the acts, principally between the first and second, the proprietor of the box regales her company with

152

iced fruits and sweetmeats... It is the custom in Italy to light the stage only... but on gala nights the theater is illuminated in every part.

The San Carlo Theater adjoins the small, irregular piazza Trento e Trieste , still generally known as San Fernando, with a modern fountain in the center. The square lies at the junction of several important streets: to the north runs the via Roma, to the west the via Chiaia. On the corner is San Ferdinando (Map 2, 13), a Jesuit church renamed, after the expulsion of the Order in 1767, in honor of Ferdinand I, whose morganatic wife Lucia Migliaccio (d. 1826) is buried within. Turning south we come immediately to the piazza del Plebiscito (Map 2, 13), a wide hemicycle with a Doric colonnade and frigid equestrian statues of Charles III and Ferdinand IV, by Antonio Canova and Antonio Calì. Here rises the church of San Francesco di Paola, founded by Ferdinand I as a votive offering for his restoration to the throne, and copied by Pietro Bianchi (1817-32) from the Roman Pantheon. The north and south sides of the piazza are occupied respectively by the *Prefecture* and the *Palazzo Salerno* (residence of the military commandant). On the east is the majestic façade of the Royal Palace, built in 1600-02 by Domenico Fontana for viceroy Ferrante di Castro, and furnished (about 1808) in the neoclassical style by Joachim Murat and Caroline Bonaparte. The first-floor apartment was the official residence of the Spanish and Austrian viceroys, then of the Bourbon kings. Following a fire of 1837, the latter with their court moved to the second-floor rooms now occupied by the National Library (visit, Route III, a). From the northwest corner of the piazza del Plebiscito the steep quarter of Pizzofalcone (Map 2, 13) is reached by the piazza Carolina and the via Serra, which lead to the piazza and church of Santa Maria degli Angeli, by Francesco Grimaldi. The church, begun in 1600, is built to one of the more daring designs of its day. The architect's clear, decisive treatment of solids and voids and his handling of architectural ornament are well ahead of contemporary developments in Naples or even in Rome. The third south chapel contains a Holy Family by Luca Giordano; the second on the north, an Immacolata by Massimo Stanzione. From the piazza, turn left and ascend the via Monte di Dio. In the Middle Ages this street was lined with convents, but in the eighteenth century it became the center of a fashionable residential area. Today it is known for its aristocratic palaces, the most noteworthy of which is the Palazzo Serra di Cassano (N° 14-15), built in the early eighteenth century to plans by Ferdinando Sanfelice and recently restored. With two courtyards and a scenographic double staircase, it is one of the most impressive of all Neapolitan palaces. Also interesting are the Palazzo Sanfelice (N° 4-5); Palazzo Capracotta (N° 74);

and Palazzo Carafa di Nola, the courtyard of which gives onto a lovely garden. The via Parisi leads west to the former convent of the Nunziatella, now a military college, with an eighteenth century church. Returning by the via Parisi and continuing along the north side of the Palazzo Serra di Cassano, we turn left into the via Egiziaca a Pizzofalcone. Just beyond the church of Santa Maria Egiziaca, attributed to Cosimo Fanzago, the via della Solitaria descends to the Istituto d'Arte, with a small museum of applied art, whence steps bring us back to the piazza del Plebiscito.

Turning to the west from the piazza Trento e Trieste we enter the via Chiaia (Map 2, 13), a busy shopping street, and pass under a bridge linking Pizzofalcone with the via Nicotera, near which an elevator ascends to Santa Maria degli Angeli. Farther on, the Palazzo Cellamare, begun in the sixteenth century and restored in the early eighteenth century, stands on a bend in the street. Here Angelica Kauffmann, Ferdinand I's official court painter, lived in 1784. The garden has a fine sixteenth century fountain; inside the palace are frescoes by Fedele Fischetti and a chapel designed by Ferdinando Fuga. Across the street from the Palazzo Cellamare (right) is the church of Santa Caterina (about 1600), with the simple tomb of Cleotilde of France (1755-1802). Hence the via Santa Caterina opens immediately into the piazza dei Martiri, the center of Naples' most fashionable shopping district. The square takes its name from a column, the work of E. Alvino (1868), to the martyrs of four revolutions (in 1799, 1820, 1848, and 1860). To the left the via Morelli leads to the west end of the *Galleria della Vittoria* (see below), whence we turn south to the waterside and follow the shore eastward along the via Partenope, a broad promenade where several of the finest hotels enjoy a magnificent view across the bay. On the right is the Borgo Marinaro, the ancient island of Megaris, once the site of the villa of Lucullus, later joined by a causeway to the shore, thus forming the little Port of Santa Lucia. Restaurants line the quay, overlooking smart yachts and modest fishing boats. On the island rises the Castel dell'Ovo (Map 4, 14), a fortress of 1154. Here in 1821 Sir R. Church, then in the Neapolitan Service, was imprisoned for having failed to make his troops do their part in quelling the Sicilian revolt in Palermo the previous year. It is now a barracks. At the end of the via Partenope stands the baroque Fontana dell'Immacolatella (1601), with statues by Bernini and caryatids by Naccherino. We turn left into the straight via Nazario Sauro, which affords a further splendid view right across to Vesuvius. Half way along a wide terrace overlooks the sea.

Reached by any of the streets leading inland is the quarter of Santa Lucia, the site of the old shell-fish market and once highly characteristic, but now much changed. It is traversed by the broad via Santa Lucia, which was once the quay-side. The Victorian novelist George Gissing, writing in 1897, helps us imagine what the quarter must have been like before urban renewal hit:

> I pass the Santa Lucia with downcast eyes, my memories of ten years ago striving against the dullness of today. The harbour, whence one used to start for Capri, is filled up . . . . They are going to make a long straight embankment from the Castel dell'Ovo to the Great Port, and before long the Santa Lucia will be an ordinary street, shut in among huge houses, with no view at all. Ah, the nights that one lingered here, watching the crimson glow upon Vesuvius, tracing the dark line of the Sorrento promontory, or waiting for moonlight to cast its magic on floating Capri.

At the end of the via Nazario Sauro, Gissing's "long straight embankment," the via Cesario Console ascends back to the piazza del Plebiscito. We descend by the via F. Acton with a view, to the right, over the Public Gardens, to the Molosiglio, embarkation point for pleasure boats. To the left, at the bottom of the hill, is the mouth of the Galleria della Vittoria, a tunnel, opened in 1929, beneath the hill of Pizzofalcone. The via Acton bears right, skirting the south side of the Palazzo Reale, to the Porto Beverello, from which ply the regular ferries for the Gulf of Naples. With the Castel Nuovo high above, we reach the wide forecourt of the *Stazione Marittima Passeggeri* (Map 3, 15), where the largest passenger liners dock; this was built on the Molo Angioino to the design of C. Bazzani in 1936 and rebuilt after 1945.

b From the Castel Nuovo to Capodimonte

Walking tour, 5 km (3 miles), bus.

This route brings us again to the via Roma (Route I, a) and its continuations, which are followed to the **Royal Palace at Capodimonte**. Side trips are suggested, along the way, to the **Conservatory of San Pietro a Maiella**, and to the **National Ceramics Museum**, which is set in a beautiful park known as the Villa Floridiana.

From the Castel Nuovo to the piazza Trento e Trieste , see Route I, a. From here the via Toledo leads north. Beyond the Galleria Umberto I (Map 2-13, 14) is the lower station of the *Funicolare Centrale*, by which we climb to the Vomero. The via Cimarosa leads west across the hillside to the Villa Floridiana. The gardens, beautifully sited on a spur overlooking the sea, are famous for camellias; the view from the terrace is particularly fine. The mansion houses the **Museo Nazionale della Ceramica Duca di Martina**. The original porcelain collection of Placido di Sangro, Duke of Martina, augmented by his nephew, Count De Marzi, was presented to the city by the widow of the latter, Maria Spinelli. The museum now contains over 6,000 pieces of European and Asiatic porcelain and pottery, as well as goldsmiths' work, ivories, and seventeenth and eighteenth century paintings.

From the foyer a stair ascends past a marble bust of Ferdinand IV. On the landing are two columns of African marble and Oriental granite, with Oriental vases and bronze decorations of the nineteenth century; eighteenth century French tapestries, and embroidered panels of local workmanship. Hence we pass through the Antecamera to Room 1, containing assorted porcelain, precious stones, ivories, and a collection of canes with interesting carved handles. Rooms 2-4 are dedicated to Meissen porcelain, including many fine miniatures. Room 5. Capodimonte and Naples porcelain. Rooms 6-7. More Meissen ware. Room 8. Viennese and Saxon porcelain. Room 9. Pieces from the Ginori works at Doccia. Room 10. French porcelain of various manufacture. Room 11. Late Saxon ware. Room 12. English (Chelsea, Wedgwood, Burslem, Bow Essex, Worcester) and Viennese porcelain. Rooms 13-14. China and Japan ware. The small room adjacent contains items of varied provenence.

Pass through the foyer to Room 16, containing European and Oriental ceramics. Room 17. Italian (Abruzzese and Neapolitan) majolica. Room 18. Faience. Rooms 19-20. Murano glass and Bohemian crystal.

The return to the via Roma may be made by following the winding via Falcone and corso Vittorio Emanuele to the church of San Sepolcro, then descending the *gradoni* of Vico San Sepolcro or via Porta Carrese. This is rather a long walk, however, and the funicular is recommended.

The via Roma continues north, passing (left) the **church of the Spirito Santo** (Map 2, 5). Designed and built between 1757 and 1774 by Marco Groffredo, it rivals Vanvitelli's **Annunziata** (Route V, a) as the most masterful expression of the new classical taste that grew up in Naples under Charles III. Inside, the powerful columns of Groffredo's main order so thoroughly dominate the nave arcade of the earlier church that the latter nearly disappears. However, the architect remains faithful to the Neapolitan tradition in such devices as the choir gallery above the main altar, the design of the altar itself, and in the overall proportions of the building. At the sides of the entrance are the tombs of Ambrogio Salvio and Paolo Spinelli, by Michelangelo Naccherino. The south transept has a Madonna and Saints by Fedele Fischetti, and the apse a

Pentecost by Francesco De Mura. The chapels of the north side contain (first chapel) a Purification, Conversion of St. Paul, and Fall of Simon Magus by Fischetti; (fourth chapel) a Madonna del Soccorso by Fabrizio Santafede, and a tomb by Michelangelo Naccherino; and (fifth chapel) a Baptism of Christ by Santafede. The façade, which is much less advanced than the interior, adheres to the contemporary Roman type.

Opposite is the Palazzo d'Angri, by Luigi and Carlo Vanvitelli (1755), where Garibaldi stayed in 1860. Continuing we pass (left) the via Tarsia which leads to Montesanto station (Cumana Rly.) and the Montesanto Funicular, opposite which, in the church of Santa Maria di Montesanto, is buried Alessandro Scarlatti, the composer. The via Roma proper ends in the piazza Dante (Map 2, 6), enclosed on the east by Luigi Vanvitelli's hemicycle, and the seventeenth century Port'Alba; the monument to the poet dates from 1872.

One block east, in the via San Pietro a Maiella, is the **Conservatory of Music** (Map 2, 6), the oldest in existence, founded in 1537 and removed here in 1826.

The conservatory grew out of the gradual merger of four institutions-Santa Maria di Loreto, the Pietà dei Turchini, Sant'Onofrio a Capuana, and the Poveri di Gesù Cristo-that grew up in the sixteenth and seventeenth centuries as home for foundlings. In these institutions catechism and singing was taught. Later on, when the private donations that were their only income dwindled or ceased altogether, the young musicians began to offer their services in churches, theaters, and the homes of nobles. In practically no time the conservatories became great markets for singers, instrumentalists, virtuosi, and composers, the demand for which was insatiable. The Conservatory of San Pietro a Maiella and its illustrious predecessors graduated Domenico Cimarosa, Nicola Antonio Porpora, Giovanni Paisello, Domenico and Alessandro Scarlatti, and Giovan Battista Pergolesi. Today the Library (with an extraordinary collection of autograph manuscripts) and the Museum (portraits of eminent musicians and historical items such as Martucci's piano and Rossini's desk) repay a visit. The church of San Pietro a Maiella, adjoining, built in 1313-16, contains a magnificent series of paintings by Mattia Preti (1656-61) depicting the life of Celestin V and the legend of St. Catherine of Alexandria.

The via Santa Maria di Costantinopoli continues northward. After a few steps, we pass (right) the little church of San Giovanni Battista, with paintings by prominent eighteenth century artists (above the entrance, St. Mary Magdalen, by Mattia Preti; south side, first chapel, Annunciation by Andrea Vaccaro and Immacolata by Bernardo Cavallino; south transept, Crowning of the Virgin by Massimo Stanzione; above the high altar, St. John the Baptist by Luca Giordano; north side, first chapel, St. Luke Painting the Virgin by Andrea Vaccaro). Across the street stands the Accademia di Belle Arti; the gallery of modern art formerly here is now at Capodimonte. The church of Santa Maria di Costantinopoli, further along on the same side, has a noteworthy ceiling by Belisario Corenzio.

We emerge at the southeast corner of the National Archaeological Museum. The museum building, first built as a barracks in 1586, was reconstructed in its present form (1738-1818) by Charles III and Ferdinand IV to receive the antiquities from Pompeii and Herculaneum, and the Farnese Collections inherited by Charles from his mother, Elisabeth Farnese. About 2 km (1,5 miles) northeast along the via Foria lies the Botanic Garden (Map 5, 3), founded by Joseph Bonaparte in 1807, now a laboratory of the University Faculty of Sciences. It may be visited by special request. Just beyond is the Albergo dei Poveri, an old-age home, orphanage, and rehabilitation center founded by Charles III. Built in 1751 to a plan by Ferdinando Fuga, this immense structure (the main façade is over 1100 ft long) represents barely one fifth of the building originally planned.

From the National Museum, the via Santa Teresa degli Scalzi and its continuation, the corso Amedeo di Savoia (which together comprise Joseph Bonaparte's Capodimonte road), climb in just over a mile to the Tondo di Capodimonte (Map 4, 2). For the approaches to the Royal Palace of Capodimonte and its magnificent Park, see Route IV, c.

c Capodimonte

The Royal Palace of Capodimonte (Map 5, 3), a plain Doric building begun in 1738 and completed in 1838, is magnificently situated in a fine park, enjoying a wide view of Campania and of Naples itself. In May 1957 the palace was opened as the new seat of the National Museum and Galleries of Capodimonte, comprising the National Gallery of Naples, formerly in the National Museum, and a large collection of Italian art of the nineteenth century, formerly in the Accademia di Belle Arti, as well as important exhibitions of armor, porcelain, and ivories from the royal collections.

The palace is situated at the north end of the via Roma and its extensions (Route Ia), about 4 km (2 miles) from the piazza del Municipio and 3,5 km from the piazza Garibaldi (Stazione Centrale). City bus services (N° 110 and 127) ply from the latter to the Tondo di Capodimonte, whence pedestrians mount the tree-lined flight of steps, whereas N° 24 from the piazza della Vittoria (Map 4, 14) continues to ascend the via di Capodimonte, in a long curve, passing the dome of a huge new church. To the left, in via Miano, is the porta Piccola, to the right, the porta Grande, the more usual entrance to the Park. The trees are magnificent and it is planned to lay out a golf course in the extensive grounds. Within the park still exist the kilns from the famous porcelain works founded by Charles of Bourbon in 1739 which were working until 1805. The entrance to the Palace is through the most northerly of the three courts.

Intended by Charles of Bourbon to be the most important summer hunting-lodge in Europe, the Royal Palace of Capodimonte was begun in 1738 by Giovanni Antonio Medrano under the direction of Canevari, and the park designed by Ferdinando Sanfelice. From 1759 to 1806 the building housed the Farnese Collections. The construction by Joachim Murat of the Sanità bridge and of a new approach road stimulated further enlargements which were completed in 1834-38. The palace became a favorite haunt of Victor Emmanuel II, and in 1906-47 of the Dukes of Aosta.

The principal royal apartments on the first floor have been preserved and lesser rooms adapted as a background to the nineteenth century art collection. The whole of the second floor, formerly servants' quarters of no special architectural or decorative merit, has been replanned to display the treasures of the National Gallery in the best possible manner, the rooms being is air-conditioned and the lighting, natural and artificial, can be controlled to suit any weather, so that every picture may be enjoyed under perfect conditions.

The National Gallery of Naples, on the Second Floor, may be reached by elevator or by an impressive marble staircase with a bronze balustrade. At the top of the staircase, Bust of Charles of Bourbon, probably by Antonio Calì, and two eighteenth century tapestries of local manufacture.

In the vestibule (Room I), Guglielmo della Porta, Infant Hercules throttling the serpents. We enter Room 3, and turn right. Room 2 contains a series of seven Tapestries (1531) from designs by Bernard van Orley of Brussels, depicting the defeat and capture of Francis I by Charles V at the Battle of Pavia (1525). The detailed view of the city in N° 5 is of remarkable interest. In the glass cases are numerous small bronzes, including Giambologna 's Rape of the Sabines. Room 3. Early (thirteenth century) Campanian Art. Room 4. Simone Martini, St. Louis of Toulouse crowning Robert of Anjou king of Naples (1317); school of Simone Martini, Blessing Christ. Room 5. Central Italian Art of the Fourteenth Century. Bernardo Daddi, Madonna and Child, Madonna and Child with Saints; Masolino, Assumption of the Virgin and Foundation of Santa Maria Maggiore in Rome, panels from a polyptych executed for that church. Room 6. Masaccio, Crucifixion (1426 - 27). Room 7. Central Italian Masters of the Fifteenth and Sixteenth Centuries. Botticelli, Madonna and Child with

Angels, a youthful work, Raphael, Eternal Father with the Virgin, from a painting executed at Città del Castello in 1501, partly by the master; Perugino, Madonna and Child ; Filippino Lippi, Annunciation with Saints; Luca Signorelli, Adoration, Pinturicchio, Assumption of the Virgin, Lorenzo di Credi, Adoration; Raffaello del Garbo, Madonna and Child with the Young St. John . Room 8. Lorenzo Lotto, Archbishop Bernardo De' Rossi of Treviso (1506), Madonna with St. Peter Martyr, Bartolomeo Vivarini, Madonna and Child with Saints (1465), a fine decorative composition; Alvise Vivarini, Madonna and Child with Sts. Francis of Assisi and Bernardino of Siena; Giovanni Bellini, Transfiguration; Andrea Mantegna, Francesco Gonzaga, St. Eufemia (1454); Mathematical lecture (Fra' Luca Pacioli and a youth) signed "Iaco. Bar." possibly a Spanish artist. Room 9. Temporary exhibits. Room 10. Fifteenth Century Neapolitan Painters. Anonymous, Triumph of Alfonso of Aragon after the battle of Ischia, Colantonio, St. Jerome and the Lion, St. Francis giving his rule to the Brothers and the Poor Clares. Room 11. Fifteenth Century Neapolitan and Ligurian Painters. Room 12. Michelangelo, Three soldiers, cartoon for the fresco, Crucifixion of St. Peter, in the Vatican (1541 - 49); Raphael, Moses, cartoon for another Vatican fresco (151-14); School of Raphael, Leo X, a copy, once attributed to Andrea del Sarto, of Raphael's portrait in Florence; Polidoro da Caravaggio, Deposition, Way to Calvary; Sebastiano del Piombo, two Portraits of Clement VII, Holy Family; Marcello Venusti, Last Judgment, a small but excellent copy of Michelangelo's painting in the Sistine Chapel. Room 13. Cesare da Sesto, Adoration, works by Andrea da Salerno, Vasari, Fabrizio Santafede, and others. Room 14. Dosso Dossi, Madonna and Child with the Young St. John, Madonna and Child with Bishop - Saint. Room 15. Sixteenth-Century Mannerists, including Fra' Bartolomeo (Assumption), Rosso Fiorentino (Portrait of a Youth), Pontormo (Scene of Sacrifice), Sodoma (Resurrection). Room 16. Sixteenth Century Lombard Masters. Giampietrino, Madonna and Child with Saints; Bernardo Luini, Madonna and Child. Room 17. Emilian Masters, notably Parmigianino, Lucretia, the so-called Portrait of Antea, Portrait of Galeazzo Sanvitale (1524), Holy Family; Michelangelo Anselmi, Madonna and Child with the Young St. John, St. Anthony of Padua, St. Clare, and others; Correggio, St. Joseph and a Devotee (1529), Marriage of St. Catherine, a charming composition with a delightful landscape, Madonna called "La Zingarella" from her headdress, Girolamo da Carpi, Portrait of Girolamo de' Vicenti (1535). Room 18. Sixteenth Century Venetian Masters. Titian, St. Mary Magdalen; Moretto, Christ at the Column ; El Greco, Portrait of G. Clovio (1577), Youth blowing on hot coals, Pordenone, Disputa of the Immaculate Conception, Leandro Bassano,

National Gallery of Capodimonte: Giovanni Bellini's Transfiguration.

San Prisco. This lovely mosaic, showing a small bird eating a grape, adorns the burial chapel of the fifth-century saint, Matrona, in the basilica of San Prisco, near Santa Maria Capua Vetere.

Ischia. The circular harbor of Ischia Porto is one of the more pleasant and colourful ports in Italy. It was made by opening the crater of an extinct volcano to the sea. Brightly painted fishing boats line the quay, beneath the balconies of the fishermens's homes.

Ischia. The harbor.

Royal Palace of Caserta, Gardens. The gardens of Caserta, laid out by Martin Biancour under the supervision of Luigi Vanvitelli, are famous for their fountains and ornamental water-works adorned with statuary groups. Here we see the myth of Diana and Actaeon, played out below an artificial cascade fed by a lofty aqueduct.

Many of the hill towns of the Neapolitan hinterland have changed little since the Middle Ages.

Resurrection of Lazarus. Room 19. Works of Titian. Paul III Farnese (1543); Paul III with his nephews Alessandro and Ottavio Farnese, sons of Pier Luigi (1545); Pier Luigi Farnese (1546); Cardinal Alessandro Farnese (1543); Charles V; Philip II of Spain, a masterpiece of expression, Lavinia Vecellio ; Danaë (1546); the bust of Paul III is by Guglielmo della Porta. Room 20. Sixteenth Century Flemish Masters. Pieter Brueghel the Elder, The Blind leading the Blind, and "Il Misantropo", and allegory of the corruption of the Church, both signed and dated 1568; Bernart van Orley, Portrait of Charles V; Joos van Clese the Elder, Adoration of the Magi , Crucifixion (both triptychs); Cornelisz van Oostsaanen, Adoration of the Shepherds ; Herri Met de Bles, four landscapes, Jean Bourdichon, triptych with the Madonna and Saints ; Lucas Cranach, Christ and the Adultress, and Hans Holbein the Younger (attrib.), Erasmus of Rotterdam .

We pass through the Sala di Sosta (Room 21; refreshments), whence a staircase leads to a terrace, affording a wonderful view of the park and the city.

In the three rooms (22-24) of the west wing are displayed Master Drawings of the Sixteenth and Seventeenth Centuries.

Rooms 25 and 27-29 are devoted to the Seventeenth Century Emilian School (Room 26 is used for lectures). Room 25. The Carracci, notably Annibale Carracci, Pietà, Marriage of St. Catherine ; Agostino Carracci, Satire (perhaps directed against Caravaggio, the smiling head in the corner is a portrait of the artist). Rooms 27-29. Works by Domenichino, Lanfranco, Claude Lorrain, and Bartolomeo Schedoni; Guido Reni, Atalanta's Race. Room 30. Caravaggio, Flagellation, from the church of San Domenico, School of Caravaggio, works by Battistello Caracciolo, Giuseppe Ribera, Massimo Stanzione, Artemisia Gentileschi, and others. Room 31. Alberto Burri, Large Black Cretto 1978, donated to the Museum by the artist. Rooms 32-39 are dedicated to Neapolitan and Northern European Painters of the Seventeenth Century, including Francesco Fracanzano, Matteus Stomer, Salvatore Rosa, Aniello Falcone, Mico Spadaro, Hans Heindrich Schoenfeld, Bernardo Cavallino, Francesco Guarino, Massimo Stanzione, Simon Vouet, Giuseppe Ribera, Andrea Vaccaro, and Anton Van Dyck. Room 40. Mattia Preti. Belshazzar's Feast, Allegories of the Plague of 1656 at Naples, The Prodigal Son, Feast of Absolom. Room 41. Luca Giordano. St. Francis Xavier and St. Francis Borgia, Marriage at Cana, Madonna of the Baldachin. Room 42. Abraham Brueghel and pupils, Still - life with fruit, flowers, and game. Hence we enter the *Sala della Raccolta del Banco di Napoli* (on permanent deposit with the museum), with paintings by Andrea da Salerno Presentation at the Temple, Belisario Corenzio Circumcision, Salvatore Rosa, Paolo Porpora, Gaspare Traversi, Francesco De Mura,

Francesco Guarino, Bernardo Cavallino, and Francesco Solimena. Rooms 43-43bis are dedicated to Flemish Genre Painters of the Sixteenth and Seventeenth Centuries and to Minor Eighteenth Century Artists. Rooms 44-45 house works by eighteenth century Neapolitan painters, including Giuseppe Maria Crespi, Sebastiano Ricci, Corrado Giaquinto, Paolo de Matteis, Giuseppe Bonito, Giacomo Del Po, the Venetian Michele Marieschi, and Giovanni Pannini.

Descend to the First Floor, the west side of which (Rooms 46-66) is occupied by the Gallery of Nineteenth Century Art; the remainder consists of the Royal Apartments with the Museum. The emphasis of the Gallery is on Southern Italian artists, and the collection reflects the merits and defects of the century. It should preferably not be visited immediately after the *Galleria Nazionale*.

In the vestibule, late eighteenth century busts representing the Four Seasons. Room 47. Neoclassicism typified by four huge canvases, including Vincenzo Camuccini (1771-1844), Death of Virginia, Death of Caesar ; Francesco Hayez (1791-1882), Ulysses at the court of Alcinous. Room 48. Paintings by Alessandro Ciccarelli and Natalino Carta; marble group, Telemachus' Departure, by Tito Angelini (1806-78). Room 49. Works by Raffaello Postiglione (1815-97) and Luigi Rocco. Room 50. Early nineteenth century paintings by Filippo Marsigli and Raffaello Spenò; tempera showing Ferdinand I returning to Naples. Room 51. Volaire, Eruption of Vesuvius. Rooms 52-54. Campanian landscapes by the Dutchman Pitloo, who profoundly influenced the "realistic landscape" school, of which Giacinto Gigante (1806-76) is perhaps the most interesting (Amalfi Coast). The full development of the Posillipo School is represented (Room 54) mainly by the Palizzi brothers, Giuseppe Palizzi (1812-88), Monk and peasant; attrib. to Filippo Palizzi (1818-99), the same subject. Academic romanticism is represented by early works by Domenico Morelli (1826-1901). Room 55. Paintings by Gioachino Toma (1836-91). Room 56. Italian artists, including Giovanni Fattori (1825-1908), Domenico Induno (1815-78), Favretto, Volpedo, and Boldini, from the Cenzato and Marino Bequests. The *Banco di Napoli* Collection follows, affording a coup d'oeil of the best of the Neapolitan nineteenth century schools. Room 66. Sala di Sosta, decorated in 1825-30 in the Pompeian manner.

From Room 66 pass to the elaborately decorated Royal Apartments, which contain many works of art of the eighteenth century and earlier. Rooms 67-71. Porcelain and majolica, a selection of some 3000 items from the royal collections, produced in Naples, Sevres, Vienna, Meissen, and elsewhere. Room 72. Foreign paintings presented by Margherita, Princess of Marsiconovo. Rooms 74-75. Neapolitan tapestries of the eighteenth century. Room 76. Prints and drawings. Beyond Room 77, a huge salon, start the Bourbon portraits, of which the most interesting are, perhaps, François Gérard, Marie Amélie, Duchess of Orleans, with the Young Duke of Chartres; and Angelica Kauffmann, Family of Ferdinand IV, both in Room 80. Here also is a fine bisquit representing Jupiter Hurling Thunderbolts at the Titans. Rooms 82-85 contain the valuable De Ciccio Collection, with over 1300 examples of European and Oriental majolica and porcelain, Renaissance bronzes, ivories, enamels, French and Swiss time pieces, liturgical vestments, precious fabrics, lace, embroidery, silver, glass (from Murano and Nevers), a small archaeological collection, paintings, and sculpture. We pass through the huge Sala delle Geste (Room 86), decorated in blue and gold by Salvatore Giusti (1835-38), with galleries at either end. Rooms 87-88. On the walls, sixteenth century Flemish and Tuscan tapestries; sculptures, including Guglielmo della Porta, Bust of Paul III ; Giambologna, Hercules and the boar of Erymanthus; Jacopo Del Duca, Tabernacle; Guido Mazzoni, Ferdinand of Aragon, and a sixteenth century Florentine bronze of Dante. In the cases are bronzes mainly of the sixteenth and seventeenth centuries, and Andrea del Pollaiuolo, David.

The famous **Armory of the Farnese family** (fifteenth to the seventeenth century) is displayed in Rooms 89-90; of the three suits of equestrian armor, that in the center (1545-47) belonged probably to Pier Luigi Farnese. In the show-cases are sporting pistols, weapons, and other firearms of the Bourbon period. Room 91. Renaissance medals. The eclectic collection of sculpture, ivories, jewellery, etc. contains several pieces of the first rank, including (Room 92) Passion scenes, English alabaster polyptych (early fifteenth century); a late tenth century Byzantine reliquary cross; a French triptych of the fourteenth century, and (Room 93) Casket with scenes from the story of Jason, from the Embriachi workshop (late fourteenth century); a silver gilt statue of Diana the Huntress by Jacob Miller the Elder; sixteenth century altar furnishings from Fontevrault. Room 94, the *Salottino di Porcellana*, a pretty little room in the Chinese style, was executed in Capodimonte porcelain in 1757-59.

The next three rooms are hung with tapestries by Pietro Duranti (eighteenth century) showing scenes from Don Quixote. Room 95. Farnese Casket, one of the finest known examples of sixteenth century goldsmiths' work; the six oval panels of crystal are by Giovanni Bernardi of Castel Bolognese, the metal-chasing is the work of the Florentine Manno di Bastiano Sbarri (1540-47). Room 96. Pier Bonacolsi, Cupid Sacrificing (fifteenth century bronze from an antique marble). In Room 99 are the sedan-chairs of Charles of Bourbon and his consort.

163

d The Royal Palace of Caserta

Road, Autostrada A2 to Caserta Nord, 28 km (18 miles); the Palace lies between the exit and the town proper.

Railway. A choice of two lines provides a good service from Naples (Centrale). Trains on the old main line via Cancello and Cassino to Rome, and on the main line via Aversa and Benevento to Foggia, both stop at Caserta station, which is directly in front of the Palace. The Cancello line is the quicker of the two (34 km in 45 min.).

The Royal Palace of Caserta, overlooking a huge square, is one of the more sumptuous buildings of its kind in Italy. It was begun by Charles III in 1752 and completed by Ferdinand I in 1774 from the plans of Luigi Vanvitelli. The first stone was laid by the king on his thirty sixth birthday, January 20, 1752: for the occasion the perimeter of the future palace was marked by several regiments of infantry and squadrons of cavalry, and two cannons with artillerymen were placed at each corner. The army of workmen engaged on the building was increased by convicts and galley-slaves. Construction proceeded with great alacrity until 1759, the year in which Charles left Naples to take the throne of Spain. Work then slowed, coming to a complete halt in 1764 when, in the midst of a severe plague and famine, the half-finished building was occupied by the poor and homeless. On the death of Vanvitelli in 1773, his son, Carlo continued the construction, but he ran up against difficulties of various kinds and was unable to complete the building according to his father's plan. Eliminated from the design were four corner towers and a central dome, which undoubtedly would have relieved the obtrusive sense of gravity which emanates from the building today, and the guards' quarters which were to enclose the vast forecourt on all sides. During the long reign of Ferdinand IV the palace, where the king held court every spring and autumn, was enlivened by balls, receptions, hunting parties, and theatrical performances. It was the favorite residence of Ferdinand II, and after the unification of Italy it was visited by the Savoyard kings. It was presented by Victor Emmanuel III to the State, in 1921. On April 29, 1945 it was the scene of the unconditional surrender of the German forces in Italy to Supreme Allied Commander in the Mediterranean Field Marshall Alexander.

The two principal façades, 787 ft long and 107 ft high, are pierced by 243 windows and several monumental entrances. The two other sides are 616 ft in length, and have 135 windows. The palace consists of five stories-a ground floor, mezzanine, first floor, second floor, and attic-containing 1200 rooms served by 43 staircases, all arranged around four monumental courtyards of which the decoration was never finished. The design of the building was controversial even in its own day. Although many contemporaries regarded it as "one of the noblest edifices of the kind in Europe for magnitude and elevation," some considered it a megalomaniac construction.

"The vast dimensions of its apartments", wrote Henry Swinburne in the 1770s, "the bold span of their ceilings, the excellence and beauty of the materials employed in building and decorating it, and the strength of the masonry, claim the admiration of all beholders, who must confess it is a dwelling spacious and grand enough to have lodged the ancient masters of the Roman world. It is a pity that its enormous bulk drowns the minuter members of its architecture, and gives too much the idea of a regular monastery, where the wealthy chief of some religious order presides over long dormitories of segregated monks; by the gigantic range, and the number of windows, too great a sameness is produced, the few breaks in the front become imperceptible, and the lines too long and uniform, consequently fatiguing to the eye; the colonnades sink into the walls, and variety is in vain sought for in the prodigious expanse; bolder and greater projections, massive towers, arcades or porticoes, would have shown the parts of this great building to more advantage, and formed those happy contrasts that are so necessary in works of so very large a dimension. Upon a nearer approach, the parts and proportions are better distinguished, and the objection ceases".

Royal Palace of Caserta, Grand Staircase. Designed in 1752, this staircase is one of the finest achievements of the prominent Neapolitan architect, Luigi Vanvitelli. Like many of his neoclassical contemporaries, Vanvitelli drew inspiration from the archaeological excavations at Pompeii and Herculaneum.

Within, the main portico is divided into three vestibules by sixty four columns. The State Staircase ascends to the first-floor vestibule, an octagon surrounded by twenty four pillars of yellow marble. Opposite the head of the stairs is the Palatine Chapel, usually closed. Modeled on the chapel of the Palace of Versailles, it contains the finest marble ornaments and several noteworthy paintings, including an Immaculate Conception by Bonito, a Presentation in the Temple by Mengs, and five works by Conca.

A door on the left gives entrance to the Royal Apartments, beautifully decorated with tapestries, paintings, frescoes, and period furniture. The Room of the Halabardiers, the first to be entered, has a Bourbon coat of arms borne by Virtues in the ceiling. The Guard Room, following, is decorated with the apotheosis of the Farnese family (of which, it will be recalled, Charles's mother was an eminent member) and the twelve provinces of the kingdom, in the ceiling; and with scenes from ancient history, in the bas-reliefs around the walls. On the right is a marble statuary group of Alexander Farnese crowned by victory, carved, according to tradition, out of a column from the Temple of Peace in Rome. Hence we enter the Room of Alexander, which corresponds to the center of the main façade; from the window there is a good view of the tree-lined high road to Naples. The ceiling fresco and the stucco reliefs show scenes from the life of Alexander Farnese; the other paintings celebrate deeds of Charles of Bourbon. The portrait medalion in porphyry over the fireplace is of Alexander the Great. The room is furnished in the Empire style; particularly noteworthy is the large clock on the right wall, made in Naples in 1828.

The New Apartment, so called because it was the last to be completed (1845), is reached by a door on the right. It consits of three rooms, furnished in the Empire style and decorated with paintings and reliefs of mythological subjects. Notice, in the center of the first room, an Oriental alabaster cup presented by Pope Pius IX to Ferdinand II. The Throne Room, the largest room of the palace (114 x 42 ft), is adorned with a frieze containing medalions of the kings of Naples from Roger the Norman to Ferdinand II (Joseph Bonaparte and Joachim Murat have been tactfully omitted). The ceiling painting shows Charles III laying the first stone of the palace.

Beyond the Throne Room extend the living quarters of the king. The Council Room contains a fine table given by the city of Naples to Francis I as a wedding present. Hence we cross an antechamber, where majolicas are displayed, to the Bedroom of Francis II, containing a magnificent mahogany bed and the first known example of a roll-top desk. The ceiling painting of Theseus Killing the Minotaur is by Giuseppe Cammarano. Adjoining the bedroom are the king's Bathroom and Study. Beyond two handsome Drawing Rooms decorated with mythological subjects lies the Bedroom of Joachim Murat, containing perhaps the finest Empire-style furniture in the palace; on the far side of the room are an antechamber and a small chapel.

Returning to the central Room of Alexander, we enter the east wing of the palace, inhabited by Ferdinand I from 1780 until his expulsion in 1806, and from 1815 until his death in 1825. The Reception Room, Drawing Room, Dining Room, and Fumoir are decorated with allegories of the Four Seasons, by Antonio De Dominici and Fedele Fischetti. Here Maria Carolina held her famous receptions, one of which was recorded in a particularly delightful manner by an English guest, Lady Anne Miller:

After mounting a staircase, you enter several large rooms, hung and adorned in the Italian taste with crimson damask, velvet, etc., and amply illuminated. The chairs are placed all round against the walls, and each sits down where they choose. These rooms were so full, that there was a double row of chairs placed back to back down the middle. Accident placed me exactly opposite the Queen, who took the first chair she found empty. There are no tables in any of the rooms; but every person being seated, the supper is served thus: The best looking soldiers, chosen from the King's guards, carry about the supper with as much order, regularity, and gravity as if they were performing a military manoeuvre. First appears a soldier bearing a large basket with napkins, followed by a page, who unfolds and spreads them on the lap of each of the company as they happen to sit; but when it comes to the Queen's turn to be served, a lord of the Court presents her majesty's napkin. The first soldier is immediately followed by a second, bearing a basket of silver plates; another carries knives and forks; then follows a fourth, with a great pâté, composed of macaroni, cheese, and butter; he is accompanied by an *écuyer tranchant*, or carver, armed with a knife a foot long, who cuts the pie, and lays a large slice on the plate (which has been placed on the lap of each of the company); then a fifth soldier, with an empty basket, to take away the dirty plates; others succeed in the same order, carrying wine, iced water, etc.; the drinkables are served between the arrival of each eatable: the rest of the supper consisted of various dishes of fish, ragouts, game, fried and baked meats, perigord-pies, boar's-heads, etc. The dessert was formed into pyramids, and carried round in the same manner; it consisted of sweetmeats, biscuits, iced chocolate, and a great variety of iced fruits, creams, etc. The Queen ate of two things only, prepared particularly for her by her German cooks; she did me the singular honour to send me some of each dish.

Beyond the public rooms is the Study, with lacquered furniture from Frankfurt am Main, and a small Drawing Room. The Bedroom of Ferdinand II follows. From here we enter the rooms of the queen: first her Sewing Room, with a small Bathroom adjacent; then a tiny Dressing Room, beyond which lie the Drawing Room and a room for the queen's ladies-in-waiting. From the latter a series of richly decorated rooms leads to the Library, containing some 10,000 volumes and a huge Presepe, with over 1200 pieces made by Giuseppe Sammartino and other eminent sculptors.

The next ten rooms comprise the Gallery, where an extensive but dull collection of still-lifes, historical scenes, and family portraits is displayed. The small **Museo Vanvitelliano** contains the architect's original drawings and models for the palace.

We return to the Ground Floor and cross the second courtyard to the Palatine Theater. This charming eighteenth century period piece hosted concerts, plays, and balls. Lady Anne Miller describes the original appearance of the theater and the use that was made of it during a ball that she attended in 1771:

There is no precedence observed at these balls, the King and Queen go in and out promiscuously, which is the reason why the company is not so numerous as one might expect to find it. None but such as the Queen esteems proper to receive and converse with, *sans cérémonie*, are ever admitted; and there are many of the Neapolitan nobility, even to the rank of dukes, who are allowed only to see the ball from the upper boxes ... The theatre is in the palace; it is approached through spacious courts, and then through large passages lined with a double row of guards under arms. The plan is circular, the proscenium appeared to me to cut off about a third from the circle; the boxes are larger than those in any other I have yet seen, they are lined, gilt, and decorated with a profusion of ornaments ... The stage was covered with the musicians upon benches, rising pyramidically one above the other, the top of the pyramid is crowned by the kettle-drums. The musicians are all in a livery, their coats blue, richly laced, their waistcoats red, and almost covered with silver, small black hats, with long scarlet feathers stuck upright in them: large wax candles are placed between, so that they form a striking *coup d'oeil* upon our entering the theatre; the whole is so artfully illuminated that the effect is equal, and seems as if the light proceeded from a brilliant sun at the top ... The pit (which is more like an antique arena) is floored with a composition colored red, very hard, and rather slippery; here it is they dance. The boxes are appropriated to the foreign ministers and great officers belonging to the Court.

Inaugurated by Ferdinand IV in 1769, the theater has been recently restored to its original form, with a horseshoe-shaped auditorium and five tiers of boxes. The ceiling painting, by Crescenzo della Gamba, shows Apollo killing the Serpents.

From the main portico entrance is gained to the Gardens, which extend to the north, east, and west side of the palace. Among the more enchanting achievements of Italian landscape architecture, they were laid out by Martin Biancour under the supervision of Luigi Vanvitelli. They are famous for their fountains and ornamental water-works adorned with statuary groups.

The crowning glory of the gardens is the Great Cascade, a waterfall some 247 ft high which can be seen clearly from the palace two miles away. The central promenade leads across a broad lower garden bordered by holm-oaks and camphor trees (paths diverge into the woods on the left and right) to the circular **Fontana Margherita**, which is linked by a bridge over a sunken highway to the impressive **Pescheria Superiore**. Beyond, a long, narrow lawn ends at the semicircular **Fontana di Aeolo**, inhabited by twenty nine zephyrs and wind gods (fifty four were originally planned). The **Fontana di Cerere**, containing seven stepped cascades and statues of Ceres, nymphs, tritons, and river gods, follows; then more lawn and the **Fontana di Venere**, with its group of Venus and Adonis. From here a scenographic staircase flanked by men and women in hunting garb leads up to a basin with groups of Diana surrounded by nymphs, and Actaeon being turned into a stag, into which plunges the Great Cascade. The water is brought from Monte Taburno by a lofty aqueduct. The view from the top of the wooded hill is attractive.

To the east of the cascade is another, later garden laid out in the so-called English style; visitors are accompanied by a custodian. Here are more modest fountains and romantic groves of holm-oaks, artificial ruins adorned with statues from Pompeii and Herculaneum, a large fishpond, a miniature fort for Prince Ferdinand's mimic battles, a swan lake, an apple orchard, a classical temple, a bath of Venus, covered walks, and greenhouses.

About 3 km (2 miles) northwest of Caserta, San Leucio was built as a model town and social experiment by Ferdinand IV. He built the Casino Reale di Belvedere (also called the Casino di San Leucio), and he introduced the culture of silk worms and silk manufacture. The industry (now artificial silk and nylon), continues in the vast *Palazzo dello Stabilimento Serico*, much of the work being done on ancient hand looms.

V Naples Today

In 1884 a terrible epidemic of cholera swept Naples, taking a high toll particularly in the crowded tenements of the medieval city center. As a result special laws were passed tohasten urban renewal. Wide thoroughfares were driven through the slums, the waters of the Serino River were brought into the city, and complete new quarters were built. Naples lost much of its picturesqueness without gaining in improved health, as the population evicted from the condemned buildings was housed in neighboring blocks, increasing density even further. The greatest achievement of the *Risanamento*, as the urban renewal program was called, was the construction of the corso Umberto I (popularly the *Rettifilo*) from the piazza Garibaldi (and the railway station) to the piazza del Municipio (the center of local government). Other "improvements" included the rebuilding of the quarter of santa Lucia, the founding of a new residential district on the hill of Vomero and the establishment of the first industries in the Vasto Arenaccia area, the most easterly link in the chain of industrial suburbs that encircles Naples today, presenting a serious obstacle to the successful expansion of the city.

Quite independently of the Risanamento, wealthier Neapolitans began, around the end of the century, to build their luxurious villas in the area around the Riviera di Chiaia (piazza Amedeo, parco Margherita). Many of these elegant dwellings, which continued to be built up till the eve of the First World War, are in a curious local variant of the art-nouveau style.

The period between the wars witnessed a revival of building without any precise guidelines. During the Fascist period both urban expansion and rebuilding activity in the city center were important. The suburban quarters grew rapidly, particularly at Fuorigrotta, where development was stimulated by the construction of the *Mostra d'Oltremare* fairgrounds, and of the tunnel under the hill of Posillipo. In central Naples the most striking changes took place in the Carità quarter, between the via Toledo, via Monteoliveto, and via Medina. Here the Central Post Office, the Provincial Office Building, and the Police Headquarters were erected, concentrating administrative services in an already overburdened area. Finally, in 1939 the need for an organic design stimulated the drafting of a general town plan, which, however, was not applied until many years after the war. Meanwhile, the events of World War II nullified many earlier improvements. Naples was heavily bombed on August 4, 1943 by the advancing Allies; and it was attacked and captured by the Germans after the armistice of September 8. A Neapolitan rising (*Le Quattro Giornate*, September 28-

October 1) drove out the Germans, who prior to retreating destroyed the port, utilities, and public archives. A typhus epidemic followed by a bad winter added to the distress and aggravated the age-old problem of the *scugnizzi*, unfortunate children who managed to survive only by resorting to crime.

Commercial and industrial development has radically changed the aspect of city in the post-war years. The Gulf coast from Pozzuoli to Castellammare di Stabia and the inland suburbs host an array of industrial plants (including iron works, food processing plants, an oil refinery, cement works, aircraft and automobile assembly plants), and residential building has expanded over the hill zones as well as to the eastern plains. This apparent burgeoning of wealth and activity is illusory, however; it does not truthfully reflect the economic condition of the city which, notwithstanding costly and elaborate plans for development, remains substantially poorer than its northern counterparts.

Overcrowding has further aggravated the century-old problem of economic malaise, creating more troubles of its own. Naples has the highest population density of any European city, and is most lacking in social services. Despite the efforts of the local authorities to provide adequate housing, many Neapolitans still live in *bassi*, street-level, single-roomed dwellings in which light and air are admitted by a double door alone. At the same time illegal building activity has altered the appearance of the town beyond recognition; and faulty construction has led to death and injury in more than one instance. A special investigatory committee of the Ministry of Public Works revealed in 1971 that almost all of what has been built in Naples since 1945 is in violation of the law, and blamed "the frivolity and the incapacity of the civil authorities, the impudence of speculators and the ever-growing greed of building contractors" for having "trampled upon the right of Neapolitans to an ordered form of civil society, blindly transforming the ancient and marvellous capital of the Mediterranean into the present, most uninhabitable provincial capital in Italy." Judiciary action in 1975 resulted in the incrimination of a former mayor; the demolition of twenty two buildings erected on lands destined for parks, schools and other public facilities; and the arrest of several contractors. In spite of intimidatory actions brought by the profiteers and their sympathisers, the effort to restore to Naples her natural grace and beauty continues.

The task is not an easy one, for even the force of nature must be taken into account. On November 22, 1980 a violent earthquake rocked Campania and the neighboring region of Basilicata, claiming more than 3000 victims and causing damage for well over 10 billion dollars. In Naples, the largest city affected by the quake, 200,000 persons were left homeless.

An effort is now being made to make reconstruction activiy coincide with an overall design for urban renewal.

When the great German poet Goethe visited the Naples in 1787, he exclaimed:

> "Naples is a paradise, in it every one lives in a sort of intoxicated self-forgetfulness. It is even so with me … Were I not impelled by the German spirit, and desire to learn and to do rather than enjoy, I should tarry a little longer in this school of a light-hearted and happy life, and try to profit from it still more".

But as the tastes (and moral philosophy) of northern visitors changed, so did their opinion of Naples. The literary historian Edward Chaney has traced this change in the minds of his fellow Englishmen:

> The climax of English enthusiasm for ancien régime Naples was probably Lady Blessington's still very readable *The Idler in Italy*, which appeared in two volumes in 1839. 'The more I see of the Neapolitans', she declared, the better I like them'. It was, however, only one year after these words were published that the headmaster of Rugby, Dr Arnold, was registering puritanical disgust with both the place and its inhabitants. In this, as in much else, he anticipated the prejudices of his fellow Victorians. Charles Dickens, visiting Naples just five years later, was little more enthusiastic, though he was more broadminded. Where Arnold had waxed indignant that Naples' stained the fame even of Nelson (who had himself scorned this country of fiddlers and poets, whores and scoundrels), Dickens was primarily concerned that 'lovers and hunters of the picturesque (should) not keep too studiously out of view the miserable depravity, degradation, and wretchedness, with which this gay Neapolitan life is inseparably associated'. Growing English concern over the increasing oppression of Ferdinand II's government was finally allayed in 1860, when Garibaldi peacefully entered the city and thus terminated the brief reign of Francesco II. With the disappearance of the Bourbons, however, Naples suddenly did become merely 'picturesque'. The lavish social life in which the English had participated so actively and for so long was at an end. With the taste for Neapolitan, or indeed any other kind of baroque, at its lowest ebb ever, the city's monuments offered no compensation for the loss. The American George S. Hillard's *Six Months in Italy* of 1853, states that 'in Naples . . . there are very few objects of interest or curiosity. In architecture, there is almost nothing that deserves a second visit. There is not a church or a

palace or a public building of any kind, of such conspicuous merit that one need regret not to have seen it' . . . . Ruskin's influential enthusiasm for the purity of early Tuscan art evolved alongside increasing prejudice against Naples as 'the most loathsome nest of human caterpillars I was ever forced to stay in'. The terrible cholera epidemic of 1884 seemed to confirm Ruskin's opinion of ten years before that Naples was, 'certainly the most disgusting place in Europe'.

In this period, as may be seen from the architecture of some of the villas and grand hotels, Sorrento, Capri, Ischia, and the hillside villages of the Amalfi coast came into their own as alternative resorts for visitors to the South. Sorrento and Ravello were favorite haunts of Wagner and Nietzsche. Residents of Capri have included Emil von Behring (1854-1917), discoverer of a successful inoculation against tetanus; Axel Munthe, the Swedish physician; Maxim Gorky (1868-1936), who lived here in 1907-13 and ran a school for revolutionaries visited by Lenin, Stalin, and Chaliapin, C. C. Coleman (1841-1928), American painter of genre scenes; and Norman Douglas (1868-1952), the writer. Positano is frequented by a certain sort of jet set, Gore Vidal spends several months of the year at Ravello, and Ischia is virtually a German colony. Today these areas, which are known principally for their natural beauty, attract hundreds of thousands of visitors each year, very few of whom venture into Naples proper. But they cannot be blamed, really; for these luxurious paradises of sea and sand, where the brilliance of the sun is equalled by the only violence of the landscape, and where men and women have lived in tranquil idleness for more than two thousand years, possess a subtle magic, under the spell of which one readily forgets oneself and the world.

Site Visits

a The Rettifilo and the Harbor

Walking tour, 4km (2,5 miles); bus.
This route takes us through the area of the city between the medieval Castel Nuovo and the modern Central Railway Station, along the busy corso Umberto I, popularly called the *Rettifilo*. This long, straight thoroughfare is a characteristic example of late nineteenth century town planning in Italy, which as a rule had little regard for local needs or traditions,

and was concerned chiefly with glorifying the ruling house of the newly formed kingdom. The Rettifilo cuts through Naples' eastern quarters in a merciless manner, destroying the area's medieval flavor and introducing a rather academic and pretentious architectural style vaguely related to the neoclassicism of the Bourbon era. The monuments that will be visited are neither numerous nor particularly interesting. They include the churches of San Pietro Martire, Gesù Vecchio, Annunziata, San Pietro ad Aram, and Santa Maria del Carmine; the marketplace, traditionally the center of political and economic life; and the harbor.

From the Piazza del Municipio the wide via Agostino Depretis, lined with banks and offices, leads straight to the piazza Giovanni Bovio (Map 2, 10). In the center of the square is the graceful Fountain of Neptune, designed in 1601, perhaps by Domenico Fontana. The sea monsters are by Pietro Bernini, and the figure of Neptune is by Michelangelo Naccherino. Cosimo Fanzago carved the lions, coats-of-arms, and balustrade. On the left rises the Palazzo della Borsa, or Stock Exchange (1895), incorporating the eighth century chapel of Sant'Aspreno al Porto, rebuilt in the seventeenth century. The columns of the vestibule were taken from the cloister of San Pietro ad Aram. The corso Umberto I begins on the northeast side of the square, whence it stretches for nearly 1400 yards to the main railway station, cutting through a maze of medieval alleys visible behind the modern façades.

Just a block from the piazza Bovio, the via Mezzocannone, on the left, leads to the steps of San Giovanni Maggiore (Map 2, 6). The church, built in the sixth century on the ruins of a pagan temple, but remodeled in 1685 and again in 1870, retains its basilican plan. The sixth century apse incorporates a colonnade that was originally surrounded by an ambulatory. A chapel on the south side contains an eighteenth century terracotta Presepe; the third chapel on the north a *Baptism of Jesus*, attributed to Giovanni da Nola. In the nave are fragments of an eleventh or twelfth century choir screen, showing Byzantine influence. The magnificent high altar (1732-43) is the work of Domenico Antonio Vaccaro. In the adjacent largo san Giovanni Maggiore stands the little church of San Giovanni dei Pappacoda, with a beautiful Gothic doorway carved by Antonio Baboccio and his followers in 1415, and an equally impressive belltower. In the neighborhood are several patrician palaces, notably the fifteenth century Palazzo Penna (24, piazzetta Teodoro Monticelli), and the eighteenth century Palazzo Palmarice (opposite), built to plans by Ferdinando Sanfelice.

Return to the corso. On the right stands the church of San Piero Martire (Map 3, 7-11), begun in 1294 by order of Charles II of Anjou, and completed in 1347. It was badly damaged by a flood in 1343, an earthquake in 1456, and bombs during the

Second World War. The interior contains numerous fifteenth, sixteenth, and seventeenth century works of art, including a naively realistic painting of the life, death, and miracles of St. Vincent Ferrer, by the fifteenth century artist Colantonio (in the third chapel on the north); as well as paintings by Solimena, Conca, and Santafede.

Immediately opposite the church is the imposing façade of the University, by Pier Paolo Quaglia and Guilielmo Melisborgo (1897-1908), with a pediment sculpted by Francesco Ierace. Founded in 1224 by Frederick II, the university was established in the former Jesuit convent behind the present building in 1777. This now houses an extensive library (700,000 volumes, 400 rare books, 119 manuscripts) and a small Mineralogical Museum, with some interesting material from Vesuvius and the Phlegraean Fields. The modern building incorporates the church of the Gesù Vecchio, built in 1564-1612 and containing a Madonna with Sts. Lorenzo and Ignatius, and a Transfiguration, by Marco Pino (third south chapel); statues of Prophets by Cosimo Fanzago (south transept); a St. Ignatius by Francesco Solimena (north transept), a St. Louis attributed to Battistello (second north chapel) and a Nativity by Marco Pino (in the sacristy).

The corso crosses the long via Duomo at the piazza Nicola Amore, named after a mayor of Naples. His statue, by Ierace, has been moved to the piazza della Vittoria. The square is popularly called *I Quattro Palazzi* on account of the four palaces of uniform design that surround it. Farther along, on the left, a narrow street of steps leads up to Sant'Agostino alla Zecca (Map 3, 7), a large and imposing church of the fourteenth century transformed in 1641 by Bartolomeo Picchiatti, and again in 1761 by Giuseppe Astarita. Within are a marble Madonna and Child by Francesco Laurana and a beautifully carved Pulpit by Annibale Caccavello (1570), both against a pillar of the nave arcade. The fine fourteenth century chapter house, opening off the baroque cloister, is reached by a door beneath the seventeenth century Bell Tower.

On the corso, to the left, farther on, is the little church of Santa Maria Egiziaca (Map 3, 7), originally of the fourteenth century, but in its present form designed by Domenico Lazzari (1684), with paintings by Andrea Vaccaro, Luca Giordano, and Francesco Solimena. The oval plan is rare in Naples. By taking the via Egiziaca to the left and then turning right into the via dell'Annunziata, we reach the santissima Annunziata (Map 3, 4), rebuilt by Luigi Vanvitelli and his son Carlo in 1761-82 after a fire, important as one of the first examples of the new classical taste which was championed by Vanvitelli and Fuga as official architects of Charles III. The interior is a Latin cross with barrel-vaulted nave and choir, and short transepts. The nave arcade is replaced by a colonnade bearing a flat entablature. The crossing, the choir, and the semicircular apse, as well as the gallery at the west end of the nave, provide interesting variants in the use of columns. The white and grey stucco underscores the severity of the design. The slender cupola, badly damaged in 1943, has been well restored.

The Treasury, containing frescoes (in a bad state) by Corenzio, and the Sacristy, on the south side (likewise decorated by Corenzio), which has sculptured sixteenth century presses, are relics of the former church of 1318, in which Joan II was buried (plain tomb before the high altar). The altars of the unusual, circular crypt are adorned with statues by Domenico Gagini and Giuseppe Sammartino. The adjacent Foundling Home, built (ca. 1500) to plans by Tommaso Malvito, preserves its original wooden doors, carved by Pietro Belverte and Giovanni da Nola (1508).

We turn right and, by the via Antonio Ranieri, regain the Rettifilo near the church of San Pietro ad Aram, with a finely stuccoed interior. The seventeenth century façade faces the via Santa Candida, but the usual entrance is by the south door from the corso. The church stand on the site where St. Peter is said to have baptized santa Candida and St. Asprenus, who later became first bishop of Naples. A fresco in the porch depicts St. Peter celebrating Mass with them. The huge high altar is decorated with mosaics and the presbytery is adorned with early works of Luca Giordano. Restorations in the crypt in 1930 uncovered remains of an aisled church of the Early Christian era.

The corso Umberto I ends in the vast piazza Garibaldi (Map 3, 4) in front of the modern Central Station (1959-70). The monument to Garibaldi at the center of the square is by Cesare Zocchi (1904). From the right side of the square, at the corner nearest us, the broad corso Garibaldi leads south to the piazza Nolana, where the massive porta Nolana, part of the ancient *enceinte*, has a fifteenth century relief of Ferdinand I of Aragon. From the piazza the corso Garibaldi continues southward, passing (left) the terminus of the Circumvesuviana Railway, to the piazza Guglielmo Pepe. Here the via del Carmine, to the right, leads through a poor neighborhood (in the via Carmignano are considerable remains of the Aragonese walls of 1484) to the church of Santa Maria del Carmine (Map 3, 8), originally of the twelfth century, rebuilt at the end of the thirteenth century, and completely redecorated in the seventeenth and eighteenth centuries. The Bell Tower was begun in the fifteenth century, but not completed until 1631, when Fra Giuseppe Nuvolo added the spire; the façade, by Giovanni del Gaizo, dates from 1766.

The interior of the church, consisting of a broad nave flanked by communicating chapels, is decorated with polychrome marble: the modern roof replaces a seventeenth-century coffered ceiling destroyed in 1943. Under the transept arch stands a fourteenth century wooden crucifix, which, according to a popular legend, avoided destruction during the Aragonese siege of Naples by dodging a cannonball, the figure of Christ losing only its crown of thorns. The paintings in the north transept and in the sixth chapel on the north side are by Solimena; in the south transept is an Assumption, also by Solimena. Also in the north transept is a fifteenth century crucifix. Behind the high altar a much-venerated fourteenth century painting, the Madonna della Bruna, occupies a sixteenth century marble shrine. Between the fifth and fourth chapels on the north side stands a monument to Conradin of Hohenstaufen, who is buried behind the altar. The monument was donated in 1847 by Crown Prince Maximilian of Bavaria.

To the west in the noisy piazza del Mercato, center of old Naples and much hit by bombing in the Second World War, Conradin and his kinsman Frederick of Baden were beheaded by Charles I of Anjou in 1269. For centuries thereafter the square was used as the official place of execution of criminals. Permanently installed here were a chopping-block for the nobility, and a gallows for the populace. Here also Masaniello's rebellion broke out in July 1647. In the church of Santa Croce al Mercato is preserved a porphyry column from a chapel erected on the site of Conradin's scaffold. On the west side stands sant'Eligio, restored after war damage, with a Gothic doorway showing French influence.

On the south side of the piazza del Carmine stand the remains of the Castello del Carmine, erected in 1382, enlarged in 1662, and demolished in 1906. The porta del Carmine, with massive pillars, gives access to the via Nuova della Marina along which we turn to the right. This busy street skirts the extensive installations of the Harbor.

The port of Naples, already famous in Greek and Roman times, was developed greatly under Charles II of Anjou, and went on expanding as the volume of shipping increased-particularly under Charles III of Bourbon, who commissioned the rococo Immacolatella office building (built to plans by Domenico Antonio Vaccaro), among other improvements. In place of the present via Nuova della Marina a wider thorough-fare to be called the via Marittima, now under construction, will give easier access to the whole basin. Among the most important new works is the Graving Dock (1955) by the Molo Cesario Console toward the east end of the harbor. Over 1000 ft long, this is able to accomodate almost any vessel in existence.

We turn right and follow the via Nuova della Marina and its continuation, via Cristoforo Colombo, along the waterfront to the Stazione Marittima Passeggieri, at the seaward end of the piazza Municipio.

b The Lungomare and Posillipo

This is the most spectacular of our in-town routes. It follows the beautiful via Francesco Caracciolo, a quayside street lined with cool gardens and elegant houses; and the via di Posillipo, a superb road framed by gardens and villas affording one of the finest sea views in the world. Visits will be made to the **Aquarium**, the first institution of its kind in Europe; to Mergellina, a port frequented by pleasure-boats; to Marechiaro, a charming little fishing village much celebrated in Neapolitan song; and to the pine-shaded heights of the **Posillipo Park**, where one may truly appreciate the maritime flavor that is Naples' greatest appeal.

Using public transport, the best way of following this route is to take a bus or taxi from the piazza della Vittoria to Capo Posillipo (rotonda) and make the tour of the park on foot.

From the Castel Nuovo, take in via San Carlo to the piazza Trento e Trieste , then the via Chiaia to the piazza dei Martiri (Map 2, 13; Route IV, a). From here the short via Calabritto leads south to the piazza della Vittoria, on the seaward side of which a *cipollino* column (from the amphitheater of Neapolis) commemorates Neapolitans who lost their lives at sea. The statues amid the palm trees represent Giovanni Nicotera (1828-94), the patriot; and Nicola Amore (1830-94), mayor of Naples during the period of the Risanamento. From the piazza della Vittoria the via Caracciolo, a broad and busy street, extends westward along the waterfront to Mergellina, offering fine views over the city and the gulf.

The street is flanked for nearly a mile by the luxurious **Villa Comunale**, a favorite public garden beautifully shaded by evergreen oak, pine, palm, and eucalyptus trees. This garden, which is bounded on the north by the elegant Riviera di Chiaia, was first developed under the Spanish viceroys, who planted a double row of trees and constructed thirteen fountains. It became a public park in 1778-80, by order of Ferdiand IV, who entrusted its design to Carlo Vanvitelli and Felice Abate. In the center is the **Zoological Station** (Map 4, 10), founded in 1872 for research into the habits of marine flora and fauna. Its chief attraction is the famous Aquarium, remarkable for the perfection of the arrangements by which water is supplied direct from the sea, enabling the most delicate marine organisms to be preserved alive. The collection includes more than 200 species from the water of the bay. Across the Riviera di Chiaia, set in a walled garden, is the neoclassical Villa Pignatelli, which houses the **Museo Principe Diego Aragona Pignatelli Cortes** (Map 4, 10), opened to the public in 1960. The collection includes Italian and European porcelain (from Capodimonte, Venice, Doccia, Vienna, Berlin, Meissen,

Thurigen, Bow, Chelsea, and Zurich), bisquits from Naples, Vienna and Sevres; Chinese vases; period furniture, and some modest works of painting and sculpture, including family portraits. In the garden is the **Carriage Museum**, with English, French and Italian carriages of the nineteenth and early twentieth centuries.

To the right of the Riviera di Chiaia rises the Rione Amedeo, a modern and fashionable quarter. Ascending the via Santa Maria in Portico, we leave to the left the church of Santa Maria in Portico (begun 1632, with a façade of 1862), and climb to that of the Ascensione a Chiaia. Begun in the fourteenth century but rebuilt by Cosimo Fanzago (1645), the church contains canvases by Luca Giordano. Farther on another church in the baroque style, Santa Teresa a Chiaia (1650-62), also contains paintings by this artist. To the west lies the piazza Amedeo, the center of the quarter, whence the parco Margherita winds up to join the corso Vittorio Emanuele.

At the end of the Villa Comunale is the piazza della Repubblica, where stands the Monumento alle Quattro Giornate (1969), a joint effort of the architect Persichetti and the sculptor Mazzacurati. From the piazza start three busy streets: the via Mergellina on the right, the Viale principessa Elena in the center, and the continuation of the via Caracciolo on the right. We follow the latter past modern aprtment buildings (right) and a landing stage for hydrofoils from Capri and Ischia (left) to reach the little **bay of Mergellina** (Map 4, 13), much sung by poets, and affording a good view back to santa Lucia. Here is the lower station of the funicular to Posillipo (via Manzoni). Above the south end of the bay rises the church of santa Maria del Parto, or del Sannazaro, founded in the sixteenth century by the Neapolitan poet Jacopo Sannazaro, whose estate (a gift of Frederick of Aragon) once spread over the hills and along the shores this once-rural area. The church contains the well-known *Diavolo di Mergellina* (St. Michael overthrowing Satan), by Leonardo da Pistoia (1542). At the back of the apse, which is well decorated with paintings and stucco, is the tomb of Sannazaro, by Fra Giovanni da Montorsoli (1537).

From the church the via Posillipo hugs the shore for some way and then leads away up the slopes of the hilly promontory known as the **Posillipo**, a name said to be derived from *Pausilypon*, a villa belonging to Vedius Pollio and afterward to Augustus. This picturesque road, begun in 1812 under Murat and completed in 1823, passes many handsome villas amid rich vegetation, and commands lovely views, especially at sunset. As we climb gently we pass a fountain of 1635 with a statue of Neptune (on the left); the neoclassical Casino del Principe d'Angri (right), the Villa Quercia (left), and the impressive Palazzo di Donn'Anna (farther along on the left). The latter was built in 1642-44 by Cosimo Fanzago for Anna Carafa, wife of the Duke of Medina, viceroy of Naples, and is perhaps the most ingeniously planned and dramatically situated of all Neapolitan palaces. Although its construction was interrupted by the death of the patron in 1642, and despite the state of general neglect into which it has fallen, it retains much of its original grandeur.

Farther on is the **Ospizio Marino**, a home for old sailors and fisherman, with a monument to Ludovico da Casoria, its founder. The view becomes increasingly fine as the road climbs to the piazza San Luigi (about 275 ft, restaurants). The road continues to climb to the Parco della Rimembranza, with a Mausoleum, the memorial to the dead of the First World War, in the Egyptian style. Beyond the piazza Salvatore di Giacomo the exceptional view gives its name to the church of Santa Maria di Bellavista. Close to the church the via Ferdinando Russo leads down in 15 minutes to the **Capo di Posillipo** (view; restaurant) near which is the sumptuous Villa Maria Pia, formerly Villa Rosebery, a residence of the President of the Republic.

The road ascends more slowly, now, reaching its highest point at the **Quadrivio del Capo**, a starting-point for walks in the enchanting surroundings.

To **Marechiaro**. To the south, a road through villas and vineyards (view), leads down to (1 km) Marechiaro, an unspoiled fishing hamlet with stone houses rising in steps from the sea. The view across the gulf to Capri and the Sorrentine Peninsula is well worth the walk. In the main square, on the right, are remains of an antique column and of the so-called Temple of Fortune. Farther down, a plaque marks the window celebrated by Salvatore di Giacomo in the song set to music by Francesco Paolo Tosti. From a balcony one may examine the tufa rock on which the village is built, and admire the play of light and color in the water below (the name, *Marechiaro*, means "clear sea"). Delightful excursions may be made by boat to the Grotta dei Tuoni and La Gaiola (see below).

To the **Posillipo Park**. About 500 yards beyond the Quadrivio del Capo, the viale Tito Lucrezio Caro, to the left, winds up to the entrance to the Parco di Posillipo (497 ft above sea level) on the summit of the Coroglio Promontory. A road encircles the park; at the point nearest the sea a Belvedere offers a splendid vista to Capri and Vesuvius, and to Ischia and Capo Miseno. Nisida lies immediately below. From the park entrance Posillipo Alto may be reached directly by the viale Virgilio (see below).

To **Pollio's Villa**. From the viale Lucrezio Caro a road on the right descends steeply, with fine views over the Gulf of Naples. At Poggio Luculliano we leave on our right a road leading to the Grotto of Sejanus (a Roman tunnel of A.D. 37) and continue to the left, on a track that reaches the beach near La Gaiola, a tiny fishing hamlet. On the right is a headland with a Roman ruin, called the Casa del Mago or Scuola di Virgilio, where, if we are to believe the medieval legend, Virgil taught the art of magic. Opposite are three rocks, the largest of which is called the Isola Gaiola. Here, in ancient times, stood a temple of Venus. In the vicinity the tufa has been eroded to form numerous caves where the waves produce thunderous echoes. The largest of these is called the Grotta dei Tuoni, and may be reached by boat from Marechiaro. In a field above La Gaiola are the scanty remains of Pollio's Villa Pausilypon. Excavations in the last century revealed a theater, an odeon, two unidentified buildings, an aqueduct, and a vaulted piscina.

To Nisida. From the via Caro we turn right (left if returning from the Parco di Posillipo), passing under the Viaduct of Montagna Spaccata, to reach the rotonda di Posillipo, another famous viewpoint overlooking the Phlegraean Fields, the Gulf of Pozzuoli, and Procida. The view is somewhat marred by the railway sidings and chemical works in the foreground. The road turns toward the sea and descends, passing the entrance to the Grotto of Sejanus (see above). At the foot of the hill a by-road crosses the modern causeway to the island of Nisida, an extinct volcano, known to the ancients as Nesis. It belonged to Lucullus and was afterwards the retreat of Marcus Brutus, who was visited here by Cicero. The conspiracy against Caesar was planned at Nesis by Brutus and Cassius; and here Brutus bade farewell to his wife Portia. The castle, now a school, was the prison of Carlo Poerio, whose plight horrified the visiting Gladstone, provoking his famous description of Bourbon rule as "the negation of God raised to a system of government."

To Posillipo Alto. The road to the right from the Quadrivio del Capo, the via Boccaccio (also reached from the park by the viale Virgilio), climbs to the via Manzoni. From the Torre Ranieri crossroads, the via Petrarca drops gradually to Mergellina, offering unimpeded views toward the sea; whereas the via Manzoni (left) runs along the whole length of the Posillipo hills through magnificent country dotted with modern villas. The road passes the upper station of the funicular from Mergellina (see above). At the Quadrivio di Posillipo Alto (520 ft above sea level) the via Stazio descends in steep bends to Mergellina. The via Manzoni continues, still affording pleasant views, to the Villa Patrizi, where a road diverges (left) for Agnano, and to the Largo Europa. Hence another road to the left, the via Tasso, drops down (with a great part of the city spread out below) to join the corso Vittorio Emanuele (Map 4, 9), while the via Falcone ascends to the Vomero (Route IV b).

c Capri

Capri, a small island 4 miles long and 2 miles wide, lies 3 miles from the Sorrentine Peninsula, of which it forms the geological prolongation. It is a mountainous island, with a precipitous and almost inaccessible coast, abounding in caves and fantastic rocks. With its perennial sunshine, its extraordinarily pure air, and its luxuriant, almost tropical vegetation, it is the pearl of the Gulf of Naples. Its beauties are however best enjoyed out of season. The chief town on the island is Capri. Anacapri, in a somewhat less sheltered position, is popular with convalescents. Monte Solaro (1914 ft) is the highest point. The principal products of the island are fruit, oil, and wine.

Capri is served by ferry-boats and hydrofoils from Naples and Sorrento (a complete timetable will be found in Chapter VII, 3). Only residents may drive automobiles on the island.

Capri was joined to the mainland and inhabited in prehistoric times, as the discovery on the island of flint tools and other interesting material (including the fossilized remains of palaeolithic animals) suggests. The origin of the name, Capri, is uncertain. Strabo speaks of *Caprea*, isle of sharp rocks; but Varro uses the name *Caprae,* deriving it from *capra* ("goat"), or *capros* ("boar"). Whether he intended this as an allusion to the island's silhouette (a reclining goat? a charging boar?), or to the wild animals that inhabit its rocky shores, is anyone's guess. A less authoritative interpretation derives the name from the Hebrew word *capraim*, meaning "two villages." The proponents of this theory suggest that Capri was once inhabited by the Phoenecians.

It is certain that the island was colonized by the Greeks, although it is not known in what year (the oldest artefacts found by archaeologists date from the fourth century B.C.). After 325 B.C. it shared the fortunes of Neapolis, together with which it was Romanized. Augustus visited the island in 29 B.C., and was so impressed by its natural beauty that he obtained it from the Neapolitans in exchange for the larger and more fertile island of Ischia. On Capri he built roads, aqueducts, and villas (29 B.C.). The wider fame of the island began with Tiberius, who retired to Capri in A.D. 27.

The historians Tacitus and Suetonius describe his ten years' residence as a period of decadence and cruelty, but their writings are undoubted exaggerations. On the dominant points of the island Tiberius erected several villas, dedicated (probably) to the major deities of the Roman Pantheon. The most important of these was the Villa Jovis; of the others remains have been found at Pianoro di Damecuta and Palazzo a Mare.

After Tiberius the island declined in importance. In 182 Commodus assigned it as a place of exile for his wife Crispina and his sister Lucilla. In 523 or 530, it seems, the Roman patrician donated the island to the Abbey of Montecassino, but when Naples became an independent duchy Capri joined in its lot. In the seventh and eighth centuries it was pillaged by the first of the Saracen corsairs whose incursions would continue up to the beginning of the nineteenth century. The islanders, terrorized by these destructive raids, abandoned the old town at the Marina and moved to the central highlands. The present towns of Capri and Anacapri date from this period, as the many defensive works (gates and archways) show. Later the island was taken by the Lombards and by the Normans. Joan I of Anjou granted the islanders many privileges, and founded the Certosa of Capri, where she died. In the sixteenth century the Saracen incursions resumed with renewed ferocity; in 1535 the Barbarossa attacked and destroyed the castle of Anacapri, which today still bears his name.

A plague of 1656 decimated the population of Capri, which had been immune to such disasters previously. It seems that the disease was brought by a servant returning to his master's household after visiting relatives on the mainland. The island was much loved by Charles of Bourbon, and it was frequented by Ferdinand IV for its superb quail hunting. Ferdinand convinced the populace to constitute a militia against pirates, exempting the inhabitants from military service. In 1806 the island was taken by the British fleet under Sir Sidney Smith and strongly fortified. Sir Hudson Lowe, who would later become famous as Napoleon's chancellor on Sant'Elena, was appointed governor. In 1808 Capri was retaken by the French, and in 1813 it was restored to Ferdinand I of the Two Sicilies.

For more than 150 years Capri has provided a home for expatriates, artists, and eccentrics. In recent years, however, it has lost its flavor as a retreat for intellectuals, to become one of the more elegant and exclusive international vacation spots.

Travelers arriving in **Capri** generally land on the north coast, in the bay of the Marina Grande. From this point the town of Capri is reached by funicular railway, by road (3 km), or by footpath (Strada Campo di Pisco).

The road winds up from the harbor, offering a series of magnificent views over the island, the gulf, and the Sorrentine peninsula. Where it passes the Bristol Hotel, the via Palazzo a Mare diverges to the right, leading in just a few yards to the Villa Williams, where ancient masonry belonging to a villa of Tiberius (see above) may be seen; adjacent is a soccer field, originally the garden of the villa, made over by the French and British as a parade ground between 1806 and 1815. Here an exedra and traces of a small private harbor remain. We continue our ascent, passing (right) the church of San Costanzo, built in the tenth or eleventh century and enlarged around 1330, with a Byzantine dome and small, characteristic bell-tower. Within, the crossing is marred by the loss of its ancient cipollino columns, four of which were removed in 1755 to decorate the Palatine Chapel at Caserta (four remain). The church contains the relics of St. Constance, patriarch of Constantinople and patron saint of the island. The road unites farther on with those from the Marina Piccola (southwest) and Anacapri (northwest); we proceed along the "backbone" of the island and enter Capri, emerging in the central piazza Umberto I.

A small and quaint town with vaulted houses and labyrinthine streets, Capri lies in the saddle between Punta del Capo on the east and Monte Solaro on the west. Hard by rise the hills of san Michele and Castiglione. In the piazza Umberto I stands the seventeenth century church of santo Stefano, approached by a flight of steps. The interior contains, at the foot of the high altar, a fragment of inlaid pavement from the Villa Jovis (see below) and the Tombs of Giacomo and Vincenzo Arcucci, by Michelangelo Naccherino. Adjacent is the Palazzo Cerio, once a residence of Joan I. Close to the upper station of the cable railway from the Marina may be seen remains of a megalithic wall. The view from the terrace embraces the entire Gulf of Naples; it is especially beautiful at night and in the early morning.

Around the square rises the picturesque medieval quarter with its steep, narrow streets. Here, it will be noticed, the original architectural flavor of the town has been carefully

Capri. The island's lush vegetation and quaint, flat-roofed houses have made a visit to the island a must for more than five generation of travelers.

preserved: the characteristic use of vaulted roofs suggests that local builders, in creating an original form and style suited to the particular geophysical conditions of the place (i.e., the scarsity of water and of wood for building), looked to late Roman and Byzantine buildings for inspiration.

Several fine walks may be taken in the environs of Capri. These are described below, in order of increasing difficulty.

The Certosa may be reached in about 6 minutes. Leave the piazza Umberto I by a vaulted passage in the south corner, and follow the via Vittorio Emanuele to the Quisisana Hotel. The via Federico Serena, to the right of the hotel, climbs, and then descends to the Certosa di San Giacomo, a Carthusian Monastery founded in 1371 by Giacomo Arcucci, secretary to Joan I; it was sacked by Torgud in 1553 and suppressed in 1807. Recently reoccupied, the sixteenth century conventual buildings house a school and a library, and the Gothic church has been restored. The fresco above the portal, showing the Madonna and Child with the founder and his queen, is possibly the work of Andrea Vanni. From the via Federico Serena (see above) the via Matteotti leads to the via Augusto, a paved path built by Friedrich Krupp, the German armaments manufacturer, which descends to the Marina Piccola.

The **Castiglione** and the **Punta del Canone** may be reached in 20 minutes by ascending the steps of santo Stefano (see above) and following (right) the via Madre Serafina. About 0,5 km beyond the church of santa Teresa, a narrow path to the right leads up to the ruins of the Castiglione (249 m; closed to public), a medieval castle constructed with ancient materials.

In summer the main square is crowded, but outlying areas are still visitable.

Bear left. More steps and a shaded path lead to the Punta Canone, which affords a super view of the Faraglioni and the Marina Piccola. On the north slope of the hill, in 1786, excavations brought to light five ancient rooms, with painted and marble decoration.

The **Punta Tragara** also lies about 20 minutes outside of town. The via Camerelle, to the left of the Quisisana Hotel (see above), skirts a series of brick vaults known as the Camerelle-probably the arches of a road connecting the villas of Tragara and Castiglione. Ascend slightly, to reach the Belvedere Tragara (view of the Faraglioni and toward Marina Piccola); steps by the café and a path lead thence to the Punta Tragara from which the view includes (east) the flat rock known as Il Monacone from a species of seal once native to Capri. From the steps another path continues east to the Arco Naturale (see below).

The **Arco Naturale** may be gained in 20 minutes, the **Grotta di Matromania** in 10 minutes more. From the northeast corner of the piazza follow the narrow via Botteghe, via Fuorlovade, and via Croce. Where the latter divides take the via Matromania (right); after 8 minutes keep to the left, and after 8 minutes more descend the steps (left) to the Arco Naturale, a fantastic archway in the rock (view). Returning to the path continue to descend to the Grotta di Matromania, which opens toward the east. The cave ends in a semicircular apse, and there are various small chambers with walls in *opus reticulatum*. This is probably a sanctuary of Cybele, the Mater Magna; the erroneous belief that it was a Mithraeum was exploded when it was learned that a Mithraic relief in the Naples museum, supposedly discovered here, had in fact been found elsewhere on the island.

A lovely walk of just under an hour leads to the **Villa of Tiberius**. From the via Croce (see above) take the rising via Tiberio (left, follow the central strip of paving) and pass the small church of Santa Croce. Farther on bear to the right, passing near the remains of a Pharos, or lighthouse, probably built by Augustus and overthrown by an earthquake after the death of Tiberius. Here is the Salto di Tiberio (296 m), the almost vertical rock from which it is fabled that Tiberius precipitated his victims. A few more paces brings us to the ruined Villa Jovis (or of Tiberius) known to the Capriotes as the Palazzo di Tiberio, and in reality a residence of palatial proportions with several stories. The villa was systematically explored for the first time in 1932-35, by which time most of its mosaic pavements and other decorative elements had already been carried off. The ruins cover an area of 7000 sq. m, centering around a rectangular zone occupied by four large cisterns hewn out of the rock and divided into intercommunicating cells. From the entrance to the park, a brick path mounts to the Vestibule, conserving the bases of four marble columns. Adjacent are the Rooms of the Guard Corps, converted during the Middle Ages into cisterns. A corridor ascends to a second Vestibule, whence a corridor on the right climbs to the Baths, consisting of a dressing room, a cold bath, a tepid bath, a warm bath (with two semicircular apses) and rooms for the heating and distribution of the water. To the east, built in a hemicycle, are the State Rooms. Retracing our steps, go along the west wing of the palace, past the Servants' Quarters to the Imperial Apartments (remains of mosaic pavement), whence a corridor and steps descend to the Loggia Imperiale or Belvedere, a long, straight porch set into the north rim of the cliff, 65 ft below the level of the palace. Steps along the west (inland) flank of the villa descend to vaulted Storerooms and to the Kitchens, set apart from the rest of the structure. At the highest point, on an ancient substructure, is the chapel of santa Maria del Soccorso, commanding the finest View in Capri, embracing the island itself, the sea, and the Punta della Campanella, and the two bays. Restored in 1979, the church is preceded by an enormous bronze Madonna brought to the site by a United States Navy helicopter and solemnly blessed by Pope John-Paul II.

The trip from **Capri to Anacapri** is a mere 3 km (2 miles), and may be made on foot or by bus. The road, constructed in 1874 and restored in 1923, ascends in long windings hewn in the rock and affords a series of beautiful views. On the way we pass the torre Quattro Venti, near which is the Palazzo Inglese,

Among the more noteworthy sights is the Villa San Michele, one time home of the Swedish physician, writer, and art collector, Axel Munthe.

built ca. 1750 by Sir Nathaniel Thorold and a key-point in the French assault of 1808. Formerly the only means of communication between Anacapri and the rest of the island was by the Scala Fenicia, a flight of 800 steps attributable to the Greeks or to Augustus, descending to the Marina Grande. This (now, however, with fewer steps) crosses the road at the chapel of Sant'Antonio, above which are the ruins of the Castello di Barbarossa, destroyed in 1535 by the corsair of that name (see above). Near the top of the steps is the Villa San Michele.

Anacapri is a pleasant village that recalls Sicily by its white houses and quasi-oriental roofs. Its setting, on a gently sloping plain planted with olives and fruit trees (which block the view of the sea) give it an overall feeling very different from that of Capri. The main via G. Orlandi crosses the entire town, opening up near its beginning to form the piazza della Vittoria. Here is the lower station of the chair-lift for Monte Solaro (see below). From the square the pleasant via san Michele mounts in 15 minutes to the Villa san Michele, built by the Swedish doctor, Axel Munthe (1857-1949), on the site of a villa of Tiberius. The interior is furnished with precious antiques, mainly of the eighteenth century, and is adorned with Roman works of art; but the villa is known above all for its subtropical gardens and its wonderful view. From the via san Michele a mule track ascends in roughly 30 minutes to the **Castello di Barbarossa** (see above), an impressive ruin set amid umbrella pines and enjoying an extensive panorama.

We return to the piazza della Vittoria. From the square, the main street bears right, passing the Museo della Torre, with a modest collection of antique weapons and sculpture. To the north, in the piazza san Nicola, the octagonal church of san Michele, finished in 1719, possesses a majolica pavement (Story of Eden), executed by Leonardo Chiaiese (1761) to a design of Solimena. The plan of the church is ascribed to Domenico Antonio Vaccaro. The four sides on the main axes are slightly longer than those on the diagonals, and the vestibule and choir are deeper than the other areas leading off the central space, imparting a longitudinal emphasis to the plan. The architect also uses pilasters at the points where the vestibule and choir join the central space to lead the eye from one area of the church to the next, placing them at an angle to the main axis. The center of the town is the piazza Armando Diaz with the Chiesa Parrocchiale (Santa Sofia; 1510, enlarged 1870), whence the street continues (left) to the smiling village of Caprile (0,5 km).

Anacapri, like Capri, offers many interesting excursions. **The plateau of Migliara** (304 m), reached in 40 minutes, commands a striking view of the Faraglioni and the precipices of Monte Solaro. To reach it, take the stony path from the road's end at Caprile, joining the mule track which leads to the

Belvedere di Migliara. The return may be made via the Torre della Guardia above the Punta Carena, and the fifteenth century Torre di Materita.

A road runs west from the Parrocchiale to the **Mulino a Vento**, which enjoys a fine view of Ischia, and to (20 minutes) Olivastra, peasantly set amid olive groves and vineyards. Here a by-road (right) brings us, in 10 minutes more, to the twelfth century Torre di Damecuta, near which lie the ruins of another Roman villa brought to light in 1937-48. Damaged by the showers of ash which followed the eruption of Vesuvius and probably abandoned in A.D. 79, the villa lost many of its mosaic pavements and other decorative fineries to the negligence and greed of early (eighteenth and nineteenth century) excavators. Nevertheless it preserves a fine belvedere similar to the one at the Villa Jovis, a few rooms of the east and west wings, and a cistern for rain water, about 500 ft inland. The view of the Phlegraean Fields is particularly fine at sunset. A path descends to the Blue Grotto (see below).

The ascent of **Monte Solaro** may be made in 1 hour (chairlift in 12 minutes). From the strada della Migliara, we skirt the garden-wall of the Villa Giulia, and reach the path (signpost) along the slope, which we follow toward the south. A steep ascent passes by remains of the English fortifications of 1806-08 to the Crocella saddle (45 minutes), with a shrine of the Virgin. From here it takes about 15 minutes more to attain the summit of Monte Solaro (1914 ft), which is crowned by a ruined castle. The wonderful panorama extends over the bays of Naples and Salerno to the Ponziane Islands (northwest), the Apennines (east), and the mountains of Calabria (south).

On the north coast of the island is the famous **Blue Grotto**, a visit to which is the most popular excursion on Capri. It may be visited either by motor-launch or by small boat from the Marina Grande. The latter skirts the north side of the island, affording a view of the ruins known as the Palazzo a Mare (described above). When a strong wind blows from the north or east, entrance to the grotto is impracticable. The light effects are best between 11 a.m. and 1 p.m..

A marine cavern, the Blue Grotto owes its marvellous geological formation to a gradual subsidence of the coast which probably took place sometime after the Roman epoch. Though known in antiquity, it seems to have then lacked the curious effects of light that are now its great charm. Its possibilities were realized in 1822 by Angelo Ferrara, a Capri fisherman, who in 1826 led Augustus Kopisch, a German poet, and some others to its "accidental" discovery. Kopisch entered the facts in the register of Pagano's hotel, and these were publicized in Hans Christian Andersen's novel, *The Improvvisatore*.

Once a nymphaeum of Tiberius, the cavern has, in recent years, yielded a wealth of archaeological material, including several large statues (these objects are awaiting collocation in the planned archaeological museum). In addition, underwater explorations in 1976 revealed the existence of niches, platforms, and broad apses hewn out of the rock, in about 6 ft of water. The opening is barely 3 ft high, so that even in calm weather heads have to be ducked. The interior of the cave is 185 ft long, 98 ft wide and 49 ft high. The sun's rays, entering not directly but through the water, fill the cave with a magical blue light. Objects in the water have a beautiful silvery appearance. Near the middle of the grotto is a ledge where one can land. An adjoining cleft, once supposed to be the begining of an underground passage to the Villa of Damecuta (compare above), has been proved to be a natural orifice. Outside the grotto is the beginning of a path ascending to Anacapri. The *giro* or "Voyage Round the Island" takes 3-4 hours, and may be begun at either the Marina Grande or the Marina Piccola.

Heading east from the Marina Grande, in succession we pass the Grotta del Bove Marino, the strangely shaped little point of Fucile (rifle), and the rock named La Ricotta (cream-cheese). After doubling round Il Capo we reach the Grotta Bianca and the Grotta Meravigliosa, both with stalactites (the second accessible also from the land). Farther on are the Faraglione di Matromania and Il Monacone, with its Roman remains. Off the Punta Tragara are the three gigantic rocks named the Faraglioni, one of which, La Stella (292 ft), is connected with the island. The outermost, Lo Scopolo (289 ft), resembles a sugar-loaf and is the habitat of a rare species of blue lizard. The boat passes through a natural arch in the central rock. Next comes the Grotta dell'Arsenale, supposed to have been used for repairing ships. Beyond the Marina Piccola, at the foot of Monte Solaro, is the Grotta Verde, with beautiful green light effects (best 10-11); inacessible in a strong south wind. Not far off comes the Grotta Rossa. The voyage along the west side of the island to the Blue Grotto is less interesting. For the Blue Grotto, and thence back to the Marina Grande.

d Procida and Ischia

Procida, Ischia, and the tiny islet of Vivara constitute the archepelago known as the **Phlegraean Isles**; they can be considered a continuation of the Phlegraean Fields, whose volcanic origin they share.

The tiny island of Procida, the ancient *Prochyta*, is formed of four craters of basaltic tufa and pumice-stone partly destroyed by the sea so as to form semicircular bays. The chief occupations are fishing and vine growing, and the islanders have long been famed for their seamanship. Perhaps because it is nearer to the mainland that the other islands in the gulf, or perhaps because it is the least dramatic, Procida has suffered less from the domesticating influence of tourism. For this reason it remains the most characteristic-the noisiest and most chaotic, but also the most colorful - of all the islands in the Gulf of Naples.

Ischia is a collection of craters and lava streams of which the highest point is the conical Monte Epomeo (2561 ft), the north side of an extinct volcano. Adjoining its slope are other craters: northeast, Monte Rottaro and Monte Montagnone, east Monte Trippiti, west, Monte Imperatore, and in the hills extending to the Punta dell'Imperatore. Lava streams also formed the promontories of Monte Caruso and Punta Cornacchia in the northwest. With a circumference of about 20 miles, Ischia is the largest island in the gulf. It has a mild climate, and its volcanic slopes are richly covered with subtropical vegetation. Its beauty, interest, and variety prompted Bishop Berkeley to describe it, in a letter to Pope (1717) as "an epitome of the whole earth". Celebrated for its hot mineral springs (season May-October; some open year-round) and for sea-bathing, boating, and its delightful walks, Ischia is everywhere well supplied with hotels, restaurants, and bathing establishments.

Both Procida and Ischia may be reached from Naples by ferry-boat and hydrofoil, and from Pozzuoli by ferry-boat. For a complete timetable, see Chapter VII, 3.

The Santuario del Soccorso, small, white, and picturesque, stand on a promontory dominating the village of Forio, on the west side of the island.

The boat trip to **Procida** offers a series of fine views over the gulf to the promontories of Posillipo and Capo Miseno, with Pozzuoli and the Phlegraean Fields in between. The little town of Procida, with flat-roofed white houses of Eastern aspect flanked by steep cliffs, stretches along the north coast of the island and rises in terraces on the hills beyond. Around the Marina, where the ferry and the hydrofoil land, the winding streets have changed little since the Middle Ages. In the piazza dei Martiri there is a tablet commemorating twelve of the inhabitants of Procida executed after the rising of 1799, and a statue of Antonio Scialoia, the statesman, who died on the island in 1877. The Castle is now a prison. The via San Michele climbs to the Terra Murata (296 ft), highest point of the island, where the abbey church of San Michele contains, in the ceiling, Luca Giordano's St. Michael defeating Lucifer. (St. Michael is patron saint of Procida; so popular is his following that his feast day is celebrated twice a year, on September 26 and May 8.) At the southwest end of the island, beyond the castle of Santa Margherita, is the Bay of Chiaiolella, which commands a superb view over the olive-clad islet of Vivara to Ischia.

According to the ancient poets Ischia was the abode of the giant Typhoeus who, when struck by Jupiter's thunderbolts, expressed his revengeful fury in volcanoes and earthquakes. The Greeks who colonized it called it *Pithecusa* or *Pithecusai*, the Latins *Aenaria* or *Inarime*. In the ninth century it was known as *Iscla*, a corruption of "insula" (i.e., the island par

The Castel of Ischia stands on a rocky connected to the town by a causeway. This once secret tunnel linked the fortress to the sea, and could be used to smuggle food and arms in, or defenders out, in times of siege.

excellence), from which its modern name is derived. The earliest recorded volcanic eruption on the island dates from about 500 B.C., the last was in 1301. Ischia was seized in 474 B.C. by Hieron of Syracuse, ca. 450 by the Neapolitans, and in 326 by the Romans. Augustus exchanged it with the Neapolitans for Capri. It was later taken by the Saracens in 813 and 947, by the Pisans in 1135, by Henri VI and Frederick II, and finally shared the fortunes of Naples. Ischia was the birthplace of the marquis of Pescara (1489), and here his widow Vittoria Colonna retired in 1525. The island was sacked by the pirate Barbarossa in 1541 and captured in 1547 by the Duke of Guise; it was occupied by Nelson, and in 1815 provided a brief refuge for Murat. The self-portrait of Allan Ramsay in the National Portrait Gallery in London was executed on the island in 1776, and the sculptor Canova was rewarded in 1816 with the title of Marquis of Ischia.

The commune of Ischia (or Ischia Porto), the chief town of the island, consists of **Ischia Ponte**, extending picturesquely along the shore for about 2 km (1 mile) north of the Castle, and the modern Ischia Porto around the harbor to the northwest, the two separated by a fine beach backed by pine woods. We land at Ischia Porto. The town rose round a crater lake, the seaward side of which was pierced in 1854 to form the circular harbor, 0,5 km (1 mile) across. The Punta san Pietro on the east, and the public park and the pier on the west side command good views. In the piazza del Redentore are the Terme Comunali, with mineral waters (65°C; 149°F) resembling those of Casamicciola (see below). The Museo dell'Isola, approached by the via Roma, has interesting local antiquities. Continuing east, the via Roma and its continuation, the via Vittoria Colonna, lead to Ischia Ponte, beyond which the Ponte Aragonese (1438), a causeway 741 ft long, leads to the rocky islet fortress of Alfonso the Magnanimour (private). On the island is the fourteenth century Cathedral. The Castle, in which Vittoria Colonna resided, rises 361 ft above the sea.

From Ischia Ponte follow the via del Seminario and the via Sogliuzzo through pine woods to the little piazza degli Eroi, where the Via Alfredo De Luca leads back to Ischia Porto. A road diverging to the south from the main road about 600 yards northwest of Ischia Porto, leads to (35 minutes) Fiaiano (view), and then (north) in 10 minutes more to the top of Monte Montagnone (1010 ft; chair-lift from Ischia Porto in 4 minutes).

A tour of the island by road (30 km or 18 miles; bus) may be made comfortably in one day. The road climbs steeply from Ischia Porto to the hamlet of Perrone, then turns southwest.

Casamicciola Terme, on the north slope of Monte Empomeo, is a pleasant bathing resort and spa, the first on Ischia to be frequented for its mineral waters. The town was rebuilt after the earthquake of 1883 in which 1700 people perished. The mineral waters (80°C; 176°F) are prescribed for arthritis and rheumatism. At the Villa Ibsen (then Piseni) Ibsen started *Peer Gynt* in 1867. The **Osservatorio Geofisico** on the Grande Sentinella commands a fine view.

At **Lacco Ameno**, another thermal resort with the most radioactive waters in Italy, is the little church of santa Restituta, patron saint (d. 284) of the island. Traces of an early sanctuary have come to light. The eighteenth century Villa Arbusto will soon house an Archaeological Museum containing finds from the excavations of Pithecusa, remains of which occupy the gardens. In addition to Greek and Italic material, the finds include Egyptian and Syrian objects which attest the colony's commercial ties with the Eastern Mediterranean. The saint's day (May 17) is celebrated by fireworks, bonfires on Monte Vico, etc. The thermal establishments of Lacco Ameno are considered the most exclusive on the island. Some are open year round; the others, from March to October.

The road now ascends steeply over the lava stream of 474 B.C. and descends to Forio, home of Epomeo wine and the center of the foreign (particularly German) colony on the island. The Pensione Nettuno occupies a convent of 1742, with a picturesque medieval tower. The Santuario del Soccorso above the village commands an enchanting view.

The road passes above the radioactive sands of Citara, traversing Cuotto, where a path diverges to the right for the Punta dell'Imperatore (754 ft; lighthouse), the southwest extremity of the island.

Panza enjoys a view of Capri. To the south lie the rich orchards of Succhivo, and Sant'Angelo (2,5 km; 2 miles), a health resort with submarine springs, from whose sandy beach, the Marina dei Maronti, issue jets of steam. Beyond Panza the road turns east and ascends, with many turns and magnificent views all the way, to Serrara Fontana (1075 ft); higher up is Parrocchia, a hamlet with a color-washed church.

Fontana (449 m) has a church of 1374. This is the best starting place for the ascent of Monte Epomeo (2561 ft; 1 hour; mules for hire), the summit of which commands a view extending from Terracina to Capri. The prominent iron crucifix commemorates 44 people killed in an air crash. The descent may be made in 2 hours to Forio, Casamicciola, or Ischia Porto.

Descend through a ravine to Buonopane, separated by another ravine from Barano d'Ischia, among its vineyards. To the south is the village of Testaccio by which a descent may be made on foot to the Marina dei Maronti (see above). Turn northeast, and Procida, Capo Miseno, and the Castle of Ischia come into sight ahead.

Beyond Molara we leave sant'Antuono on the right, and, following the Lava dell'Arso, regain the coast between Ischia Ponte and Ischia Porto at the piazzetta di Ferrocavallo.

VI The Gourmet Guide to Naples

No Italian city has contributed more to the national cuisine of Italy than Naples. Indeed, many Neapolitan dishes-such as spaghetti, lasagne, and pizza-can be enjoyed not only throughout Italy, but all over the world, thanks to the many thousands of Neapolitans who carried their culinary tradition along with them when they emigrated to foreign lands.

Neapolitan food is usually good and inexpensive. The least pretentious restaurant often provides the best value. Prices on the menu do not include a cover charge (*coperto*, shown separately on the menu) which is added to the bill. The service charge is now almost always automatically added at the end of the bill. Tipping is therefore not strictly necessary, but a few thousand lire are appreciated. The menu displayed outside the restaurant indicates the kind of charges the customer should expect. However, many simpler establishments do not offer a menu, and here, although the choice is usually limited, the standard of cuisine is often very high. The price for a meal (in 1985) per person, in a luxury restaurant can be from 30,000-100,000 lire, in an average restaurant from 20,000-40,000, and in a *trattoria* from 15,000-30,000. Lunch is around 1 p.m., and is the main meal of the day, dinner is around 8 or 9 p.m.

Snacks and light lunches are served in a *Pizzeria*, *Rosticceria*, and *Tavola Calda*. A *Vinaio* often sells wine by the glass and simple food for very reasonable prices. *Bars* (which are open from early morning to late at night) serve numerous varieties of excellent refreshments that are usually taken standing up. The customer generally pays the cashier first, and presents a receipt to the barman in order to get served. It has become customary to leave a small tip for the barman. If a customer sits at a table he should not pay first, as he will be given waiter service and the charge will be considerably higher.

Black coffee (*caffé* or *expresso*) can be ordered diluted (*alto* or *lungo*), with a liquor (*corretto*), or with hot milk (*cappuccino*). In summer, many customers take cold coffee (*caffé freddo*), or cold coffee and milk (*caffé- latte freddo*).

In Naples as elsewhere in Italy, pasta is an essential part of most meals. Pasta is classified according to its composition and shape. Experts draw a distinction between *pasta comune* (spaghetti, rigatoni, lasagne, etc.) produced industrially and made of a simple flour and water paste; and *pasta all' uovo* (tortellini, ravioli, etc.), made with an egg batter. The forms that pasta may assume are virtually numberless. An ordinary Italian supermarket usually stocks about 50 different shapes, but some experts estimate that there are more than 600 shapes in all. *Pasta corta* (i.e. rigatoni) is much more varied than *pasta lunga* (i.e. spaghetti). The latter may be tubular (like ziti or macaroni), or threadlike (spaghetti, vermicelli, capellini); smooth (fettucce, tagliatelle, linguine), ruffled (lasagne, ricce), or twisted (fusilli). Pasta corta comes in a virtually limitless variety of shapes-shells (conchiglie), stars (stelle), butterflies (farfalle), etc. - and may be smooth (penne) or fluted (rigatoni). The differences of shape translate into differences of flavor, even when the pasta is made from the same dough, or by the same manufacturer. The reason for this is that the relation between the surface area and the weight of the pasta varies from one shape to another, causing the sauce to adhere in different ways and to different degrees. But even when pasta is served without a sauce, experts claim to perceive considerable differences in flavor due to the fact that different shapes cook in different ways.

Naples is the classical home of *pasta asciutta*, which is quite different from the *pasta fresca* preferred in Northern Italy. The latter is usually homemade, from a dough composed of flour, eggs and just a little water; and it is soft and pliable both before and after cooking. Pasta asciutta is generally factory-made, from a simple flour and water paste that is rolled into sheets, cut and molded in the desired shape, and then air dried. It is hard and brittle when bought, and when correctly cooked it remains *al dente* (chewy; never soft), additional moisture being provided by the sauce. An early American appreciator of pasta asciutta was Thomas Jefferson, who in 1787 brought a spaghetti-making machine from Italy to the United States.

Whereas the invention of egg pasta is generally credited to the Chinese, the origin of pasta asciutta may well be Italian. The Etruscan Tomb of the Reliefs at Cerveteri, near Rome, has stucco decorations representing pasta-making tools: a board and a rolling pin for rolling out the dough, knives, even a toothed cutting-wheel for making decorative borders. References to *lasagne* may be found in Cicero and other Roman writers; the name itself is probably derived from the Latin *lagana* or *lasana*, a cooking pot. By the end of the Middle Ages pasta was known throughout Italy. The fourteenth century *Codex of the Anonymous Tuscan* preserved in the library of Bologna University contains several serving suggestions; and the poet Boccaccio, in his masterpiece, the *Decameron*, describes an imaginary land of grated parmesan cheese inhabited by people whose only pastime is the making of "maccheroni e raviuoli." Of course tomato sauce was unheard of until the discovery of America; Boccaccio's contemporaries cooked their macaroni and ravioli in chicken broth, and dressed them with fresh butter.

A Neapolitan Menu

Characteristic dishes of Italian cuisine, to be found all over the country, are included in the menu given below. Many of the best dishes to be had in Naples are regional specialites; these are given in a separate section at the end.

Antipasti, Hors d'oeuvre

Prosciutto crudo o cotto, Ham, raw or cooked
Prosciutto e melone, Ham (raw) and melon
Salame, Salami
Salsicce, Sausage
Tonno, Tuna fish
Fagioli e cipolle, Beans with onions
Carciofi o finocchi in pinzimonio, Raw artichokes or fennel with a dressing
Antipasto misto, Mixed cold hors d'oeuvre
Antipasto di mare, Seafood hors d'oeuvre

Minestre e Pasta, Soups and Pasta

Minestre, zuppa, Thick soup
Brodo, Clear soup
Minestrone, Vegetable soup
Spaghetti al sugo o al ragù, Spaghetti with a meat sauce
Spaghetti al pomodoro, Spaghetti with a tomato sauce
Tagliatelle, Flat spaghetti-like pasta, almost always made with egg
Lasagne, Layers of pasta with meat filling and cheese and tomato sauce
Cannelloni, Rolled pasta "pancakes" with meat filling and cheese and tomato sauce
Ravioli, Filled with spinach and ricotta cheese
Tortellini, Small coils of pasta, filled with a rich stuffing served either in broth or with a sauce
Agnolotti, Ravioli filled with meat
Fettuccine, Ribbon noodles
Spaghetti alla carbonara, Spaghetti with bacon, beaten egg, and black pepper
Spaghetti alle vongole, Spaghetti with clams
Pappardelle alla lepre, Pasta with hare sauce
Gnocchi, Dumplings, made from potatoes, flour, and eggs

Risotto, Rice dish
Fagioli all'uccelletto, White beans in tomato sauce

Pesce, Fish

Zuppa di pesce, Mixed fish usually in a sauce (or soup)
Fritto misto di mare, Mixed fried fish
Fritto di pesce, Fried fish
Pesce arrosto, Pesce alla griglia, Roast, grilled fish
Pescespada, Swordfish
Aragosta, Lobster (an expensive delicacy)

Calamari, Squid
Sarde, Sardines
Coda di Rospo, Angler fish
Dentice, Dentex
Orata, Bream
Triglie, Red mullet
Sgombro, Mackerel

Baccalà, Salt cod
Anguilla, Eel
Sogliola, Sole
Tonno, Tuna fish
Trota, Trout
Cozze, Mussels
Gamberi, Prawns

Pietanze, Main Dishes

Bistecca alla fiorentina, Beef rib steak (grilled over charcoal)
Vitello, Veal
Manzo, Beef
Agnello, Lamb
Maiale (arrosto), Pork (roast)
Pollo (lesso), Chicken (boiled)
Costolette alla milanese, Veal cutlets, fried in breadcrumbs
Costoletta alla bolognese, Veal cutlet with ham, covered with melted cheese
Saltimbocca, Rolled veal with ham
Bocconcini, As above, with cheese
Ossobuco, Stewed shin of veal
Spezzatino, Veal stew, usually with pimento, tomatoes, onions, peas, and wine
Petto di pollo, Chicken breasts
Pollo alla cacciatora, Chicken with herbs and (usually) tomato and pimento sauce
Cotechino e Zampone, Pig's trotter stuffed with pork and sausages
Stracotto, Beef cooked in a sauce, or in red wine
Trippa, Tripe
Fegato, Liver
Tacchino arrosto, Roast turkey
Cervella, Brains

Bollito, Stew of various boiled meats
Fagiano, Pheasant
Coniglio, Rabbit
Lepre, Hare
Cinghiale, Wild boar

Contorni, Vegetables

Insalata verde, Green salad
Insalata mista, Mixed salad
Pomodori ripieni, Stuffed tomatoes
Funghi, Mushrooms
Spinaci, Spinach
Broccoletti, Tender broccoli
Piselli, Peas
Fagiolini, String beans
Asparagi, Asparagus
Zucchine, Zucchini squash
Melanzane alla parmigiana, eggplant in a cheese sauce
Carciofi, Artichokes
Finocchi, Fennel
Patatine, diced potatoes

Dolci, Sweets

Torta, Cake
Monte Bianco, Chestnut pudding
Zuppa inglese, Trifle
Gelato, Ice cream

Frutta, Fruit

Fragole (con panna), Strawberries (with cream)
Mele, Apples
Pere, Pears
Arance, Oranges
Ciliege, Cherries
Pesche, Peaches
Albicocche, Apricots
Uva, Grapes
Macedonia di frutta, Fruit salad
Fichi, Figs

Regional Dishes

The number and variety of regional dishes is so great, that to describe them all in detail would require·several hundred pages. What follows is therefore a brief summary.

Antipasti

Crostini alla napoletana, are among the simplest and tastiest of all *crostini*. Small, thin slices of bread are covered with mozzarella, chopped anchovies and tomatoes; seasoned with salt and oregano; then lightly toasted in the oven.

Gattò di patate. The gattò (which harks back to the days of the Angevins) is fairly common in Neapolitan cooking, althouth the ingredients often change. It has nothing to do with the *gâteaux* of French haute cuisine. On the contrary, it is a humble dish, a sort of dumpling made of mashed potatoes, eggs, prosciutto, mozzarella, and whatever else happens to be on hand. It is usually served piping hot.

Impepata di cozze. is a simple plate of fresh mussels, poached and dressed with lemon juice, chopped parsley, and olive oil.

Mozzarella in carrozza translates as "mozzarella in a carriage". It consists of a slice of mozarella fried between two slices of bread that are dipped in an egg batter, like French toast.

Pagnottine Santa Chiara, as the name suggests, were invented by the nuns of Santa Chiara. They are savory cakes made with anchovies, tomatoes, parsley and oregano.

Panzanella alla napoletana is a favorite salad dish made of crumbled bread, onions, tomatoes, anchovies, basil, and garlic (sometimes peppers and green olives are added)-all dressed with olive oil.

Peperoni farciti. Another Neapolitan favorite, this peasant dish-stuffed baked peppers-exists in a variety of versions. Three common fillings are: olives, capers, parsley, and anchovies; egg-plant and tomatoes; macaroni in a savory sauce.

Taralli col pepe are rings of crisp bread flavored with pepper and almonds. Another version uses fennel seeds.

Zucchine e scapece. This may be either an antipasto or a *contorno* (see below). Zucchini squash are sliced and fried in olive oil, then seasoned with vinegar and fresh mint leaves. Served cold.

Soups and Pastas

Fusilli alla napoletana are served in a rich sauce made with meat drippings, tomatoes, onions, celery, carrots, ricotta, salame, bacon, garlic and seasoned pecorino cheese. Sometimes spaghetti or macaroni are used instead of fusilli.

Lasagne di Carnevale. An especially rich dish, popular at Carnival time. Square lasagne are baked in a sauce containing sausages and meat balls; mozzarella, ricotta, and other cheeses; and hard-boiled eggs.

Minestra maritata. A very old, very typical Neapolitan specialty, also known as *pignato grasso.* It is a classical winter dish consisting chiefly of beet greens or cabbage boiled with a ham bone and sausages, served hot as a soup.

Minestrone napoletano. This is similar to all other Italian minestroni, with a predominance of yellow zucchine over all the other ingredients. Usually served with macaroni.

Maccheroni cacio e uova are simply macaroni in a cheese and egg sauce, sprinkled with chopped parsley before serving.

Pasta fritta. Originally a way of getting good mileage out of leftovers, pasta fritta is now a classic first course in its own right. Vermicelli or macaroni are seasoned with a rich sauce made with meat balls, chopped prosciutto, and cheese. The whole concoction, bound together by a few well-beaten eggs, becomes a fragrant and savory omlette. Often considered a complete meal.

Pasta e fagioli all'ischitana. This specialty of the island of Ischia is made with spaghetti, tripolini, bucatini and linguine, or whatever leftovers one happens to have on hand. The sauce is made with lots of fresh beans, and is seasoned with *peperoncino.*

Pasta alla sorrentina. The tradition in Sorrento is to add diced scamorza cheese to one's tomato sauce, to make it thick and stringy. The pasta thus seasoned is served with lots of grated caciocavallo or parmesan cheese.

Pizza is today at least as well known as spaghetti, and perhaps even more so. Suffice it to recall here that there are an infinite variety of pizza recipes, all based on bread dough. The secret of a successful pizza is a blazing hot oven. Only violent heat, in fact, is capable of cooking the pizza in such a way that it is soft, yet crunchy at the same time; if the oven is not hot enough the dough becomes tough as shoe leather. A wood-fired oven is best, although it is possible to produce an acceptable pizza in an electric or gas oven.

Ragù alla napoletana. This is the famous *rraù*, a special sauce for special occasions, which is traditionally placed on the stove at dawn and left to simmer slowly all day. It is prepared by melting lard and ham fat in a pan, then adding slices of veal rolled around a filling of grated cheese, garlic, parsley, raisins, and pine-nuts. As the sauce cooks, red wine and tomatoes are added. At the end the sauce is used to dress the pasta, while the meat rolls are served as an entrée.

Sartù. This is the richest of all Neapolitan dishes. Today only a few Neapolitan restaurants make it regularly, and to taste it at its best one should order it ahead of time. It is a rice pie stuffed with meat balls, sausage, chicken livers, mozzarella, mushrooms, peas, etc. Baked in a mold, it is not only tasty, but also very theatrical.

Spaghetti aglio e olio are served in a sauce consisting of olive oil, garlic, parsley, and sometimes peperoncino. Best enjoyed after midnight.

Spaghetti alle vongole is spaghetti in a clam sauce flavored with onions, tomatoes, cheese, and aromatic herbs. When rice is used instead of spaghetti the result is *risotto alle vongole*.

Timballo di maccheroni. Like Sartù, this is a classical dish of the Neapolitan aristocracy. It gradually spread throughout the kingdom of the Two Sicilies to become one of the more characteristic dishes of Southern Italy. It is made with macaroni baked in a pie with a sauce of chicken livers, mushrooms, and black truffles.

Vermicelli alla carrettiera (teamsters'vermicelli) belong to a category of pasta (like *spaghetti alla bucaniera*, pirates' spaghetti, and *maccheroni alla zappatora*, ditchdiggers' macaroni) whose names suggest that their seasoning is so strong that only he-men can be expected to cope with them. In vermicelli alla carrettiera a distinctive element is provided by the breadcrumbs that are sprinkled over the pasta instead of parmesan cheese.

Zite ripiene. The basic ingredient of this specialty of Caserta is the pasta known as *zite*, although *conchiglie* or *lumaconi* (both called shells in English) can also be used. The pasta is filled with diced pork, onions, salame or sausage, cheese, spices, and eggs; then covered with more cheese and baked. In a Lenten version the filling is made of ricotta, fresh basil, and other herbs.

Zuppa di cardoni. This is a rich and tasty dish from the Campanian hinterland. It is made of cardoons (an edible thistle) cooked in chicken broth with meat balls, mozzarella, the boned chicken, and sausages.

Zuppa alla marinara is made with as many varieties of fish as possible, which are stewed together with clams and mussels in lots of tomato sauce, olive oil, garlic, and hot peppers.

Main dishes

Agnello pasquale is a roast of lamb seasoned with rosemary, bayleaf, and sage; and accompanied by tender new onions and potatoes. Considered traditional in the Easter period, it appears the year round on the menus of many restaurants.

Anguilla in umido is a common dish in the Caserta area, where it is still fairly easy to find eels (*anguille*) in the irrigation canals. The eels are cooked in tomato sauce and served on toast. *Anguilla alla griglia* is grilled and basted with a sauce of olive oil, garlic, vinegar, and fresh mint leaves.

Baccalà alla napoletana. In this traditional dish, fillets of salt cod are first floured and fried, then stewed with tomatoes, capers, black olives, rasins, pine nuts, and, of course, garlic.

Braciole alla napoletana is a rich dish usually reserved for special occasions. An immense slice of beef or pork is covered with chopped provolone, prosciutto, rasins, and eggs; then tightly rolled, tied with string, and cooked in tomato sauce.

Cecenielli literally means little chick peas; but if one orders cecenielli in a Neapolitan trattoria what one gets is quite different: spicy little fish cooked in a flour and water paste, or served on a pizza.

Cervella alla napoletana is brain of veal or lamb baked with capers, black olives, pepper, and bread crumbs.

Coniglio all'ischitana. Breeding rabbits (conigli) seems to be a favorite pastime on Ischia, where the delicate meat of this animal is greatly appreciated. Cut into pieces and browned in olive oil, it is cooked in white wine, tomato sauce, and rosemary.

Costata alla pizzaiola is a T-bone steak served in a tomato sauce flavored with garlic and oregano.

Genovese. Neapolitans use this name to indicate a particular kind of beef stew-cooked slowly with much onion, olive oil, lard, and tomato sauce-which crept into the local culinary tradition through the colony of Genoese merchants who lived in Naples.

Polpo alla luciana. It seems that this manner of stewing octopus-with tomatoes, olive oil, garlic, and hot peppers - was developed by the wives of the fishermen of santa Lucia. When small octopi are used the dish is called *purpetielle affocate*.

Vegetables

Carciofi ripieni alla napoletana are baked artichokes with a delicious filling of meat, mushrooms, onions, and tomatoes.

Cianfotta is a sort of vegetable stew made with potatoes, yellow peppers, onions, tomatoes, eggplant, zucchini, and celery.

Insalata di rinforzo. This traditional Christmas dish is a hodge-podge of cauliflower, olives various pickled vegetables, anchovies, and capers, mixed together and dressed with olive oil and vinegar. The name comes from the fact that the dish is eaten in more than one day, and is continually "reinforced" with other ingredients which take the place of the ones eaten the day before.

Melanzane alla partenopea is an eggplant casserole, like melanzane alla parmigiana (which, despite its name, is a Campanian invention). Ingredients: eggplant, cacciocavallo and parmesan cheese, tomato sauce, spices.

Peperoni in teglia alla napoletana are yellow peppers fried in olive oil with capers and anchovies.

Desserts

Coviglie (*al caffe* or *al ciocolato*) is a traditional Neapolitan dessert much like a mousse.

Pastiera. This classic dessert can be found in Campanian *pasticcerie* from November to March. It is a pie filled with fresh ricotta, grains of wheat, rice, or barley boiled in milk, candied fruit, eggs, sugar, spices, and other ingredients. Some famous Neapolitan bakers make pastiera to order, packing it in such a way that it can stand up to long journeys.

Sfogliatelle are perhaps the most famous of Neapolitan breakfast pastries. There are two types, one made with a thin ribbon of crisp dough wound in tight spiral layers (*sfogliatelle ricce*); the other a simple envelope of soft dough. Both types are filled with fresh ricotta, chopped candied fruit, cinnamon, vanilla, and other ingredients.

Sproccolati are sun-dried figs filled with fennel seeds and preserved on wooden sticks. They are a specialty of Ravello and the Amalfi Coast.

Struffoli. This traditional Christmas dessert has all the characteristics typical of ancient Greek sweets: it calls for very little sugar, relying for its sweetness on honey, and, to a lesser extent, on candied fruit. It comes in two shapes: the traditional cone, and the more modern ring.

Susamelli. These "s" shaped cookies were once made with flour, sesame seeds, sugar, honey, and candied orange and lemon peals. The fusion of the Italian words for sesame and honey (*sesamo, miele*) gave rise to the name. Today the sesamo seeds are often substituted by ground almonds.

Wines of Campania

Campanian wines fall into three categories: *D.O.C.* (the initials stand for *denominazione di origine controllata*, which means that they are recognized by the President of the Republic); *D.O.S.* (*denominazione di origine semplice*, which means that their names are established by tradition); and *denominazione di vitigno*, which simply receive their names from their growers.

The most famous of the wines of Vesuvius is the *White Lacrima Christi*, a dry wine with an exquisite aroma; but the less known *Red Lacrima Christi* is equally good, especially when matured. *Red Vesuvio* and other varieties are grown in the region of Vesuvius. On the Phlegraean Hills, at Pozzuoli and Cumae, grow the vines which yield *Falerno*, which has inherited at least the name of the famous wine of the ancients, the

Falernum of Latium. This is a full-bodied, richly colored red wine, and like the straw-colored *White Falerno*, improves with age. But excellent white and red wines are produced all over Campania: at Posillipo and in the peninsula of Sorrento; on Ischia, practically one productive vineyard; on the hills of Formia and Sessa, where fine varieties of Falerno are likewise produced; near Aversa, the typical wine of which is the Asprinio; and in the environs of Salerno. On Capri is produced the famous *Capri*, a topaz - colored wine, clear as crystal, with a delicate bouquet and an agreeable dry flavor. *Red Capri*, scarcely inferior, with an exquisite aroma, assumes with age a tawny port-like hue. The production of *Solopaca*, palatable white or red, centers on the town of that name in the province of Benevento; and from the upper Calore, near Avellino, comes *Taurasi*, a superior red wine.

Vini a D.O.C:

Capri Bianco	white
Capri Rosso	red
Greco di Tufo	white
Ischia Bianco	white
Ischia Rosso	red
Lamezia	white
Solopaca Bianco	white
Taurasi	red

Vini a D.O.S.:

Calore degli Alburni	red	Gragnano	red
Campi Flegrei Bianco	white	Irno Bianco	white
Campi Flegrei Rosso	red	Irno Rosso	red
Castellabate Rosato	rosé	Irpinia Bianco	white
Castellabate Rosso	red	Irpinia Rosato	rosé
Cilento Rosato	rosé	Irpinia Rosso	red
Cilento Rosso	red	Lacrima Christi	red
Colli del Sannio Bianco	white	Mondragone Bianco	
white			
Colli del Sannio Rosso	red	Mondragone Rosso	
red			
Corbara	red	Pannarano	red
Falerno Bianco	white	Ravello Bianco	white
Falerno Rosso	red	Ravello Rosato	rosé
Gran Furore della Divina		Ravello Rosso	red
Costiera	white	Tramonti	red
		Vesuvio	red

Vini con denominazione di vitigno

Acinato	red
Aglianichello	red
Asprinio	white
Biancolella	white
Fiano	white
Forastera	white
Pellagrello Bianco	white
Pellagrello Rosso	red
Per ' e' Palummo	red
Sanginella	white

Wines of Campania

VII Practical Information

1 Approaches to Naples

Direct air services operate between Northern Europe and Naples throughout the year. There are also scheduled flights from New York, Los Angeles, etc. to Rome, where connecting flights may be found for Naples. Night trains, with sleeping cars and couchettes (seats converted into berths at night) run between Paris, Amsterdam, etc. and Rome, where there are connecting trains for Naples. The easiest approaches to Italy by road are through the Mont Blanc, Saint Bernard, Frejus, or Moncenisio tunnels, or over the Brenner pass. General information may be obtained from the Italian State Tourist Office (E.N.I.T.) in New York, who issue free an invaluable *Traveler's Handbook* (revised almost every year). Your nearest travel agent sells travel tickets and books accomodation, and may also organize inclusive tours and charter trips to Italy. The official Italian agency, C.I.T., has offices in New York (666 Fifth Avenue, Tel. 397-2666), Chicago, and Los Angeles.

Passports are necessary for all American visitors entering Italy, and may be obtained from the passport office in most cities, or, for an additional fee, through any travel agent. No visa is required for American travelers to Italy.

Currency Regulations. There are no restrictions on the amount of dollars the traveler may take out the United States. However, there are frequent variations in the amount of Italian notes that may be taken in or out of Italy. As there are normally strict limitations, the latest regulations should be checked before departure.

Money. In Italy the monetary unit is the Italian *lira* (plural, *lire*). Notes are issued for 1000, 2000, 5000, 10,000, 20,000, 50,000, and 100,000 lire. Coins are of 10, 20, 50, 100, 200, and 500 lire. The rate of exchange in 1989 is approximately 1400 lire to the U.S. dollar.

Customs Regulations. The following articles are admitted without formality (beyond oral declaration) for personal use (but may not be disposed of in Italy): camping equipment, fishing tackle, two cameras with 10 rolls of film each, one movie camera with 10 rolls of film, one canoe or similar boat, sport equipment (skis, rackets, etc.), one portable typewriter, one phonograph with a "reasonable" number of records, one tape recorder with a "reasonable" number of tapes, one portable radio and one portable television set (subject to a licence fee to be paid at Customs), one musical instrument, binoculars, one bicycle, sporting guns and 200 cartridges (a hunting permit is required and must be obtained beforehand from an Italian Consulate). Other items essential for the owner's profession or trade. The duty-free allowance for U.S. residents going to or returning from Italy varies from time to time; information is obtainable from travel agents or at airports. Items bought in Italy, up to a maximum value of one million lire, can be exported free of duty, but special permits are necessary (and the payment of a tax) for the exportation of antiques and modern art objects.

Police Registration. Police Registration is required within three days of entering Italy. For travelers staying at a hotel the management will attend to the formality. The permit lasts three months, but can be extended on application.

2   Hotels and Restaurants

Hotels in Italy are classified into five categories: de luxe, first, second, third, and fourth. Pensions are classified into three categories, first, second, and third. In country districts there will occasionally be found the modest *Locanda*, or graded below the fourth class. De Luxe hotels compare favorably with their counterparts in other countries, and first-class hotels usually live up to their name. In some localities, the second-class hotels deserve upgrading; in others they may disappoint. The difference between third-and fourth-class hotels is mainly of size and number of public rooms, and either class may give first-rate accomodation and service. Pensions in most towns are usually clean and are to be recommended to visitors staying more than a few days in one place. However, those that provide board are entitled to impose half-pension terms.

In this guide hotels have not been indicated in the text because it can now be taken for granted that almost every small center in the country will be provided with adequate accomodation. Hotels and pensions of every class will be found in the larger towns. The Italian State Tourist Office publishes an annual official list of all Italian hotels and pensions (*Annuario Alberghi*) which can be consulted at travel agents or E.N.I.T. in Italy; each Provincial Tourist Board (Ente Provinciale Turismo) issues a free list of hotels giving category, price, and facilities; and local tourist offices help travelers to find accomodation on the spot. Charges vary according to class, season, services available, and locality. Every hotel or pension has its fixed charges agreed with the Provincial Tourist Board. In all hotels the service charges are included in the rates. Sales tax is added in all hotels. However, the total charge is exhibited on the back door of the hotel room.

The average prices for a double room in 1989 ranged from 40.000 lire in an economic hotel, to 450.000 lire and up in one of the De Luxe class.

Naples is least noisy near the sea or on the hill. The *Azienda Autonoma di Soggiorno Cura e Turismo* makes the following recommendations:

Near the sea

De Luxe	Excelsior	48	via Partenope	Tel.	417-111
	Vesuvio	45	via Partenope		417-044
1 Class	Royal	38	via Partenope		400-244
	Santa Lucia	46	via Partenope		116-566
2 Class	Miramare	24	via Sauro		416-775
	Rex	12	via Palepoli		416-388
	Galles	5	via Sannazaro		668-344
	Le fontane al mare	14	via Tommaseo		416-354

On the hill

1 Class	Britannique	133	corso Vitt. Emanuele	660-933
	Parker's	135	corso Vitt. Emanuele	684-866
2 Class	Paradiso	11	via Catullo	660-233
	Sant'Elmo	21	via Bonito	377-775
	Splendid	96	via Manzoni	645-462
3 Class	Belvedere	51	via Angelin	364-540
	Camaldoli	586	via Nuova Camaldoli	466-836
Pensione 2	Villa Deriana	146	via Manzoni	645-382

Downtown

1 Class	Jolly Ambassador	70	via Medina	416-000
	Majestic	68	largo Vasto a Chiaia	416-500
	Mediterraneo	25	via Ponte di Tappia	312-240
	Oriente	44	via Diaz	312-133
	Terminus	91	piazza Garibaldi	286-011
2 Class	Torino	123	via Depretis	322-410
	Cavour	32	piazza Garibaldi	285-929
	Grilli	40	via Ferraris	264-344
	Palace	9	piazza Garibaldi	264-575

3 Class	Lago Maggiore	10	via del Cerriglio	320-611
	Pinto Storey	72	via Martucci	681-260
	Bristol	61	piazza Garibaldi	281-780
	Coral	12	via Pica	260-944
	Eden	9	corso Novara	285-690
	Esedra	12	piazza Cantani	339-465
	Europa	15	corso Meridionale	267-511
	Guiren	114	via Bologna	286-530
	Mignon	7	corso Novara	204-812
	Nuovo Rebecchino	356	corso Garibaldi	268-026
	Prati	4	via Rosaroll	268-898
	Pugliese	14	via Pica	269-766
	San Giorgio	27	vico III Duchessa	281-602
	San Pietro	18	via San Pietro ad Aram	200-855
	Sayonara	59	piazza Garibaldi	220-313
	Washington	311	corso Umberto I	286-729
Pensione 2	Dei Mille	15	piazza Amedeo	411-725

Camping is very popular in Italy. The Local Tourist Bureau of the nearest town will give information and particulars of the most suitable sites. There are over 1600 official camping sites in Italy. Full details of the sites are published by the Touring Club Italiano in *Campeggi in Italia* (from C.I.T.). A list and location map can be obtained free from the Federazione Italiana del Campeggio at their headquarters, P.O. Box 649, Florence. In Naples, the *Città di Napoli* campground (viale Giochi del Mediterraneo, 2 km from the Agnano Terme exit of the Tangenziale, tel. 760-5169) is open year round; as is the *Averno*, near Pozzuoli (via Domiziana, km 55; Tel. 866-1202.

Restaurants. For a detailed description of Neapolitan cuisine, see Chapter VI. The following list of restaurants in Naples has been compiled by the Azienda Autonoma di Soggiorno e Turismo:

Near the sea

Casanova Grill Bar				
(Excelsior Hotel)	48	via Partenope	Tel.	417-111
Bersagliera		borgo Marinaro		415-692
Ciro		borgo Marinaro		415-66
Starita		borgo Marinaro		404-349
Transatlantico		borgo Marinaro		412-646
Zi Tore		piazza della Repubblica		663-707
Al Sarago		piazza Sannazaro		685-587
Ciro a Mergellina	21	via Mergellina		681-780
Marino	118	via Santa Lucia		416-280

De Peppino	8	via Palepoli	415-582
Da Ferdinando	7/9	via Campanella	684-455
Da Salvatore alla Riviera	91	riviera di Chiaia	680-490
Dal Delicato	34	largo Sermonta	667-047
Il Drago	270	riviera di Chiaia	403-692
Don Salvatore	5	via Mergellina	681-817
La Cantinella	23	via Sauro	404-884
San Carlo	18	via Cesario Console	417-206
Giuseppone a Mare		via Russo	769-6002
Finestrella	23	via Marechiaro	769-0020
Il Galeone	16A	via Posillipo	684-581
Rosiello		Discesa Marechiaro	769-4401
La Fazenda	58	via Marechiaro	769-7420
Il Galletto	29	Discesa Coroglio	769-7225

On the hill

Belvedere	51	via Angelini	364-540
La Sacrestia	116	via Orazio	664-186
D'Angelo	203	via Falcone	365-363
Le Arcate	249	via Falcone	683-380
Renzo e Lucia	13	via Angelini	365-004

Downtown

Al 53	53	piazza Dante	341-124
Da Bergantino		via Sanfelice	310-369
Da Ciro	71	via Santa Brigida	324-072
Dante e Beatrice	44/45	piazza Dante	349-905
Da Giovanni	14	via Morelli	416-849
Da Umberto	30	via Alabardieri	418-555
El cucciolo	59	via De Cesare	407-902
Mattozzi	2	piazza Carità	324-322
Rugantino	45	via dei Fiorentini	325-491
Sangirè		via San Pasquale	413-259
Da Giovanni il Ferroviere	28	via Carriera Grande	268-828

3 Transport

Airlines. *Alitalia*, 41-42 via Medina, tel. 325-325; reservations tel. 312-200. *Air France*, via Vittorio Emanuele III, tel. 312-547. *British Airways*, 2 piazza Municipio, tel. 444-144. *Iberia*, 55 via Cervantes, tel. 322-080. *KLM*, 45 via De Gasperi, tel. 325-702. *Lufthansa*, 72 piazza Municipio, tel. 315-440. *Olympic Airways*, 47 via Ponte di Tappa, tel. 320-172. *Pan American World Airways*, 55 via Cervantes, tel. 209-456.

SAS, 32 via san Giacomo, tel. 321-059. *Swissair*, 3 piazza Francese, tel. 311-440. *TWA*, 23 via Partenope, tel. 412-834.

Capodichino, 4 km (2 miles) north of Naples, is the airport for both international and internal air services. Direct flights from London, Frankfurt, Munich and Zurich. Internal services to Bologna, Milan, Pisa, Turin, Rome, Venice, Palermo, Catania, Genoa and other cities. *Airport Terminal*, 78 via Cervantes (Map 2, 10); bus services in connection with flights, 800 lire.

Railways. The Italian State Railways (F.S.-Ferrovie dello Stato) run five main categories of trains. (1) *T.E.E.*, luxury first-class express trains running between the main Italian (and European) cities. A special supplement is charged and seat reservation is obligatory. (2) *Rapidi*, fast trains running between main towns. A special supplement is charged (approximately 30% of the normal single fare). Some rapido trains carry only first class and seats must be booked in advance. (3) *Espressi*, long-distance express trains (often international). They stop only at main stations and carry both classes. (4) *Diretti*, although not stopping at every station, are usually a good deal slower than the Espressi. (5) *Locali*, local trains stopping at all stations.

There are limitations on traveling short distances on the first-class express trains. Trains in Italy are usually crowded, especially in summer; seats can be booked from the main cities at the station booking office. Fares are still much lower than in most other European countries. A *Biglietto turistico di libera circolazione*, obtainable only outside Italy, gives freedom of the Italian railways for 8, 15, 21, or 30 days. A *Chilometrico* ticket is valid for 3000 kilometers (and can be used by up to five people at the same time).

Restaurant cars are attached to some international and internal long-distance trains. A lunch tray brought to the compartment (including three courses and wine, and costing 25000-30000 lire) is a convenient way of having a meal while traveling. Some trains now also have self-service restaurants. Also, snacks, hot coffee and drinks are sold throughout the journey from a cart wheeled down the train. At every large station snacks are on sale from carts on the platform, and can be bought from the train window. Carrier-bags with sandwiches, drinks, and fruit (*cestini da viaggio*), or individual sandwiches (*panini*) are available.

The principal railway stations in Naples are *Centrale* (Map 3, 4) and *piazza Garibaldi* (at a lower level), piazza Garibaldi, for all State Railway services to the south and east, and for all except a few of the fastest services to Rome and the north, which start from *Mergellina* (Map 4, 13), piazza Piedigrotta. From the *Stazione Vesuviana*, corso Garibaldi (Map 3, 4-8) the Circumvesuviana Railway runs several times daily to Pompeii,

Sarno, Sorrento, Nola, and Baiano. From the *Stazione di Montesanto* (Map 2, 5), piazza Montesanto, the Circumflegrea Railway serves Pozzuoli and Torregaveta (departures every twenty minutes). Tickets must be bought at the station before the journey, otherwise a fairly large supplement has to be paid to the ticket-collector on the train. Porters are entitled to a fixed amount for each piece of baggage. At present (1989) the tariff is 2000 lire.

Metropolitana. A frequent subway service runs from piazza Garibaldi to Pozzuoli Solfatara in about 30 minutes. Intermediate halts: piazza Cavour (Map 2, 2), Montesanto (Map 2, 5), piazza Amedeo (Map 4, 10), Mergellina (Map 4, 13), Fuorigrotta, Campi Flegrei, Bagnoli, Agnano Terme.

Maritime Connections. Ocean liners usually moor at the Molo Angioino (Stazione Marittima Passeggeri; Map 3, 15); other vessels at the Molo Pisacane (Immacolatella Nuova; Map 3, 11), or within the inner harbor between the two. Ferries connect Naples with Catania, Syracuse, Palermo, Cagliari, Messina, the Aeolian Islands, Malta, and Tunis; and hydrofoils run daily to Lipari. For services in the Gulf of Naples, see below.

Hydrofoils

CAREMAR (Molo Beverello, piazza Municipio, tel. 313.882)

Capri-Napoli	6.55	9.40	13.55	16.15
Napoli - Capri	7.50	13.00	14.50	17.15
Ischia - Napoli	6.50	9.30	14.10	16.00
Napoli - Ischia	7.50	11.00	15.05	16.55
Procida - Napoli	6.50	9.00	14.10	16.15
Napoli - Procida	7.45	11.50	15.00	17.1

ALILAURO (via Caracciolo 13, tel. 684.288)

Giorni feriali

Napoli - Ischia	7.20	9.00	10.30	12.10	13.00	14.00	17.50
Ischia - Napoli	.10	9.10	10.30	12.00	13.00	15.10	17.00

Giorni festivi

Napoli - Ischia	9.00	10.30	12.10	14.00	16.20
Ischia - Napoli	.50	11.10	13.00	15.10	17.00

SNAV (via Caracciolo 10, tel. 660.444)

Napoli - Capri	07.10*	08.40**	09.30	10.30	11.00	12.40	14.20
	15.30**	16.00					
Capri - Napoli	08.00*	09.25	10.20	11.50	12.50	13.40	
	16.20**	17.20	18.50				

*Monday thru Saturday **Sundays and holidays

Ferries

Da Napoli (Molo Beverello) per Capri - Caremar: 6.40
(festivi 7.00) - 9.00 - 11.10 - 15.00 - 18.30; N.L.G: 9.15 - 13.45
(feriale).
Da Capri per Napoli (Molo Beverello) - Caremar: 7.15 - 8.40
- 10.40 - 16.00 - 18.00; N.L.G: 11.30 (feriale) - 15.45.
Da Napoli (Molo Beverello) per Ischia - Caremar: 6.30
(festivi 7.05) - 8.55 - 10.30 - 14.15 (festivi 15.00) - 17.30 -
19.30; Libera Navigazione Lauro: 8.35 - 13.45 - 19.00.
Da Ischia per Napoli (Molo Beverello) - Caremar: 7.00 -
10.40 - 14.45 (festivi 16.00) - 17.25 - 19.15 - 21.15**; Libera
Navigazione Lauro: 6.40 - 8.15 - 10.20 - 14.00** - 15.15** -
16.55 - 18.45**.
Da Napoli (Molo Beverello) per Procida - Caremar 6.30
(feriali) - 9.20 - 14.00 - 19.00 - 23.00.
Da Procida per Napoli (Molo Beverello) - Caremar: 7.00 -
11.15 - 17.30.
Da Pozzuoli per Ischia - Traghetti: 5.10 - 6.30 p. - 7.15 pc -
8.30 p - 9.10*** - 10.10 - 11.30 pc. - 12.20 pc - 13.10 - 14.50 -
15.30 p. - 16.10 - 17.30 p. - 18.45 c.; Libera Navigazione
Lauro: 5.50 - 7.10 - 8.00 - 9.20 - 10.40 - 11.40 - 12.40 - 13.15 -
14.20 - 15.30 - 16.20 - 18.30 - 19.30 (feriali); Motonave Adria:
9.55 - 15.20 - 18.30 - 21.25.
Da Ischia per Pozzuoli - Traghetti: 3.30 - 6.40 p. - 7.20 -
10.00 p. - 10.40 - 11.40 - 14.00 p. - 14.35*** - 16.00 p.; Libera
Navigazione Lauro: 3.50 - 5.20 - 6.25 - 7.20 - 8.40 - 9.50 -
10.30 - 11.15 - 12.30 - 15.00 - 17.00 - 18.00 (feriali); Motonave
Adria: 7.50 - 12.40 - 16.55 - 20.00.
Da Pozzuoli per Procida - Caremar: 9.35 - 13.40 - 16.40 -
19.45.
Da Procida per Pozzuoli - Caremar: 8.10 - 12.10 - 15.50 -
18.50.
Da Pozzuoli per Procida-Ischia - Caremar: 9.35 - 13.40 -
16.40 - 19.45.
Da Ischia per Procida-Pozzuoli - Caremar: 7.30 - 11.30 -
15.10 - 18.10.
Da Ischia per Capri - Libera Navigazione Lauro: 8.30.
Da Capri per Ischia - Libera Navigazione Lauro: 16.00.
Da Pozzuoli per Casamicciola - Traghetti: 7.10 - 10.55 -
15.00 (solo feriale) - 18.50 - 22.00 (venerdì e domenica).
Da Casamicciola per Pozzuoli - Traghetti: 5.30 - 8.50 - 13.10
(solo feriale) - 17.20 - 20.30 (venerdì e domenica).
Da Procida per Ischia - Caremar: 10.10 - 14.15 - 17.15 -
20.15.
Da Ischia per Procida - Caremar: 7.30 - 11.30 - 15.10 - 18.10.

*Weekdays - via Procida - on Sundays and holidays the boat

departs at 7.05 a.m. and does not stop at Procida.

**via Procida

***Monday thru Saturday

****Suspended Wednesdays and Fridays

*Saturdays and holidays

**Weekdays

City Buses.

15 TRIBUNALI - MERGELLINA
Tribunali - via P. Coletta - corso Umberto - piazza Municipio - via Vittorio Emanuele - via santa Lucia - piazza dei Martiri - via Filangieri - via Crispi - corso Vittorio Emanuele - Salita Piedigrotta - Mergellina.

24 PIAZZA VITTORIA - PONTI ROSSI
piazza Vittoria - via Partenope - via santa Lucia - via Vittorio Emanuele - piazza Municipio - via Medina - via Monteoliveto - piazza Dante - **Museo Nazionale -** via santa Teresa - **Museo di Capodimonte** - porta Grande - via Ponti Rossi.

47 PIAZZA G.B. VICO - PIAZZA VANVITELLI
piazza G.B.Vico - via Tanucci - via Foria - **Museo Nazionale** - via Salvator Rosa - via M.B. Imbriani - via Giacinto Gigante - piazza Medaglie d'Oro - piazza degli Artisti - via Luca Giordano - via Scarlatti - piazza Vanvitelli (Vomero).

49 PIAZZA G. PEPE. Vomero - SAN MARTINO
piazza G. Pepe - Stazione Centrale - corso Umberto - via G. Sanfelice - via Monteoliveto - piazza Dante - **Museo Nazionale** - via Salvator Rosa - via M.B. Imbriani - via Giacinto Gigante - via Niutta - piazza Medaglie d'Oro - piazza degli Artisti - via Luca Giordano - via Scarlatti - via Morghen - **Museo San Martino**.

102 PARCO CASTELLO - AGNANO
parco Castello - piazza Vittoria - Riviera di Chiaia - **Aquarium** - Fuorigrotta - Terme di Agnano - Ippodromo di Agnano.

106 MERGELLINA - PIAZZA G.B. VICO
Mergellina - via Mergellina - Riviera di Chiaia - piazza Vittoria - via Partenope - via santa Lucia - via Vittorio Emanuele - piazza Municipio - piazza Bovio - corso Umberto - Stazione Centrale - via Milano - corso Garibaldi - piazza Carlo III - piazza G.B. Vico.

118 VIA DIAZ - MERGELLINA
via Diaz - via Monteoliveto - piazza Dante - via Pessina - **Museo Nazionale** - via Salvator Rosa - via M.R. Imbriani - via Battistello Caracciolo - piazza Mazzini - corso Vittorio Emanuele - via Mergellina - Mergellina.

122 CORSO VITT. EM. - PIAZZA CAVOUR
corso Vittorio Emanuele (Cumana) - via Schipa - piazza Amedeo - Riviera di Chiaia - **Aquarium** - piazza Vittoria - via Partenope - via santa Lucia - via Vittorio Emanuele - via Medina - via Monteoliveto - via Pessina - via Conte di Ruvo - piazza Cavour.

C.A. CIRCOLARE
Stazione Centrale - corso Umberto - via G. Sanfelice - via C. Battisti - piazza Carità - via Roma - piazza Trieste e Trento - via Vittorio Emanuele - piazza Municipio - via Medina - corso Umberto - Stazione Centrale.

C.D. CIRCOLARE DESTRA
Stazione Centrale - corso Umberto - via G. Sanfelice - via Monteoliveto - piazza Dante - via Pessina - via Conte di Ruvo - via Foria - corso Garibaldi - Stazione Centrale.

C.S. CIRCOLARE SINISTRA
Stazione Centrale - via Milano - piazza Principe Umberto - corso Garibaldi - via Foria - via Pessina - piazza Dante - via Roma - via Diaz - piazza Bovio - corso Umberto - Stazione Centrale.

P.T. (red)
piazza Plebiscito - via santa Lucia - via Chiatamone - piazza Martiri - piazza Amedeo - corso Vittorio Emanuele - via Tasso - piazza Europa - via Manzoni - via del Casale - via Petrarca - via Orazio - piazza Sannazaro - via Mergellina - Riviera Chiaia - piazza Vittoria - via Partenope - via santa Lucia - piazza Plebiscito.

P.T. (black)
piazza Plebiscito - via Chiatamone - piazza Vittoria - via Orazio - via Petrarca - via Manzoni - corso Vittorio Emanuele - piazza Amedeo - Riviera di Chiaia - via Partenope - piazza Plebiscito.

128 PIAZZA PLEBISCITO - VOMERO
piazza Plebiscito - via santa Lucia - via Chiatamone - piazza dei Martiri - via dei Mille - piazza Amedeo - parco Margherita - corso Vittorio Emanuele - via Tasso - via Aniello Falcone - via Scarlatti - via Bernini - viale Michelangelo - piazza Leonardo - piazza Medaglie d'Oro - piazza Muzli - via Piscicelli - via Altamura - via Simone Martini.

139 PIAZZA S. DOM. MAGG. - PIAZZA AMEDEO
piazza San Domenico Maggiore - via Mezzocannone - via Depretis - via Verdi - via santa Brigida - via Vittorio Emanuele - via Chiaia - via Filangieri - via dei Mille - piazza Amedeo.

140 PIAZZA DEL GESU' - POSILLIPO
piazza del Gesù - via Monteoliveto - via Medina - via Verdi - via santa Brigida - via santa Lucia - via Chiatamone - via Arcoleo - piazza Vittoria - Riviera di Chiaia - viale Ellena - via Mergellina - via Posillipo - Posillipo Capo.

143 PIAZZA OLIVELLA - TRIBUNALI
piazza Olivella - via Montesanto - via Tarsia - via Roma - via Diaz - via G. Sanfelice - corso Umberto - Stazione Centrale - via Poerlo - Tribunali.

150 STAZIONE CENTRALE - BAGNOLI
Stazione Centrale - corso Umberto - piazza Municipio - via Verdi - via Vittorio Emanuele - via santa Lucia - via Chiatamone - piazza Vittoria - Riviera di Chiaia - **Aquarium** - viale Augusto - via Diocleziano - via Cavallegeri Aosta - via Cattolica - via Coroglio - Bagnoli (Dazio).

152 CORSO NOVARA - POZZUOLI
corso Novara - corso Garibaldi - via Marina - via Cristoforo Colombo - via Acton - piazza Vittoria - Riviera di Chiaia - via Mergellina - piazza Italia - viale Augusto - Mostra d'Oltremare - via Nuova Agnano - strada san Gennaro - corso Terracciano -

via Domiziana - **Solfatara** - Arco Felice - via Miliscola - Pozzuoli.

Trolley - Buses.
253 PIAZZA MUNICIPIO - ERCOLANO SCAVI
piazza Municipio - via Depretis - via Marina - via Vespucci - corso san Giovanni a
Teduccio - Croce del Lagno - Portici - **Herculaneum**.

255 PIAZZA MUNICIPIO - TORRE DEL GRECO
piazza Municipio - via Depretis - via Marina - via Vespucci - corso san Giovanni a
Teduccio - Croce del Lagno - corso Garibaldi - Portici - **Herculaneum**.

Tramways.
1 POGGIOREALE - BAGNOLI (Dazio)
Poggioreale - via N. Poggioreale - corso Garibaldi - piazza Garibaldi - via Marina - via
C. Colombo - via Acton - Riviera di Chiaia - **Aquarium** - piazza sannazaro - via G.
Cesare - via Diocleziano - Mostra d'Oltremare - Stadio san Paolo - via Nuova Bagnoli
- Bagnoli.

Country Buses. Ordinary services to *Salerno*, *Eboli*,
Pompeii, *Nocera*, *Vietri*, *Castellammare di Stabia* and *Amalfi*
from via Pisanelli (Map 0, 00); to *Fiuggi*, *Benevento*, *Agropoli*
and *Pozzuoli* from piazza Garibaldi (Map 3, 4); to *Avellino* and
Pompeii from the Circumvesuviana Station (Map 3, 8), to
Caserta from porta Capuana (Map 3, 4), to *Cosenza*, *Isernia*,
Chieti, and *Pescara* from the Central Station (Map 3, 4). Most
Grand Tour services (including *Pompeii - Sorrento - Amalfi -
Positano*, etc.) start from piazza Municipio (Map 2, 10).
Sorrento, *Capri*, *Procida*, and *Ischia* are linked to Naples by
Car Ferries and Hydrofoils, which moor at the Molo Beverello
and Mergellina (see above).

Funicular Railways climb to the Vomero from piazza
Montesanto (Map 2, 5), from via Toledo (Map 2, 9) and from
via del Parco Margherita (Map 0, 00); the last two with
intermediate halts at the corso Vittorio Emanuele. Also: from
Mergellina to Posillipo.

Taxis. Taxicabs cannot be hailed, but must be hired at a taxi
stand (in all the main squares). Before engaging a taxi it is
advisable to make sure it has a meter in working order. Fares
vary from city to city, but are generally cheaper than New York
taxis. No tip is expected, but a few hundred lire can be given.
Fixed supplements are charged for night (10:00 p.m. - 7:00
a.m.) service, for excessive (more than one piece) or oversize
luggage, and for radio calls (in Naples: 364-444). A return fare
must be paid for taxis dismissed beyond the city limits. In
Naples, as elsewhere in Italy, the horse-drawn carozza is by no
means extinct. Fares are rather high; when hiring a vehicle it is
advisable to see that the meter is working or, for sightseeing, to
make an exact agreement in advance as to charges.

Taxi Stands

Zona Amedeo

piazza Amedeo	680.700
piazza Mergellina	680.900
piazza Piedigrotta	680.600
piazza della Repubblica	683.400
via Nisco	400.900

Zona Arenella

piazza Arenella	360.600
piazzale Cardarelli	461.000

Zona Centro

piazza Bovio	206.500
piazza Carità	320.700
piazza Municipio	320.200
piazza Nicola Amore	200.200

Zona Chiaia

piazza Carolina	415.600
(piazza san Pasquale)	400.940
piazza Trieste e Trento	414.500
piazza Vittoria	415.200
via Partenope	415.700

Zona Colli Aminei

via Nicolardi	743.50.00

Zona Fuorigrotta

piazzale Tecchio	616.000
piazza s. Vitale	616.200

Zona Museo

piazza Cavour	454.800
piazza Dante	210.200
piazza Mazzini	340.600
piazza Museo	340.700

Zona Nolana

piazza Carlo III	294.400
piazza Garibaldi (via Mancini)	338.700
piazza Guglielmo Pepe	220.100
piazza Nazionale	220.400
piazza s. Francesco	220.900

Zona Posillipo

piazza s. Luigi	769.12.00
via Petrarca	769.56.00
via s. Strato	769.62.22

4   Automobile Travel

Motorists intending to visit Italy will save trouble by joining the American Automobile Association, the American Automobile Touring Alliance, or other club accredited by the

Automobile Club d'Italia (A.C.I.) or the Touring Club Italiano. Temporary membership of the A.C.I. can be taken out on the frontier or in Italy. The headquarters of the A.C.I. is at 8 via Marsala, Rome. Concessions gained from membership include parking facilities, legal assistance, and discounts on tolls and car hire. Also, a free breakdown service is provided for foreign motorists by the Soccorso A.C.I.

It is obligatory to carry a red triangle in the car in case of accident or breakdown. This serves as a warning to other traffic when placed on the road at a distance of 50 m (160 ft) from the stationary car. It can be hired from the A.C.I. for a minimal charge, and returned at the frontier. In case of breakdown, the nearest A.C.I. office can be contacted by telephone number 116. On the Autostrada del Sole (Milan - Rome), there is an emergency press button box on the right of the road every 2 km (1,5 miles).

Gasoline Coupons. Foreign motorists in Italy with a vehicle registered outside the country are entitled to purchase a certain number of gasoline coupons at a fraction of the market price of gasoline in Italy. Travelers are advised to check with the Italian State Tourist Office or one of the motoring organizations. The normal cost of gasoline in 1989 is 1370 lire.

Car Rental. Rental cars are available in most Italian cities and the cost varies from about 40000 lire a day plus about 400 lire per km upwards according to the size of the vehicle. Arrangements for the hire of cars in Italy can be made in the United States through Alitalia, Pan Am, TWA, etc. (in conjunction with their flights) or through any of the principal car rental firms. It should be noted that travelers renting cars in Italy are not entitled to gasoline coupons.

Italian Superhighways (*Autostrade*). Italy has the finest superhighways in Europe. There are about 6000 km of them and more are under construction. Tolls are charged according to the rating of the vehicle and the distance covered. Service areas are found on all autostrade. There are reduced speed limits on montainous sections. On some superhighways (including the *Autostrada del Sole*) cars with foreign licence plates qualify for reduced tolls which correspond to the lowest tariff (applicable to motorcycles). The *Autostrada del Sole* is toll-free from Naples to Reggio Calabria.

Maps. The Italian Touring Club publishes several sets of maps including the *Carte Stradali* on a scale of 1: 350,000, each dedicated to a specific region. Those regarding *Lazio*, *Molise*, and *Campania* refer to the area dealt with in this guide. The sheets are on sale at all Italian Touring Club offices and at many booksellers. The *Atlante Automobilistico*, an atlas in three volumes on a scale of 1: 200,000, is more detailed and less bulky.

The *Istituto Geografico Militare* of Florence (14 viale

Strozzi) publishes a map of Italy on a scale of 1: 100,000 in 272 sheets, and a field survey (*levate di campagna*) partly 1: 50,000, partly 1: 25,000, which are invaluable for the detailed exploration of the country, especially its more mountainous regions; the coverage is, however, still far from complete.

5   General Information

Seasons. The weather in Italy, and even in the South, is less uniformly reliable than is generally believed by northern visitors. It can, even in spring, be unexpectedly cold and wet, and inland in the mountains there is risk in winter of snow and ice. In general, however, the climate of coastal resorts in the Naples area is agreeable for much of the year; save in winter a succession of more than two or three bad days is unusual except in places much affected by mountains. The heat in July and August is unpleasant in the towns and may be excessive on coasts sheltered from cooling breezes. Naples is subject to winds and to abrupt changes of temperature. The best months for traveling are April, May, and early June, and September and October; accomodation is more easily found in autumn.

Language. Familiarity with the Italian language will add greatly to the traveler's profit and enjoyment, but those who know no language but English can get along quite comfortably on the main tourist routes. Even a few words of Italian, however, are a great advantage, and the attempt in itself will enlist the native courtesy of the Italian people to the assistance of the visitor in difficulties. Local dialects vary very much and are usually unintelligible to the foreigner, but even where dialect is universally used nearly everybody can speak and understand Italian. Below is a simple series of instructions for pronouncing Italian words.

Words should be pronounced well forward in the mouth, and no nasal intonation exists in Italian. Double consonants call for special care as each must be sounded.

Consonants are pronounced roughly as in English with the following exceptions: *c* and *cc* before *e* and *i* have the sound of *ch* in *chess*; sc before *e* and *i* is pronounced like *sh* in *ship*; *ch* before *e* and *i* has the sound of *k*; *g* and *gg* before *e* and *i* are always soft, like *j* in *jelly*; *gh* is always hard, like *g* in *get*; *gl* in nearly always like *lli* in *million* (there are a few exceptions, e.g. *negligere*, where it is pronounced as in English); *gn* is like *ny* in *lanyard*; *gu* and *qu* are always like *gw* and *kw*. *S* is hard like *s* in *six* except when it occurs between two vowels, when it is soft like the English *z* or the *s* in *rose*, ss in always hard. Z and *zz* are usually pronounced like *ts*, but occasionally have the sound of *dz* before a long vowel.

Vowels are pronounced openly and are given their full value. There are no true diphthongs in Italian, and every vowel should be articulated separately. The vowel sounds in Italian are as follows: *a* is like *o* in *hot*; *e* and *é* are like *a* in *cake*; *è* is like *e* in *bed*; *i* is like *ee* in *feet*; *o* is usually like *o* in *tone*, but in certain instances (e.g., *tonno*) is like *augh* in *taught*; u is like *oo* in *fool*.

The stress normally falls on the last syllable but one, in modern practice an accent - sign is written regularly only when the stress is on the last syllable, e.g. *città*, or to differentiate between two words similarly spelled with different meaning: e.g. *e* (*and*) , and *è* (*is*).

Manners and Customs. Attention should be paid by the traveler to the more formal manners of Italians. It is customary to open conversation in shops, etc., with the courtesy of *buon giorno* (good day) or *buona sera* (good evening). The deprecatory expression *prego* (don't mention it) is everywhere the obligatory and automatic response to *grazie* (thank you). The phrases *per piacere* or *per favore* (please), *permesso* (excuse me), used when pushing past someone (essential on public vehicles), *scusi* (sorry; also, I beg your pardon, when something is not heard), should not be forgotten. A visitor will be wished *Buon appetito!* before beginning a meal, to which he should reply *Grazie, altrettanto*. This pleasant custom may be extended to fellow passengers taking a picnic meal on a train. Shaking hands is an essential part of greeting and leave-taking. In shops and offices a certain amount of self-assertion is taken for granted, as lines are not the general rule and it is incumbent on the inquirer or customer to get himself a hearing.

Begging and uninvited offers of guidance should be met with firmness but without harshness or rudeness. It should be borne in mind that in the south of Italy begging is regarded as a necessary stimulus to the virtue of charity, even the poor will give something, if only a few lire, to a beggar. In Naples the persistent attentions of small boys, rarely innocent whatever their age, should be firmly but kindly discouraged; outside the city, however, the local school-children are frequently knowledgeable and genuinely anxious to show the beauties of their home town. Where this is done in the name of hospitality no reward will be accepted.

Photography. There are few restrictions on photography in Italy, but permission is necessary to photograph the interiors of churches and museums and may sometimes be withheld. Care should also be taken before photographing individuals, notably members of the armed forces and the police. Photography is forbidden on railway stations and civil airfields as well as in frontier zones and near military installations.

Churches are normally closed for a considerable period during the middle of the day (12 to 3, 4, or 5 p.m.), although cathedrals and some of the large churches may be open without a break during daylight hours. Smaller churches and oratories are often open only in the early morning, but the sacristan may usually be found by inquiring locally. The sacristan will also show closed chapels, crypts, etc., and a small tip should be given. Some churches now ask that sightseers do not enter during a service, but normally visitors may do so, provided they are silent and do not approach the altar (s) in use. At all times they are expected to cover their legs and arms, and generally dress with decorum. An entrance fee is becoming customary for admission to treasuries, bell-towers, etc. Lights (coin operated) have now been installed in many churches to illuminate frescoes and altarpieces. In Holy Week most of the pictures are covered and are on no account shown.

Museums are usually open six days a week, the commonest closing day being Monday. Many museums are open from 9:30 - 16 on weekdays and 9:30 - 13 on Sundays and holidays. Most of the State museums have recently adopted standard opening hours for the summer and winter, namely 9-14 on weekdays, and 9-13 on Sundays and holidays. However, hours of admission are constantly being altered and shortened, and great care should be taken to allow enough time for variations in the hours shown below when planning to visit a museum. On Sundays and holidays, most museums are open in the mornings only, either free or at half price. Entrance fees vary.

Hours of Admission to the Museums, Collections, and Monuments of Naples and Environs

Name	Open
Aquarium	09.00-17.00; Sun 10.00-19.00
Acquario	Closed Mon
Cappella Sansevero	10.30-13.30, 17.00-19.00 (Jul-Sept)
Catacombs of St. Gaudiosus	Apply to sacristan
Catacombe di San Gaudioso	
Catacombs of St. Januarius	Sat, Sun, and Holidays
Catacombe di San Gennaro	09.30, 10.15, 11.00, 11.45
Conservatory Museum	09.00-13.00
Museo Storico - Musicale	
del Conservatorio	
Duke of Martina	09.00-14.00; Sun 09.00-13.00
National Ceramics Museum	closed Mon
Museo Nazionale della Ceramica	09.00-14.00; Sun 09.00-13.00
Duca di Martina	closed Mon; Collection
Filangieri Museum	09.00-14.00; Sun 09.00-13.00
Museo Civico Filangieri	closed Mon
National Archeological Museum	09.00-14.00; Sun 09.00-13.00

Museo Archeologico Nazionale	closed Mon
National Library *Biblioteca Nazionale*	Mon-Fri 09.00-19.30
National Museum and Gallery of Capodimonte *Museo e Galleria Nazionali* *di Capodimonte*	09.00-14.00; Sun 09.00-13.00 closed Mon closed for restoration from 01.04.1990
Capodimonte Park *Parco del Museo di Capodimonte*	09.00 to one hour before sunset
National Museum of San Martino *Museo Nazionale di San Martino* San Martino Museum Gardens *Giardini del Museo di San Martino*	09.00-14.00; Sun 09.00-13.00 closed Mon; Collection as above
Parco di Posillipo	09.00 to one hour before sunset
Pinacoteca dei Girolamini	closed indefinitely
Pinacoteca Pio Monte *della Misericordia*	Tue, Thu, Sat 10.00-13.00
Prince Diego Aragona *Pignatelli Cortes Museum* *Museo Principe Diego Aragona* Pignatelli Cortes	09.00-14.00; Sun 09.00-13.00 closed Mon
Royal Palace *Palazzo Reale*	09.00-14.00; Sun 09.00-13.00 closed Mon; Collection
San Carlo Theater *Teatro San Carlo*	09.00-12.00
Villa Floridiana	09.00 to one hour before sunset
Zoo	09.00-17.00 winter; 09.00-19.00 summer

***

Amalfi Arsenal *Grotta di Smeraldo*	10.00-13.00; 17.00-22.00 (AA871107) 09.30-17.00; winter 10.00-16.00
Anacapri *Villa San Michele*	10.00 to sunset (AA 8371524)
Avellino *Museo del Duomo* *Museo Irpino*	09.00-13.00 09.00-12.00; 16.00-18.00
Bacoli *Piscina Mirabile*	09.00 - 16.00 (Custody at farmhouse at beginning of path)
Baia Excavations (*Scavi*)	09.00 to two hours before sunset

Benevento	
Museo del Sannio	09.00- 13.00; closed Mon (AA21818)
Capua	
Museo Campano	09.00-14.00; Sun 09.00-13.00 (AA961402)
Caserta	
Royal Palace (*Reggia*)	09.00-13.30; closed Mon
Palace Gardens (*Parco*)	09.00 to one hour before sunset
Cassino	
Abbey of Montecassino	09.30-12.30; 15.30 to sunset
Abbazia di Montecassino	
Castellamare di Stabbia	
Antiquarium	09.00-13.00 closed Mon (AA 8711334)
Catanzaro	
Museo Archeologico Provinciale	Thu 09.00-12.00
Cumae	
Excavations (*Scavi*)	09.00 to two hours before sunset
Formia	
Antiquarium	09.00-19.00; closed Mon
Gaeta	
Museo Diocesano	Sun 09.00-13.00
Herculaneum	
Excavations (*Scavi*)	09.00 to two hours before sunset
Antiquarium	closed
Minturnae	
Antiquarium	09.00 to one hour before sunset closed Mon
Minori	
Roman Villa	08.00-12.00, 16.00-19.00
Antiquarium	08.00-12.00, 16.00-19.00
Nicotera	
National Archeological Museum	09.30-12.30, 16.30-19.30
Museo Archeologico Nazionale	09.00-14.00; winter
Ninfa	Apr-Oct 1st Sat-Sun of month
Ruins	09.00-12.00; 14.30-18.00
Padula	
Museo della Lucania Occ.	09.00-14.00, 15.00-19.00
Paestum	
Excavations (*Scavi*)	08.30 to one hour before sunset
Museum	09.00-14.00, Sun. 09.00-13.00 closed Mon.

Palmi
Museo Civico   Mon-Sat 09.00-13.00 (0966.23618)

Pertosa
Grotta   08.30-12.30, 14.30-19.00

Pietrassa
Museo Nazionale Ferrovie   09.00-1200
Pontecagnano
Museo Archeologico Nazionale   09.00-13.30, Sun 09.00-14.00 closed Mon
Pompei
Excavations (*Scavi*)   09.00 to two hours before sunset

Positano
Grotta di Smeraldo   08.30-18.00, (Jul-Sept)
                                                10.00-16.00, (Oct-Feb)
                                                09.00-17.00, (Mar-May)

Potenza
Museo Archeologico Provinciale   closed

Pozzuoli
Solfatara   07.00 to sunset
Amphitheater   closed indefinitely

Ravello
Palazzo Rufolo   9.30-13.30, 15.00-19.00, (Jun-Sept)
                                                9.30-13.00, 15.00-17.00, (Oct-May)

Reggio Calabria
National Archeological Museum   Thu-Sat 09.00-13.30; 15.00-19.00
Museo Archeologico Nazionale   09.00-12.30, (Sun-Mon); Collection
Salerno
Museo del Duomo   9.30-12.30, 16.00-18.00; closed 1990
Museo Provinciale   09.00-13.00, 17.00-19.30

Santa Maria Capua Vetere
Amphitheater   09.00 to one hour before sunset

S. Cons
Antiquarium   08.00-14.00; Sun 09.00-13.30

Sezze
Antiquarium   09.00-12.00, 16.00-19.00; closed Mon
Sorrento
Museo Correale di Terranova   9.30-12.30, 16.00-19.00 (Apr-Sept)
                                                8.30-12.30, 15.00-17.00
                                                Sun. 9.30-12.30 (Oct-March); closed Tue

Sperlonga
Grotte di Tiberio   09.00 to one hour before sunset

SS Bruno
Monastero   11.00-12.00, 16.00-17.00
                                                closed for restoration 1990

Stilo
Cattolica   Key 16 V. Salerno

Terracina	
Archeological Museum	09.00-13.00, 17.00-19.00 (May-Sept)
Museo Archeologico	closed Mon;
	09.00-14.00 (Oct.-April) closed Sun

Torre Annunziata	
Oplontis	09.00 to two hours before sunset

Torre del Greco	
Scuola Corallo	09.00-13.00; weekdays

Trinità di Cava	
Monas	09.00-12.30, Sun 09.00-10.30

Velia	
Excavations (*Scavi*)	09.00 to one hour before sunset

Vibo Valentia	
National Archeological Museum	09.00-13.00, 15.00-17.00
Museo Archeologico Nazionale	Sun 09.00-13.00; in Castel June 1990

Vico Equense	
Antiquarium	09.00-14.00 (AA 8798343)

On national holidays Sunday opening hours are observed.

Museum Cards (available from the C.I.T. for a small fee) will allow the visitor free entrance to all the State-owned museums. Students holding the International Student Identity Card issued by the National Union of Students are also entitled to free entrance to all State-owned museums.

Public Holidays. The number of Italian National Holidays when offices, shops, and schools are closed have recently been reduced. They are now as follows: January 1 (New Year) Easter Monday, April 25 (Liberation Day), May 1 (Labor Day), August 15 (Assumption), November 1 (All Saints' Day), December 8 (Conception), Christmas Day and December 26 (St. Stephen). Each town keeps its Patron Saint's day as a holiday, e.g. 19 September (St. Januarius) in Naples.

Entertainments. The opera season in Naples usually begins in December and continues until April or May. Major operas and ballets are performed at the *San Carlo*; the *Auditorio della Radiotelevisione Italiana*, via Marconi, and *Conservatorio di Musica San Pietro a Maiella*, via san Pietro a Maiella, offer concerts. The principal Neapolitan theaters are the *Politeama*, 80 via Monte di Dio; *Mediterraneo*, at Fuorigrotta; *San Fernando*, piazza Teatro San Fernando; *Cileo*, via San Domenico; *Sannazaro*, 157 via Chiaia, with dialect plays; *Bracco*, 40 via Tarsia; *Sancarluccio*, 49 via Pasquale. Cinemas abound in all towns, and it is usual to tip the usher who shows you to your seat in theaters and cinemas.

Annual Music, Drama and Film Festivals take place in many towns; among the most famous are the classical drama festival in the Roman Theater at Pompeii (*Centenario dell'Eruzione Vesuviana* ; July and August), and the International Cinema Convention in Sorrento (*Incontri Internazionali del Cinema*; October). Traditional festivals are celebrated in most towns and villages in commemoration of a local historical or religious event, and are often very spectacular. Among the more famous are the festival of Piedigrotta, featuring a series of colorful and spectacular events (September), in Naples. **Religious and Popular Festivals**. The importance of Neapolitan festivals has diminished in recent years. The most interesting are: the *Feast of St. Anthony Abbot* (January 17); horses and other animals are blessed at Sant'Antonio. *Liquefaction of the Blood of St. Januarius* on September 19 and December 16 in the Cathedral and on the first Saturday in May at Santa Chiara where the phials are borne in colorful procession (late afternoon). *Return of the Pilgrims from Montevergine* (Easter Monday); interesting costumes and harness in the streets near the harbor; participants carry staves decorated with fruit and flowers as in ancient baccanalia. *Struscio*, so called from the rustling of the silk dresses worn on the occasion; draws a large crowd in the via Toledo on the Thursday and Friday before Easter to view the season's novelties in the shops. *Festival of Piedigrotta* (night of September 7-8), in commemoration of the Battle of Velletri (1744); a popular assembly gathers at the Grotta Nuova and songs written expressly for the occasion are sung. Saturday and Sunday nights, in summer, are turned into *Neighborhood Festivals*, with processions, fireworks, sports, and performances by local bands. *Festival of the Neapolitan Song* in June.

Sports. Horse racing at the *Ippodromo di Agnano*, with the "Gran Premio" in April and harness racing in the summer. Motor racing: *Rally della Campania*, in April-May. Cycling: *Giro della Campania*, also in April-May. International Regatta (*One Ton Cup*) in June. Tennis: *Tennis Club Mergellina*, 249 via Aniello Falcone. International Tournament in Naples at the end of April. Swimming Pool at the *Mostra d'Oltremare*, where many other sporting facilities may also be found. The Assessorato al Turismo sponsors an annual horse show at Monte Faito, above Castellammare di Stabia, in July.

Telephones and Postal Information. Stamps are sold at tobaconists (displaying a blue T sign) and Post Offices. Correspondence can be addressed c/o the Post Office by adding "Fermo Posta" to the name of the locality. There are numerous public telephones all over Italy in cafés, restaurants, phone booths, etc. These are usually operated by metal discs known as *gettone*, which are bought (200 lire each) from tobacconists, bars, some newspaper stands, and Post Offices. Coin-operated phones are increasingly common in metropolitan areas.

Newspapers. The most widely read Italian newspapers are the *Corriere della Sera* of Milan, the *Stampa* of Turin, and the *Messaggero* and *Repubblica* of Rome. The principal paper in Naples is the *Mattino*. Foreign newspapers are obtainable at central newsstands and railway stations.

United States Consulate, piazza della Repubblica (Map4, 13).

Shops generally open from 08.30 or 09.00 a.m. to 13.00 p.m., and from 15.30 or 16.00 p.m. to 19.30 or 20.00 p.m.

Banks are open from 08.30 to 13.20 every day except Saturdays and Sundays. Some banks reopen in the afternoon between 14.30 and 15.30, ca. Travelers' checks can be changed at most hotels (at a slightly lower rate of exchange), and foreign money can be changed at main railway stations and airports.

For Further Information: *Ente Provinciale di Turismo* (E.P.T.), 10A via Partenope; Central Station; Mergellina Station, Capodichino Airport; viale Kennedy; along the Autostrada at the san Nicola (Caserta) and Tre Ponti ovest (Marigliano) service areas; as well as at "La Pineta" car park in Torre del Greco. *E.N.I.T.*, at the airport. *Azienda Autonoma di Soggiorno e Turismo*, Palazzo Reale. The latter publishes the useful monthly magazine *Qui Napoli* in Italian and English (free). Travel Agents: *C.I.T.*, 70 piazza Municipio.

Bibliography

Harold Acton, *The Bourbons of Naples*. London, Methuen and Co., 1959.

_____, *The Last Bourbons of Naples*. London Methuen and Co., 1961.

Paul Blanchard, *Blue Guide to Southern Italy*. 5th ed. London, Ernest Benn, 1984.

Wolfgang Leppmann, *Pompeii in Fact and Fiction*. London, Elek Books, 1968.

Touring Club Italiano, ed., *Napoli e Dintorni*. 5th ed. Milano, 1976.

_____, *Campania*. 3rd ed. Milano, 1963

_____, *Lazio*. 3rd ed. Milano, 1964.

Manuscript contents

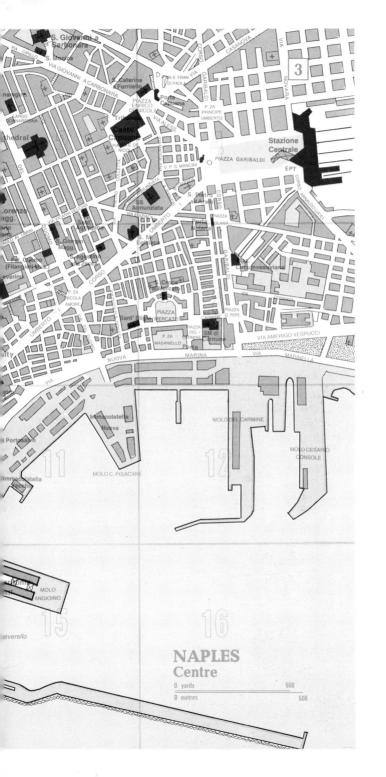

NAPLES
Centre

0 yards 500
0 metres 500

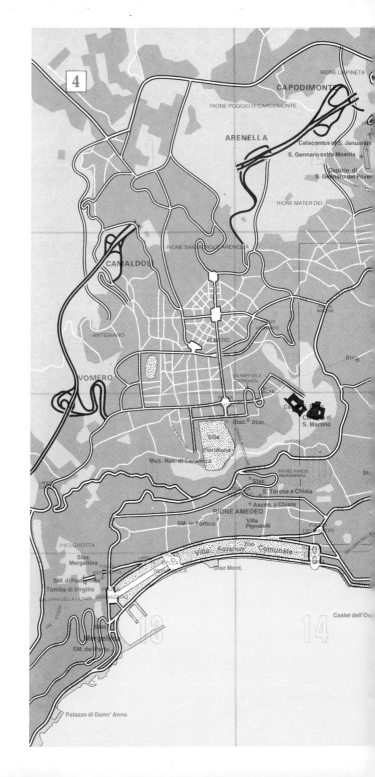

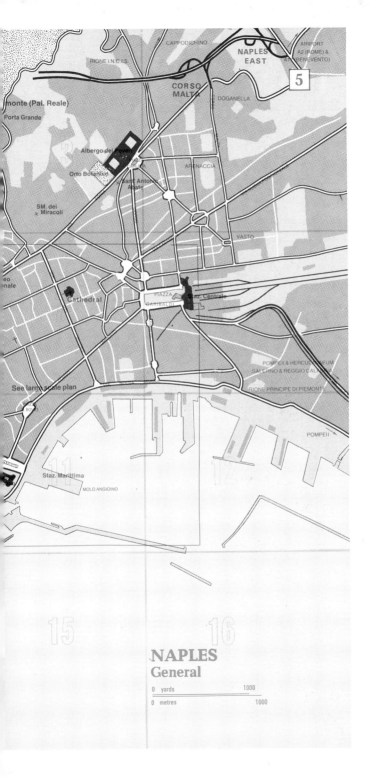

CAPPODICHINO

NAPLES
EAST

AIRPORT
A2 (ROME) &
A (BENEVENTO)

RIONE I N C I S.

5

CORSO
MALTA

DOGANELLA

monte (Pal. Reale)

Porta Grande

Albergo dei Poveri

ARENACCIA

Orto Botanico

Sant'Antonio
Abate

SM. dei
x Miracoli

VASTO

eo
nale

Cathedral

PIAZZA
GARIBALDI

Staz. Centrale

POMPEII & HERCULANEUM
SALERNO & REGGIO CAL

See large scale plan

RIONE PRINCIPE DI PIEMONTE

BOVIO

POMPEII

11

14

Staz. Marittima

MOLO ANGIOINO

15

16

NAPLES
General

| 0 | yards | | 1000 |
| 0 | metres | | 1000 |

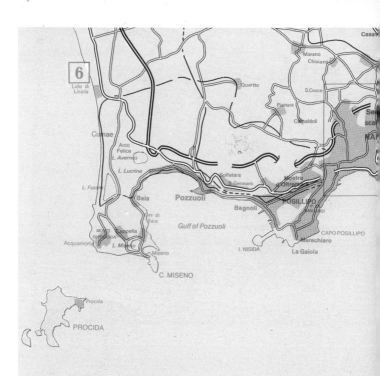

6

Lido di
Licola

Casa V

Marano
Chiaiano

Quartto

S.Croce

Pianura

Camaldoli

Se
sca

KAP

Cumae

Arco
Felice
L. Averno

L. Lucrine

Solfatara

Nostra
d'Oltrem

POSILLIPO

L. Fusaro

Baia

Pozzuoli

Bagnoli

Gulf of Pozzuoli

CAPO POSILLIPO

Marechiaro

MONTE
DI PROCIDA
Acquamorta

Cappella

Das di
Baia

L. Miseno

Miseno

I. NISIDA

La Gaiola

C. MISENO

Procida

PROCIDA

Gulf of Naples

BAY OF NAPLES

| 0 | miles | 5 |
| 0 | kilometres | 8 |

Marina
Grande

Anacapri   CAPRI   Capri

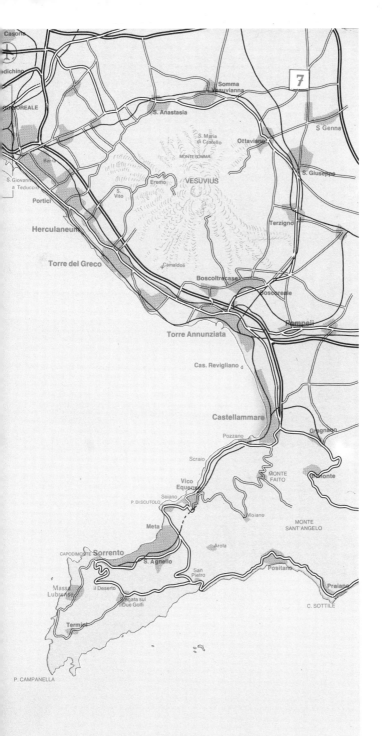

Casoria

adichino

MOREALE

Barra

S. Giovanni
a Teduccio

Portici

Herculaneum

Torre del Greco

S. Anastasia

Somma
Vesuvianna

S. Maria
di Castello

MONTE SOMMA

Eremo

S.
Vito

VESUVIUS

Ottaviano

S Genna

S. Giuseppe

Terzigno

Camaldoli

Boscoltrecase

Boscoreale

Pompeii

Torre Annunziata

Cas. Revigliano

Castellammare

Gragnano

Pozzano

Scraio

MONTE
FAITO

Monte

Vico
Equense

Seiano

P. DI SCUTOLO

Moiano

MONTE
SANT'ANGELO

Meta

CAPODIMONTE Sorrento

S. Agnello

Arola

San
Pietro

Positano

Praiano

Massa
Lubrense

il Deserto

Agata sui
Due Golfi

C. SOTTILE

Termini

P. CAMPANELLA

Notes

....

....

....

....

....

....

....

....

....

....

....

....

....

....

....

....

....

....

....